EXCAVATING BUDDHISM
A HISTORICAL PERSPECTIVE

Excavating Buddhism

A Historical Perspective

By

Madhusudan Sakya

CYBER TECH PUBLICATIONS
4264/3, Ansari Road, Daryaganj, New Delhi-110002 (India)
Ph.: 011-23244078. Fax: 011-23280028
E-Mail: cyberpublicationsdelhi@yahoo.com

Excavating Buddhism
A Historical Perspective

Madhusudan Sakya

First Edition 2011

Asian Offset Printers

Published by
G.S. Rawat for Cyber Tech Publications
4264/3, Ansari Road, Daryaganj, New Delhi-110002 (India)
Ph.: 011-23244078, 011-43559448 Fax: 011-23280028
E-Mail: cyberpublicationsdelhi@yahoo.com
cyberpublications@gmail.com
Website: www.cybertechpublications.com

Contents

Preface

"Virtues are learned at mother's knee, vices are picked up at some other joint.."

Buddhism is an ancient religion, propounded by Lord Gautama Buddha and has a large number of followers in Asia and far east as well as in western countries.

Buddhism, its doctrines, philosophy, tenets, practices, schools, and scriptures are researched and debated by academics and philosophers all across the world. A plethora of literature is available in various forms.

As the name of the title suggests, this book encompasses vital information on Buddhism in historical perspective. We have gathered here vital information under the following chapters—Buddhism: An Overview; Buddhism Through Ages; Gautama Buddha: A Life Sketch; Buddhism in Historical Perspective; Mahayana School; Theravada School of Buddhism; Pure Land Buddhism School; Pre-sectarian Buddhism; Nichiren Buddhism; Shingon Buddhism; Tibetan Buddhism; Concept of God in Buddhism and Bibliography etc.

Definitely, this venture will prove successful in furnishing vital authentic information on Buddhism, and scholars and laymen will be benefitted by it.

In course of gathering authoritative information we have consulted piles of literature on Buddhism, in form of encyclopaedias, books, articles, research papers, reports, discourses etc. available in printed and digital forms. In fact the real credit for this exercise ought go to the original contributors on whose works this project is devised and developed. I am deeply beholden to them all and the web sources also.

I was also immensely benefitted by the guidance, assistance and inspiration of my former teachers, colleagues and friends. I am grateful to them also. I am equally grateful to my publishers for evincing interest in this project and materialising this elegantly in the present form, that too within shortest possible time.

—Author

1

Buddhism: An Overview

> An important development in the Mahayana [was] that it came to separate nirvana from bodhi ('awakening' to the truth, Enlightenment), and to put a lower value on the former (Gombrich, 1992d). Originally nirvana and bodhi refer to the same thing; they merely use different metaphors for the experience. But the Mahayana tradition separated them and considered that nirvana referred only to the extinction of craving (passion and hatred), with the resultant escape from the cycle of rebirth. This interpretation ignores the third fire, delusion: the extinction of delusion is of course in the early texts identical with what can be positively expressed as gnosis, Enlightenment.
>
> —*Richard F. Gombrich, How Buddhism Began*

Asia is the cradle of civilisation. Many great world religions took birth here. Buddhism is one of these ancient religions having a large number of followers in India, Tibet, China, Sri Lanka, Korea, Japan and many more countries. Gautama Buddha was the founder of this religion.

Buddhism is a religion and philosophy encompassing a variety of traditions, beliefs and practices, largely based on teachings attributed to Siddhartha Gautama, commonly known as the Buddha (meaning "the awakened one"). The Buddha lived and taught in the northeastern Indian subcontinent sometime between the 6th and 4th centuries

BCE. He is recognized by adherents as an awakened teacher who shared his insights to help sentient beings end suffering (or dukkha), achieve nirvana, and escape what is seen as a cycle of suffering and rebirth.

Two major branches of Buddhism are recognized: Theravada ("The School of the Elders") and Mahayana ("The Great Vehicle"). Theravada—the oldest surviving branch—has a widespread following in Sri Lanka and Southeast Asia, and Mahayana is found throughout East Asia and includes the traditions of Pure Land, Zen, Nichiren Buddhism, Tibetan Buddhism, Shingon, Tendai and Shinnyo-en. In some classifications Vajrayana, a subcategory of Mahayana, is recognized as a third branch.

While Buddhism remains most popular within Asia, both branches are now found throughout the world. Various sources put the number of Buddhists in the world at between 230 million and 500 million, making it the world's fourth-largest religion.

It is remarkable that Buddhist schools vary significantly on the exact nature of the path to liberation, the importance and canonicity of various teachings and scriptures, and especially their respective practices. The foundations of Buddhist tradition and practice are the Three Jewels: the Buddha, the Dharma (the teachings), and the Sangha (the community). Taking "refuge in the triple gem" has traditionally been a declaration and commitment to being on the Buddhist path and in general distinguishes a Buddhist from a non-Buddhist. Other practices may include following ethical precepts, support of the monastic community, renouncing conventional living and becoming a monastic, meditation (this category includes mindfulness), cultivation of higher wisdom and discernment, study of scriptures, devotional practices, ceremonies, and in the Mahayana tradition, invocation of buddhas and bodhisattvas.

The evidence of the early texts suggests that the Buddha was born in a community that was on the periphery, both geographically and culturally, of fifth century BCE northeast India. This community seems to have had two categories of people, masters and servants. It was either a small republic, in which case his father was an elected chieftain or an oligarchy, in which case his father was an oligarch. This community was likely not yet absorbed into Brahmanical culture (the tradition that would evolve into Hinduism), and it is even possible that the Buddha's mother tongue was not Indo-Aryan.

Following the Buddha's death, Buddhist tradition built up an alternative biography, the Buddhist tradition mythologized some aspects of his early life. According to the Theravada Tipitaka scriptures, the Buddha was born in Lumbini, around the year 563 BCE, and raised in Kapilavastu, both situated in modern-day Nepal.

According to this narrative, shortly after the birth of young prince Siddhartha Gautama, an astrologer visited the young prince's father—King Œuddhodana—and prophesied that Siddhartha would either become a great king or renounce the material world to become a holy man, depending on whether he saw what life was like outside the palace walls. Suddhodana was determined to see his son become a king so he prevented him from leaving the palace grounds. But at age 29, despite his father's efforts, Siddhartha ventured beyond the palace several times. In a series of encounters—known in Buddhist literature as the four sights he learned of the suffering of ordinary people, encountering an old man, a sick man, a corpse and, finally, an ascetic holy man, apparently content and at peace with the world. These experiences prompted Gautama to abandon royal life and take up a spiritual quest.

Gautama first went to study with famous religious teachers of the day, and mastered the meditative attainments they taught. But he found that they did not provide a permanent end to suffering, so he continued his quest. He next attempted an extreme asceticism, which was a religious pursuit common among the Shramanas, a religious culture distinct from the Vedic one. Gautama underwent prolonged fasting, breath-holding, and exposure to pain. He almost starved himself to death in the process. He realized that he had taken this kind of practice to its limit, and had not put an end to suffering. So in a pivotal moment he accepted milk and rice from a village girl and changed his approach.

He devoted himself to anapanasati meditation, through which he discovered what Buddhists call the Middle Way: a path of moderation between the extremes of self-indulgence and self-mortification. Gautama was now determined to complete his spiritual quest.

At the age of 35, he famously sat in meditation under a sacred fig tree—known as the Bodhi tree—in the town of Bodh Gaya, in Bihar, and vowed not to rise before achieving enlightenment. After many days, he finally destroyed the fetters of his mind, thereby liberating himself from the cycle of suffering and rebirth, and arose as a fully enlightened being. Soon thereafter, he attracted a band of followers and instituted a monastic order.

Now, as the Buddha, he spent the rest of his life teaching the path of awakening he discovered, traveling throughout the northeastern part of the Indian subcontinent, and died at the age of 80 (483 BCE) in Kushinagar, India.

It is pertinent to note that the above narrative draws on the early scriptures. However, later texts, such as the Mahayana *Lalitavistara Sutra*, give different accounts. Scholars are hesitant to make unqualified claims about the historical facts of the Buddha's life. Most accept that he lived, taught and founded a monastic order but do not consistently accept the details in his biographies.

According to Michael Carrithers, while there are good reasons to doubt the traditional account, "the outline of the life must be true: birth, maturity, renunciation, search, awakening and liberation, teaching, death." In writing her biography of Buddha, Karen Armstrong noted, "It is obviously difficult, therefore, to write a biography of the Buddha that will meet modern criteria, because we have very little information that can be considered historically sound... [but] we can be reasonably confident Siddhartha Gotama did indeed exist and that his disciples preserved the memory of his life and teachings as well as they could."

Major Concepts

Karma (Action): Karma in Buddhism is the force that drives sansâra—the cycle of suffering and rebirth for each being. Good, skillful deeds ("kusala") and bad, unskillful ("akusala") actions produce "seeds" in the mind which come to fruition either in this life or in a subsequent rebirth. The avoidance of unwholesome actions and the cultivation of positive actions is called shîla (from Sanskrit: "ethical conduct"). In Buddhism, karma specifically refers to those actions (of body, speech, and mind) that spring from mental intent ("cetana"), and which bring about a consequence (or fruit, "phala") or result ("vipâka").

Every time a person acts there is some quality of intention at the base of the mind and it is that quality rather than the outward appearance of the action that determines its effect.

Notably, in Theravada Buddhism there can be no divine salvation or forgiveness for one's karma, since it is a purely impersonal process that is a part of the make up of the universe. Some Mahayana traditions however hold different views. For example, the texts of certain Mahayana sutras (such as the *Lotus Sutra*, the *Angulimaliya Sutra* and the *Nirvana Sutra*) claim that reciting or merely hearing their texts can expunge great swathes of negative karma. In like fashion, some forms of Buddhism (e.g. Vajrayana) regard the recitation of mantras as a means for cutting off previous negative karma. Similarly, the Japanese Pure Land teacher Genshin taught that Amida Buddha has the power to destroy the karma that would otherwise bind one in sansara.

Rebirth: Rebirth refers to a process whereby beings go through a succession of lifetimes as one of many possible forms of sentient life, each running from conception to death. However, Buddhism rejects concepts of a permanent self or an unchanging, eternal soul, as it is called in Hinduism or even Christianity. As there ultimately is no such thing as a self (the doctrine of anatta) according to Buddhism, rebirth in subsequent existences must rather be understood as the continuation of a dynamic, ever-changing process of "dependent arising" ("pratîtyasamutpâda") determined by the laws of cause and effect (karma) rather than that of one being, transmigrating or incarnating from one existence to the next. Each rebirth takes place within one of five realms, according to Theravadins, or six according to other schools.

1. Naraka beings: those who live in one of many Narakas (Hells)

2. Animals: sharing some space with humans, but considered another type of life
3. Preta: sometimes sharing some space with humans, but invisible to most people; an important variety is the hungry ghost
4. Human beings: one of the realms of rebirth in which attaining Nirvana is possible
5. Asuras: variously translated as lowly deities, demons, titans, antigods; not recognized by Theravâda (Mahavihara) tradition as a separate realm.
6. Devas including Brahmas: variously translated as gods, deities, spirits, angels, or left untranslated

Remarkably, Rebirths in some of the higher heavens, known as the Úuddhâvâsa Worlds (Pure Abodes), can be attained only by skilled Buddhist practitioners known as anâgâmis (non-returners). Rebirths in the arupa-dhatu (formless realms) can be attained only by those who can meditate on the arûpajhânas, the highest object of meditation.

It is pertinent to note that to East Asian and Tibetan Buddhism, there is an intermediate state (Tibetan "Bardo") between one life and the next. The orthodox Theravada position rejects this; however there are passages in the *Samyutta Nikaya* of the Pali Canon (the collection of texts on which the Theravada tradition is based), that seem to lend support to the idea that the Buddha taught of an intermediate stage between one life and the next.

Sansara: Sentient beings crave pleasure and are averse to pain from birth to death. In being controlled by these attitudes, they perpetuate the cycle of conditioned existence and suffering (sansâra), and produce the causes and conditions of the next rebirth after death. Each rebirth repeats this process in an involuntary cycle, which Buddhists strive to end by eradicating these causes and conditions, applying the methods laid out by the Buddha and subsequent Buddhists.

The Four Noble Truths: According to the Pali Tipitaka, the Four Noble Truths were the first teaching of Gautama Buddha after attaining Nirvana. They are sometimes considered as containing the essence of the Buddha's teachings and are presented in the manner of a medical diagnosis and remedial prescription—a style common at that time:

1. Life as we know it ultimately is or leads to suffering/uneasiness (dukkha) in one way or another.
2. Suffering is caused by craving. This is often expressed as a deluded clinging to a certain sense of existence, to selfhood, or to the things or phenomena that we consider the cause of happiness or unhappiness. Craving also has its negative aspect, i.e. one craves that a certain state of affairs not exist.
3. Suffering ends when craving ends. This is achieved by eliminating delusion, thereby reaching a liberated state of Enlightenment (bodhi);
4. Reaching this liberated state is achieved by following the path laid out by the Buddha.

Notably, this method is described by early Western scholars, and taught as an introduction to Buddhism by some contemporary Mahayana teachers (e.g., the Dalai Lama). According to other interpretations by Buddhist teachers and scholars, lately recognized by some Western non-Buddhist scholars, the "truths" do not represent mere statements, but are categories or aspects that most worldly phenomena fall into.

1. Suffering and causes of suffering
2. Cessation and the paths towards liberation from suffering.
   1. "The noble truth that is suffering"
   2. "The noble truth that is the arising of suffering"
   3. "The noble truth that is the end of suffering"
4. "The noble truth that is the way leading to the end of suffering"

The early teaching and the traditional Theravada understanding is that the Four Noble Truths are an advanced teaching for those who are ready for them. The East Asian Mahayana position is that they are a preliminary teaching for people not yet ready for the higher and more expansive Mahayana teachings. They are little known in the Far East. However, within the Nalanda/Tibetan tradition of Mahayana Buddhism, the Four Noble Truths remain essential to the path.

Ashthamarga (The Noble Eightfold Path) the fourth of the Buddha's Noble Truths—is the way to the cessation of suffering (dukkha). It has eight sections, each starting with the word "samyak" (Sanskrit, meaning "correctly", "properly", or "well", frequently translated into English as "right"), and presented in three groups known as the three higher trainings.

- Prajñâ is the wisdom that purifies the mind, allowing it to attain spiritual insight into the true nature of all things. It includes:
  1. Drishti—viewing reality as it is, not just as it appears to be.
  2. Sankappa—intention of renunciation, freedom and harmlessness.

- Sîla is the ethics or morality, or abstention from unwholesome deeds. It includes:
  3. vac (vâca): speaking in a truthful and non-hurtful way
  4. karman: acting in a non-harmful way
  5. ajivana: a non-harmful livelihood.
- Samâdhi is the mental discipline required to develop mastery over one's own mind. This is done through the practice of various contemplative and meditative practices, and includes:
  6. Vâyâma: making an effort to improve
  7. Smriti: awareness to see things for what they are with clear consciousness, being aware of the present reality within oneself, without any craving or aversion
  8. Samadhi: correct meditation or concentration, explained as the first four jnânas.

The practice of the Eightfold Path is understood in two ways, as requiring either simultaneous development (all eight items practiced in parallel), or as a progressive series of stages through which the practitioner moves, the culmination of one leading to the beginning of another.

Madhya Marga

An important guiding principle of Buddhist practice is the Middle Way (or Middle Path), which is said to have been discovered by Gautama Buddha prior to his enlightenment. The Middle Way has several definitions:

1. The practice of non-extremism: a path of moderation away from the extremes of self-indulgence and self-mortification

2. The middle ground between certain metaphysical views (e.g., that things ultimately either do or do not exist)
3. An explanation of Nirvana (perfect enlightenment), a state wherein it becomes clear that all dualities apparent in the world are delusory (see Seongcheol)
4. Another term for emptiness, the ultimate nature of all phenomena (in the Mahayana branch), a lack of inherent existence, which avoids the extremes of permanence and nihilism or inherent existence and nothingness.

It is pertinent to note that Buddhist scholars have produced a remarkable quantity of intellectual theories, philosophies and world view concepts (see, e.g., Abhidharma, Buddhist philosophy and Reality in Buddhism). Some schools of Buddhism discourage doctrinal study, some regard it as essential, but most regard it as having a place, at least for some persons at some stages in Buddhist practice. In the earliest Buddhist teachings, shared to some extent by all extant schools, the concept of liberation (Nirvana)—the goal of the Buddhist path—is closely related to the correct understanding of how the mind causes stress. In awakening to the true nature of clinging, one develops dispassion for the objects of clinging, and is liberated from suffering (dukkha) and the cycle of incessant rebirths. To this end, the Buddha recommended viewing things as characterized by the three marks of existence.

On Existence

Anicca is one of the three marks of existence. The term expresses the Buddhist notion that all compounded or conditioned phenomena (all things and experiences) are inconstant, unsteady, and impermanent. Everything we can experience through our senses is made up of parts, and its existence is dependent on external conditions. Everything is in constant flux, and so conditions and the thing itself are constantly changing. Things are constantly coming into being, and ceasing to be. Since nothing lasts, there is no inherent or fixed nature to any object or experience.

According to the impermanence doctrine, human life embodies this flux in the aging process, the cycle of rebirth (sansâra), and in any experience of loss. The doctrine further asserts that because things are impermanent, attachment to them is futile and leads to suffering (dukkha).

Again, Suffering or dukkha is a central concept in Buddhism, the word roughly corresponding to a number of terms in English including suffering, pain, unsatisfactoriness, sorrow, affliction, anxiety, dissatisfaction, discomfort, anguish, stress, misery, and frustration. Although dukkha is often translated as "suffering", its philosophical meaning is more analogous to "disquietude" as in the condition of being disturbed.

As such, "suffering" is too narrow a translation with "negative emotional connotations" which can give the impression that the Buddhist view is one of pessimism, but Buddhism seeks to be neither pessimistic nor optimistic, but realistic.

Thus in English-language Buddhist literature "dukkha" is often left untranslated, so as to encompass its full range of meaning. Anatta (Pâli) or anâtman (Sanskrit) refers to the notion of "not-self". Upon careful examination, one finds that no phenomenon is really "I" or "mine"; these concepts are in fact constructed by the mind. In the *Nikayas* anatta is not meant as a metaphysical assertion, but as an approach for gaining release from suffering.

In fact, the Buddha rejected both of the metaphysical assertions "I have a Self" and "I have no Self" as ontological views that bind one to suffering. When asked if the self was identical with the body, the Buddha refused to answer. By analyzing the constantly changing physical and mental constituents (skandhas) of a person or object, the practitioner comes to the conclusion that neither the respective parts nor the person as a whole comprise a self.

Further, the doctrine of pratîtyasamutpâda is an important part of Buddhist metaphysics. It states that phenomena arise together in a mutually interdependent web of cause and effect. It is variously rendered into English as "dependent origination", "conditioned genesis", "dependent co-arising", "interdependent arising", or "contingency". The best-known application of the concept of pratîtyasamutpâda is the scheme of Twelve Nidânas (from Pâli "nidâna" meaning "cause, foundation, source or origin"), which explain the continuation of the cycle of suffering and rebirth in detail.

The Twelve Nidânas describe a causal connection between the subsequent characteristics/conditions of cyclic existence, each giving rise to the next:

1. Avidyâ: ignorance, specifically spiritual
2. Sanskaras: literally formations, explained as referring to karma.
3. Vijñâna: consciousness, specifically discriminative
4. Nâmarûpa: literally name and form, referring to mind and body
5. baâyatana: the six sense bases: eye, ear, nose, tongue, body and mind-organ
6. Sparsha: variously translated contact, impression, stimulation (by a sense object)

7. Vedanâ: usually translated feeling: this is the "hedonic tone", i.e. whether something is pleasant, unpleasant or neutral
8. Trishna: literally thirst, but in Buddhism nearly always used to mean craving.
9. Upâdâna: clinging or grasping; the word also means fuel, which feeds the continuing cycle of rebirth
10. Bhava: literally being (existence) or becoming. (The Theravada explains this as having two meanings: karma, which produces a new existence, and the existence itself.)
11. Jâti: literally birth, but life is understood as starting at conception
12. Jarâmarasa: (old age and death) and also (sorrow, lamentation, pain, sadness, and misery).

Sentient beings always suffer throughout sansâra, until they free themselves from this suffering by attaining Nirvana. Then the absence of the first Nidâna—ignorance—leads to the absence of the others.

Mahayana Buddhism received significant theoretical grounding from Nagarjuna (perhaps c. 150–250 CE), arguably the most influential scholar within the Mahayana tradition. Nagarjuna's primary contribution to Buddhist philosophy was the systematic exposition of the concept of úûnyatâ, or "emptiness," widely attested in the *Prajñâpâramitâ* sutras which were emergent in his era. The concept of emptiness brings together other key Buddhist doctrines, particularly anatta and pratîtyasamutpâda (dependent origination), to refute the metaphysics of Sarvastivada and Sautrantika (extinct non-Mahayana schools).

For Nagarjuna, it is not merely sentient beings that are empty of âtman; all phenomena (dharmas) are without any svabhava (literally "own-nature" or "self-nature"), and thus without any underlying essence; they are "empty" of being independent; thus the heterodox theories of svabhava circulating at the time were refuted on the basis of the doctrines of early Buddhism. Nagarjuna's school of thought is known as the Mâdhyamaka. Some of the writings attributed to Nagarjuna made explicit references to Mahayana texts, but his philosophy was argued within the parameters set out by the agamas.

He may have arrived at his positions from a desire to achieve a consistent exegesis of the Buddha's doctrine as recorded in the Canon. In the eyes of Nagarjuna the Buddha was not merely a forerunner, but the very founder of the Mâdhyamaka system.

Sarvastivada teachings—which were criticized by Nâgârjuna—were reformulated by scholars such as Vasubandhu and Asanga and were adapted into the Yogachara (yoga practice) school. While the Mâdhyamaka school held that asserting the existence or non-existence of any ultimately real thing was inappropriate, some exponents of Yogacara asserted that the mind and only the mind is ultimately real (a doctrine known as cittamatra). Not all Yogacarins asserted that mind was truly existent; Vasubandhu and Asanga in particular did not. These two schools of thought, in opposition or synthesis, form the basis of subsequent Mahayana metaphysics in the Indo-Tibetan tradition.

Besides emptiness, Mahayana schools often place emphasis on the notions of perfected spiritual insight (prajñâpâramitâ) and Buddha-nature (tathâgatagarbha, meaning "Buddha embryo" or "Buddha-matrix"). According to the *Tathâgatagarbha Sutras*, the Buddha revealed the reality of the deathless Buddha-nature, which is said to be inherent in all sentient beings and enables them all eventually to reach complete enlightenment, i.e. Buddhahood. Buddha-nature is stated in the Mahayana *Angulimaliya Sutra* and *Mahaparinirvana Sutra* to not be úûnya, but to be replete with eternal Buddhic virtues. In the *Tathâgatagarbha Sutras* the Buddha is portrayed proclaiming that the teaching of the tathâgatagarbha constitutes the "absolutely final culmination" of his Dharma—the highest presentation of truth (other sûtras make similar statements about other teachings) and it has traditionally been regarded as the highest teaching in East Asian Buddhism. However, in modern China all doctrines are regarded as equally valid. The Mahayana can also on occasion communicate a vision of the Buddha or Dharma which amounts to mysticism and gives expression to a form of mentalist panentheism.

Buddhist Epistemology

Decisive in distinguishing Buddhism from other schools of Indian philosophy is the issue of epistemological justification. While all schools of Indian logic recognize various sets of valid justifications for knowledge (pramana) Buddhism recognizes a smaller set than do the others. All accept perception and inference, for example, but for some schools of Buddhism the received textual tradition is an equally valid epistemological category. According to the scriptures, during his lifetime the Buddha remained silent when asked several metaphysical questions.

These regarded issues such as whether the universe is eternal or non-eternal (or whether it is finite or infinite), the unity or separation of the body and the self, the complete inexistence of a person after Nirvana and death, and others. One explanation for this silence is that such questions distract from activity that is practical to realizing enlightenment and bring about the danger of substituting the experience of liberation by conceptual understanding of the doctrine or by religious faith.

Another explanation is that both affirmative and negative positions regarding these questions are based on attachment to and misunderstanding of the aggregates and senses. That is, when one sees these things for what they are, the idea of forming positions on such metaphysical questions simply does not occur to one. Another closely related explanation is that reality is devoid of designations, or empty, and therefore language itself is *a priori* inadequate.

Thus, the Buddha's silence does not indicate misology or disdain for philosophy. Rather, it indicates that he viewed these questions as not leading to true knowledge. Dependent arising provides a framework for analysis of reality that is not based on metaphysical assumptions regarding existence or non-existence, but instead on direct cognition of phenomena as they are presented to the mind. This informs and supports the Buddhist approach to liberation via the Noble Eightfold Path.

The Buddha of the earliest Buddhists texts describes Dharma (in the sense of "truth") as "beyond reasoning" or "transcending logic", in the sense that reasoning is a subjectively introduced aspect of the way humans perceive things, and the conceptual framework which underpins it is a part of the cognitive process, rather than a feature of things as they really are. Being "beyond reasoning" means in this context penetrating the nature of reasoning from the inside, and removing the causes for experiencing any future stress as a result of it, rather than functioning outside of the system as a whole.

Most Buddhists agree that, to a greater or lesser extent, words are inadequate to describe the goal of the Buddhist path, but concerning the usefulness of words in the path itself, schools differ radically.

In the Mahayana *Mahaparinirvana Sutra*, the Buddha insists that while pondering upon Dharma is vital, one must then relinquish fixation on words and letters, as these are utterly divorced from liberation and the Buddha-nature. The Tibetan tantra entitled the "All-Creating King" (*Kunjed Gyalpo Tantra*) also emphasizes how Buddhist truth lies beyond the range of discursive/verbal thought and is ultimately mysterious.

Samantabhadra, states there: "The mind of perfect purity ... is beyond thinking and inexplicable..." Also later, the famous Indian Buddhist practitioner and teacher, mahasiddha Tilopa discouraged any intellectual activity in his six words of advice.

C.D. Sebastian describes the nature of enlightenment according to one Mahayana text:

> *Bodhi* is the final goal of a Bodhisattva's career and it is indicated by such words as *buddha-jnana* (knowledge of Buddha), *sarvjnata* (omniscience), *sarvakarajnata* (the quality of knowing things as they are), ... and *acintyam jnanam* (inconceivable knowledge) ... *Bodhi* is pure universal and immediate knowledge, which extends over all time, all universes, all beings and elements, conditioned and unconditioned. It is absolute and identical with Reality and thus it is *Tathata*. *Bodhi* is immaculate and non-conceptual, and it, being not an outer object, cannot be understood by discursive thought. It has neither beginning, nor middle nor end and it is indivisbile. It is non-dual

> (*advayam*)... The only possible way to comprehend it is through *samadhi* by the yogin.

The early texts, in contrast, contain explicit repudiations of attributing omniscience to the Buddha. Furthermore, the non-duality ascribed to the nature of enlightenment in the early texts is not ontological.

Mahayana often adopts a pragmatic concept of truth: doctrines are "true" in the sense of being spiritually beneficial. In modern Chinese Buddhism, all doctrinal traditions are regarded as equally valid.

Theravada promotes the concept of vibhajjavada (Pâli, literally "Teaching of Analysis") to non-Buddhists. This doctrine says that insight must come from the aspirant's experience, critical investigation, and reasoning instead of by blind faith.

As the Buddha said according to the canonical scriptures:

> Do not accept anything by mere tradition ... Do not accept anything just because it accords with your scriptures ... Do not accept anything merely because it agrees with your pre-conceived notions ... But when you know for yourselves—these things are moral, these things are blameless, these things are praised by the wise, these things, when performed and undertaken, conduce to well-being and happiness—then do you live acting accordingly.

Liberation (Nirvana)

Nirvana means "cessation", "extinction" (of craving and ignorance and therefore suffering and the cycle of involuntary rebirths, "extinguished", "quieted", "calmed"; it is also known as "Awakening" or "Enlightenment" in the West. The term for anybody who has achieved *nirvana*, including the Buddha, is *arahant*.

Bodhi is a term applied to the experience of Awakening of arahants. *Bodhi* literally means "awakening", but it is more commonly translated into English as "enlightenment". In Early Buddhism, *bodhi* carried a meaning synonymous to *nirvana,* using only some different metaphors to describe the experience, which implies the extinction of *raga* (greed, craving), *dosa* (hate, aversion) and *moha* (delusion).

In the later school of Mahayana Buddhism, the status of *nirvana* was downgraded in some scriptures, coming to refer only to the extinction of greed and hate, implying that delusion was still present in one who attained *nirvana,* and that one needed to attain *bodhi* to eradicate delusion:

Therefore, according to Mahayana Buddhism, the *arahant* has attained only *nirvana,* thus still being subject to delusion, while the *bodhisattva* not only achieves *nirvana* but full liberation from delusion as well. He thus attains *bodhi* and becomes a *buddha.* In Theravada Buddhism, *bodhi* and *nirvana* carry the same meaning as in the early texts, that of being freed from greed, hate and delusion.

The term *parinirvana* is also encountered in Buddhism, and this generally refers to the complete *nirvana* attained by the *arhat* at the moment of death, when the physical body expires.

In Theravada doctrine, a person may awaken from the "sleep of ignorance" by directly realizing the true nature of reality; such people are called *arahants* and occasionally *buddhas.* After numerous lifetimes of spiritual striving, they have reached the end of the cycle of rebirth, no longer reincarnating as human, animal, ghost, or other being.

TYPES OF AWAKENED BEINGS

- *Sammasambuddha,* usually just called Buddha, who discovers the truth by himself and teaches the path to awakening to others
- *Paccekabuddha,* who discovers the truth by himself but lacks the skill to teach others
- *Savakabuddha,* who receive the truth directly or indirectly from a Sammasambuddha

Bodhi and *nirvana* carry the same meaning, that of being freed from craving, hate, and delusion. In attaining *bodhi,* the *arahant* has overcome these obstacles. As a further distinction, the extinction of only hatred and greed (in the sensory context) with some residue of delusion, is called *anagami.*

Mahayana

In the Mahayana, the Buddha tends not to be viewed as merely human, but as the earthly projection of a beginningless and endless, omnipresent being beyond the range and reach of thought. Moreover, in certain Mahayana sutras, the Buddha, Dharma and Sangha are viewed essentially as One: all three are seen as the eternal Buddha himself.

Celestial Buddhas are individuals who no longer exist on the material plane of existence, but who still aid in the enlightenment of all beings.

Nirvana came to refer only to the extinction of greed and hate, implying that delusion was still present in one who attained Nirvana. Bodhi became a higher attainment that eradicates delusion entirely. Thus, the *Arahant* attains Nirvana but not Bodhi, thus still being subject to delusion, while the Buddha attains Bodhi.

The method of self-exertion or "self-power"—without reliance on an external force or being—stands in contrast to another major form of Buddhism, Pure Land, which is characterised by utmost trust in the salvific "other-power" of Amitabha Buddha. Pure Land Buddhism is a very widespread and perhaps the most faith-orientated manifestation of Buddhism and centres upon the conviction that faith in Amitabha Buddha and the chanting of homage to his name will liberate one at death into the "happy land" or "pure land" of Amitabha Buddha. This Buddhic realm is variously construed as a foretaste of Nirvana, or as essentially Nirvana itself. The great vow of Amitabha Buddha to rescue all beings from samsaric suffering is viewed within Pure Land Buddhism as universally efficacious, if only one has faith in the power of that vow or chants his name.

Nearly all Chinese Buddhists accept that the chances of attaining sufficient enlightenment by one's own efforts are very slim, so that Pure Land practice is essential as an "insurance policy" even if one practises something else.

Buddha Eras

According to popular belief of the Buddhists Gautama Buddha was the first to achieve enlightenment in this Buddha era and is therefore credited with the establishment of Buddhism. A Buddha era is the stretch of history during which people remember and practice the teachings of the earliest *known* Buddha. This Buddha era will end when all the knowledge, evidence and teachings of Gautama Buddha have vanished. This belief therefore maintains that many Buddha eras have started and ended throughout the course of human existence.

The Gautama Buddha, then, is *the Buddha of this era*, who taught directly or indirectly to all other Buddhas in it.

In addition, Mahayana Buddhists believe there are innumerable other Buddhas in other universes. A Theravada commentary says that Buddhas arise one at a time in this world element, and not at all in others.

The idea of the decline and gradual disappearance of the teaching has been influential in East Asian Buddhism. Pure Land Buddhism holds that it has declined to the point where few, if any, are capable of following the path, so most or all must rely on the power of the Buddha Amitabha. Zen and Nichiren traditionally hold that most are incapable of following the "complicated" paths of some other schools and present what they view as a simple practice instead.

Bodhisattvas

Mahayana Buddhism puts great emphasis and, in fact, encourages anybody to follow the path of a Bodhisattva.

Bodhisattva means either "enlightened (bodhi) existence (sattva)" or "enlightenment-being" or, given the variant Sanskrit spelling *satva* rather than *sattva*, "heroic-minded one (satva) for enlightenment (bodhi)". Another translation is "Wisdom-Being".

The various divisions of Buddhism understand the word Bodhisattva in different ways. Theravada and some Mahayana sources consider a Bodhisattva as someone on the path to Buddhahood, while other Mahayana sources speak of Bodhisattvas renouncing Buddhahood, but especially in Mahayana Buddhism, it mainly refers to a being that compassionately refrains from entering nirvana in order to save others. So the Bodhisattva is a person who already has a considerable degree of enlightenment and seeks to use their wisdom to help other sentient beings to become liberated themselves.

While Theravada regards it as an option, Mahayana encourages everyone to follow a Bodhisattva path and to take the Bodhisattva vows. With these vows, one makes the promise to work for the complete enlightenment of all sentient beings.

A famous saying by the 8th-century Indian Buddhist scholar-saint Shantideva, which the 14th Dalai Lama often cites as his favourite verse, summarizes the Bodhisattva's intention (Bodhicitta) as follows: "For as long as space endures, and for as long as living beings remain, until then may I too abide to dispel the misery of the world." According to the Mahayana, a Bodhisattva practices in the six perfections: giving, morality, patience, joyous effort, concentration and wisdom.

Buddhism in Practice

Devotion: Devotion is an important part of the practice of most Buddhists. Devotional practices include bowing, offerings, pilgrimage, and chanting. In Pure Land Buddhism, devotion to the Buddha Amitabha is the main practice. In Nichiren Buddhism, devotion to the Lotus Sutra is the main practice.

Refuge in the Three Jewels: Traditionally, the first step in most Buddhist schools requires taking refuge in the Three Jewels (Sanskrit: *tri-ratna*, Pâli: *ti-ratana*) as the foundation of one's religious practice. The practice of taking refuge on behalf of young or even unborn children is mentioned in the *Majjhima Nikaya,* recognized by most scholars as an early text (cf. Infant baptism). Tibetan Buddhism sometimes adds a fourth refuge, in the *lama*. In Mahayana, the person who chooses the *bodhisattva* path makes a vow or pledge, considered the ultimate expression of compassion. In Mahayana, too, the Three Jewels are perceived as possessed of an eternal and unchanging essence and as having an irreversible effect: "The Three Jewels have the quality of excellence. Just as real jewels never change their faculty and goodness, whether praised or reviled, so are the Three Jewels (Refuges), because they have an eternal and immutable essence. These Three Jewels bring a fruition that is changeless, for once one has reached Buddhahood, there is no possibility of falling back to suffering."

THREE JEWELS

- The Buddha. This is a title for those who have attained Nirvana. See also the Tathâgata and Gautama Buddha. The Buddha could also be represented as a concept instead of a specific person: the perfect wisdom that understands *Dharma* and sees reality in its true form. In Mahayana Buddhism, the Buddha can be viewed as the supreme Refuge: "Buddha is the Unique Absolute Refuge. Buddha is the Imperishable, Eternal, Indestructible and Absolute Refuge."
- The *Dharma*. The teachings or law of nature as expounded by the Gautama Buddha. It can also, especially in Mahayana, connote the ultimate and sustaining Reality which is inseparable from the Buddha. Further, from some Mahayana perspectives, the Dharma embodied in the form of a great sutra (Buddhic scripture) can replace the need for a personal teacher and can be a direct and spontaneous gateway into Truth (Dharma). This is especially said to be the case with the Lotus Sutra. Dr. Hiroshi Kanno writes of this view of the *Lotus Sutra*: "it is a Dharma-gate of sudden enlightenment proper to the Great Vehicle; it is a Dharma-gate whereby one awakens spontaneously, without resorting to a teacher".
- The *Sangha*. Those who have attained to any of the Four stages of enlightenment, or simply the congregation of monastic practitioners.

According to the scriptures, Gautama Buddha presented himself as a model. The Dharma offers a refuge by providing guidelines for the alleviation of suffering and the attainment of Nirvana. The Sangha is considered to provide a refuge by preserving the authentic teachings of the Buddha and providing further examples that the truth of the Buddha's teachings is attainable.

Ethics

Sîla (Sanskrit) or *sîla* (Pâli) is usually translated into English as "virtuous behavior", "morality", "ethics" or "precept". It is an action committed through the body, speech, or mind, and involves an intentional effort. It is one of the *three practices* (*sila*, *samadhi*, and *panya*) and the second *pâramitâ*. It refers to moral purity of thought, word, and deed. The four conditions of *úîla* are chastity, calmness, quiet, and extinguishment.

Sîla is the foundation of *Samadhi / Bhâvana* (Meditative cultivation) or mind cultivation. Keeping the precepts promotes not only the peace of mind of the cultivator, which is internal, but also peace in the community, which is external. According to the Law of Karma, keeping the precepts are meritorious and it acts as causes which would bring about peaceful and happy effects. Keeping these precepts keeps the cultivator from rebirth in the four woeful realms of existence.

Sîla refers to overall principles of ethical behavior. There are several levels of *sila*, which correspond to "basic morality" (five precepts), "basic morality with asceticism" (eight precepts), "novice monkhood" (ten precepts) and "monkhood" (*Vinaya* or *Patimokkha*). Lay people generally undertake to live by the five precepts, which are common to all Buddhist schools. If they wish, they can choose to undertake the eight precepts, which add basic asceticism.

PRECEPTS FOR MEDITATION

1. To refrain from taking life (non-violence towards sentient life forms), or *ahimsâ*
2. To refrain from taking that which is not given (not committing theft)
3. To refrain from sensual (including sexual) misconduct
4. To refrain from lying (speaking truth always)
5. To refrain from intoxicants which lead to loss of mindfulness (specifically, drugs and alcohol)

The precepts are not formulated as imperatives, but as training rules that laypeople undertake voluntarily to facilitate practice. In Buddhist thought, the cultivation of dana and ethical conduct will themselves refine consciousness to such a level that rebirth in one of the lower heavens is likely, even if there is no further Buddhist practice. There is nothing improper or un-Buddhist about limiting one's aims to this level of attainment.

In the eight precepts, the third precept on sexual misconduct is made more strict, and becomes a precept of celibacy. The three additional precepts are:

6. To refrain from eating at the wrong time (only eat from sunrise to noon)
7. To refrain from dancing and playing music, wearing jewelry and cosmetics, attending shows and other performances
8. To refrain from using high or luxurious seats and bedding

The complete list of ten precepts may be observed by laypeople for short periods. For the complete list, the seventh precept is partitioned into two, and a tenth added:

6. To refrain from taking food at an unseasonable time, that is after the mid-day meal
7. To refrain from dancing, music, singing and unseemly shows
8. To refrain from the use of garlands, perfumes, ointments, and from things that tend to beautify and adorn (the person)
9. To refrain from (using) high and luxurious seats (and beds)
10. To refrain from accepting gold and silver

Monastic Life: Vinaya is the specific moral code for monks and nuns. It includes the Patimokkha, a set of 227 rules for monks in the Theravadin recension. The precise content of the vinayapitaka (scriptures on Vinaya) differ slightly according to different schools, and different schools or subschools set different standards for the degree of adherence to Vinaya. Novice-monks use the ten precepts, which are the basic precepts for monastics.

Regarding the monastic rules, the Buddha constantly reminds his hearers that it is the spirit that counts. On the other hand, the rules themselves are designed to assure a satisfying life, and provide a perfect springboard for the higher attainments. Monastics are instructed by the Buddha to live as "islands unto themselves". In this sense, living life as the vinaya prescribes it is, as one scholar puts it: "more than merely a means to an end: it is very nearly the end in itself."

In Eastern Buddhism, there is also a distinctive Vinaya and ethics contained within the Mahayana Brahmajala Sutra (not to be confused with the Pali text of that name) for Bodhisattvas, where, for example, the eating of meat is frowned upon and vegetarianism is actively encouraged (see *vegetarianism in Buddhism*). In Japan, this has almost completely displaced the monastic vinaya, and allows clergy to marry.

Meditation

Buddhist meditation is fundamentally concerned with two themes: transforming the mind and using it to explore itself and other phenomena. According to Theravada Buddhism the Buddha taught two types of meditation, *samatha* meditation (Sanskrit: *samatha*) and *vipassanâ* meditation. In Chinese Buddhism, these exist (translated *chih kuan*), but Chan (Zen) meditation is more popular. According to Peter Harvey, whenever Buddhism has been healthy, not only monks, nuns, and married lamas, but also more committed lay people have practiced meditation. According to Routledge's Encyclopedia of Buddhism, in contrast, throughout most of Buddhist history before modern times, serious meditation by lay people has been unusual. The evidence of the early texts suggests that at the time of the Buddha, many male and female lay practitioners did practice meditation, some even to the point of proficiency in all eight jhânas.

Samâdhi (Meditative Cultivation)

In the language of the Noble Eightfold Path, *samyaksamâdhi* is "right concentration". The primary means of cultivating *samâdhi* is meditation. Upon development of *samâdhi*, one's mind becomes purified of defilement, calm, tranquil, and luminous.

Once the meditator achieves a strong and powerful concentration *(jhana, dhyana)*, his mind is ready to penetrate and gain insight (vipassanâ) into the ultimate nature of reality, eventually obtaining release from all suffering.

The cultivation of mindfulness is essential to mental concentration, which is needed to achieve insight.

Samatha Meditation starts from being mindful of an object or idea, which is expanded to one's body, mind and entire surroundings, leading to a state of total concentration and tranquility (*jhâna*) There are many variations in the style of meditation, from sitting cross-legged or kneeling to chanting or walking. The most common method of meditation is to concentrate on one's breath (anapanasati), because this practice can lead to both *samatha* and *vipassana*'.

In Buddhist practice, it is said that while *samatha* meditation can calm the mind, only *vipassanâ* meditation can reveal how the mind was disturbed to start with, which is what leads to knowledge (*jñâna*;) and understanding and thus can lead to *nirvâha*. When one is in jhana, all defilements are suppressed temporarily. Only understanding (*prajñâ* or *vipassana*) eradicates the defilements completely. Jhanas are also states which *Arahants* abide in order to rest.

In Theravâda Buddhism, the cause of human existence and suffering is identified as craving, which carries with it the various defilements. These various defilements are traditionally summed up as greed, hatred and delusion. These are believed to be deeply rooted afflictions of the mind that create suffering and stress. In order to be free from suffering and stress, these defilements need to be permanently uprooted through internal investigation, analyzing, experiencing, and understanding of the true nature of those defilements by using *jhâna*, a technique which is part of the Noble Eightfold Path. It will then lead the meditator to realize the Four Noble Truths, Enlightenment and *Nibbana*. Nibbana is the ultimate goal of Theravadins.

Prajñâ (Wisdom)

Prajñâ means wisdom that is based on a realization of dependent origination, The Four Noble Truths and the three marks of existence. *Prajñâ* is the wisdom that is able to extinguish afflictions and bring about *bodhi*. It is spoken of as the principal means of attaining through its revelation of the true nature of all things as *dukkha* (unsatisfactoriness), *anicca* (impermanence) and *anatta* (not-self). *Prajñâ* is also listed as the sixth of the six *pâramitâs* of the Mahayana.

Initially, *prajñâ* is attained at a conceptual level by means of listening to sermons (dharma talks), reading, studying, and sometimes reciting Buddhist texts and engaging in discourse. Once the conceptual understanding is attained, it is applied to daily life so that each Buddhist can verify the truth of the Buddha's teaching at a practical level. Notably, one could in theory attain Nirvana at any point of practice, whether deep in meditation, listening to a sermon, conducting the business of one's daily life, or any other activity.

Zen

Zen Buddhism, pronounced *chán* in Chinese, *seon* in Korean or *zen* in Japanese (derived from the Sanskrit term *dhyâna*, meaning "meditation") is a form of Buddhism that became popular in China, Korea and Japan and that lays special emphasis on meditation. Zen places less emphasis on scriptures than some other forms of Buddhism and prefers to focus on direct spiritual breakthroughs to truth.

Zen Buddhism is divided into two main schools: Rinzai and Soto the former greatly favouring the use in meditation on the koan , as a device for spiritual break-through, and the latter (while certainly employing koans) focusing more on *shikantaza* or "just sitting".

Zen Buddhist teaching is often full of paradox, in order to loosen the grip of the ego and to facilitate the penetration into the realm of the True Self or Formless Self, which is equated with the Buddha himself. According to Zen master, Kosho Uchiyama, when thoughts and fixation on the little 'I' are transcended, an Awakening to a universal, non-dual Self occurs: ' When we let go of thoughts and wake up to the reality of life that is working beyond them, we discover the Self that is living universal non-dual life (before the separation into two) that pervades all living creatures and all existence.'. Thinking and thought must therefore not be allowed to confine and bind one. Nevertheless, Zen does not neglect the scriptures.

Vajrayana and Tantra

Though based upon Mahayana, Tibeto-Mongolian Buddhism is one of the schools that practice *Vajrayâna* or "Diamond Vehicle" (also referred to as Mantrayâna, Tantrayâna, Tantric Buddhism, or esoteric Buddhism). It accepts all the basic concepts of Mahâyâna, but also includes a vast array of spiritual and physical techniques designed to enhance Buddhist practice.

Tantric Buddhism is largely concerned with ritual and meditative practices. One component of the Vajrayâna is harnessing psycho-physical energy through ritual, visualization, physical exercises, and meditation as a means of developing the mind. Using these techniques, it is claimed that a practitioner can achieve Buddhahood in one lifetime, or even as little as three years. In the Tibetan tradition, these practices can include sexual yoga, though only for some very advanced practitioners.

Philosophical Roots

Historically, the roots of Buddhism lie in the religious

thought of Ancient India during the second half of the first millennium BC. That was a period of social and religious turmoil, as there was significant discontent with the sacrifices and rituals of Vedic Brahmanism. It was challenged by numerous new ascetic religious and philosophical groups and teachings that broke with the Brahmanic tradition and rejected the authority of the Vedas and the Brahmans.

These groups, whose members were known as shramanas, were a continuation of a non-Vedic strand of Indian thought distinct from Indo-Aryan Brahmanism. Scholars have reasons to believe that ideas such as samsara, karma (in the sense of the influence of morality on rebirth), and moksha originated in the shramanas, and were later adopted by Brahmin orthodoxy. At the same time, they were influenced by, and in some respects continued, earlier philosophical thought within the Vedic tradition as reflected e.g. in the Upanishads.

These movements included, besides Buddhism, various skeptics (such as Sanjaya Belatthiputta), atomists (such as Pakudha Kaccayana), materialists (such as Ajita Kesakambali), antinomians (such as Purana Kassapa); the most important ones in the 5th century BC were the Ajivikas, who emphasized the rule of fate, the Lokayata (materialists), the Ajnanas (agnostics) and the Jains, who stressed that the soul must be freed from matter. Many of these new movements shared the same conceptual vocabulary - atman ("Self"), buddha ("awakened one"), dhamma ("rule" or "law"), karma ("action"), nirvana ("extinguishing"), samsara ("eternal recurrence") and yoga ("spiritual practice").

The shramanas rejected the Veda, and the authority of the brahmans, who claimed to be in possession of revealed truths not knowable by any ordinary human means; moreover, they declared that the entire Brahmanical system was fraudulent: a conspiracy of the brahmans to enrich themselves by charging exorbitant fees for the performance of bogus rites and the giving of futile advice. A particular criticism of the Buddha's was Vedic animal sacrifice. Their leaders, including Buddha, were often known as œramaGas. The Buddha declared that priests reciting the Vedas were like blind leading the blind. According to him, those priests who had memorized the Vedas really knew nothing. He also mocked the Vedic "hymn of the cosmic man".

He declared that the primary goal of Upanishadic thought, the Atman, was in fact non-existent, , and, having explained that Brahminical attempts to achieve liberation at death were futile, proposed his new idea of liberation in life. At the same time, the traditional Brahminical religion itself gradually underwent profound changes, transforming it into what is recognized as early Hinduism. In particular, the brahmans thus developed "philosophical systems of their own, meeting the new ideas with adaptations of their doctrines".

Indian Buddhism

The history of Indian Buddhism may be divided into five periods: Early Buddhism (occasionally called Pre-sectarian Buddhism), Nikaya Buddhism or Sectarian Buddhism: The period of the Early Buddhist schools, Early Mahayana Buddhism, Later Mahayana Buddhism, and Esoteric Buddhism (also called Vajrayana Buddhism).

Pre-Sectarian: Pre-sectarian Buddhism is the earliest phase of Buddhism, recognized by nearly all scholars. Its main scriptures are the Vinaya Pitaka and the four principal Nikayas or Agamas. Certain basic teachings appear in many places throughout the early texts, so most scholars conclude that Gautama Buddha must have taught something similar to the Three marks of existence, the Five aggregates,

Dependent origination, Karma and Rebirth, the Four Noble Truths, the Noble Eightfold Path, and Nirvana. Some scholars disagree, and have proposed many other theories.

Early Buddhist Schools

According to the scriptures, soon after the parinirvGa (from Sanskrit: "highest extinguishment") of Gautama Buddha, the first Buddhist council was held. As with any ancient Indian tradition, transmission of teaching was done orally. The primary purpose of the assembly was to collectively recite the teachings to ensure that no errors occurred in oral transmission. In the first council, Ânanda, a cousin of the Buddha and his personal attendant, was called upon to recite the discourses (*sûtras*, Pâli *sutta*s) of the Buddha, and, according to some sources, the abhidhamma. Upâli, another disciple, recited the monastic rules (*vinaya*). Scholars regard the traditional accounts of the council as greatly exaggerated if not entirely fictitious.

According to most scholars, at some period after the Second Council the *Sangha* began to break into separate factions. The various accounts differ as to when the actual schisms occurred. According to the *Dipavamsa* of the Pâli tradition, they started immediately after the Second Council, the Puggalavada tradition places it in 137 AN, the Sarvastivada tradition of Vasumitra says it was in the time of Asoka and the Mahasanghika tradition places it much later, nearly 100 BCE.

The root schism was between the Sthaviras and the MahâsâEghikas. The fortunate survival of accounts from both sides of the dispute reveals disparate traditions. The Sthavira group offers two quite distinct reasons for the schism. The Dipavamsa of the Theravâda says that the losing party in the Second Council dispute broke away in protest and formed the Mahasanghika. This contradicts the Mahasanghikas' own *vinaya*, which shows them as on the same, winning side. The MahâsâEghikas argued that the Sthaviras were trying to expand the *vinaya* and may also have challenged what they perceived to be excessive claims or inhumanly high criteria for arhatship. Both parties, therefore, appealed to tradition.

The Sthaviras gave rise to several schools, one of which was the Theravâda school. Originally, these schisms were caused by disputes over vinaya, and monks following different schools of thought seem to have lived happily together in the same monasteries, but eventually, by about 100 CE if not earlier, schisms were being caused by doctrinal disagreements too.

Following (or leading up to) the schisms, each SaEgha started to accumulate an Abhidharma, a detailed scholastic reworking of doctrinal material appearing in the Suttas, according to schematic classifications. These Abhidharma texts do not contain systematic philosophical treatises, but summaries or numerical lists. Scholars generally date these texts to around the 3rd century BCE, 100 to 200 years after the death of the Buddha. Therefore the seven Abhidharma works are generally claimed not to represent the words of the Buddha himself, but those of disciples and great scholars. Every school had its own version of the Adhidharma, with different theories and different texts. The different Adhidharmas of the various schools did not agree with each other. Scholars disagree on whether the Mahasanghika school had an Abhidhamma Pitaka or not.

Early Mahayana Buddhism

The period of Early Mahayana Buddhism concerns the origins of Mahayana and the contents of early Mahayana

Sutras. The development of the various Early Buddhist Schools and the arising of Mahayana were not always consecutive. For example, the early schools continued to exist alongside Mahayana.

The commonly expressed misconception that Mahayana started as a lay-inspired movement is based on a selective reading of a very tiny sample of extant Mahayana Sutra literature.

Currently scholars have moved away from this limited corpus, and have started to examine early Mahayana literature, which is very ascetic and expounds the ideal of the monks' life in the forest. A scholarly consensus about the origin of the Mahayana has not yet been reached, but it has been suggested that when Mahayana became popular, in the 5th century CE, it had become something it had previously objected to: a landed monastic institution with a lay orientation.

Prior to this, the movement may well have been either a marginalized ascetic group of monks living in the forest, or a group of conservatives embedded in mainstream, socially engaged early Buddhist monasteries. Most scholars conclude that Mahayana remained a marginal movement until the 5th century AD.

The earliest Mahayana Sutras are called the Proto-Mahayana Sutras such as the Ajitasena Sutra which contains a mixture of Mahayana and pre-Mahayana ideas. It occurs in a world where monasticism is the norm, which is typical of the Pali Suttas; there is none of the usual antagonism towards the followers of the Early Buddhist Schools or the notion of Arahantship, which is typical of many Mahayana Sutras such as the White Lotus, or Vimalakirti Nirdesha.

However, the sutra also has an Arahant seeing all the Buddha fields, it is said that reciting the name of the sutra will save beings from suffering and the hell realms, and a meditative practice is described which allows the practitioner to see with the eyes of a Buddha, and to receive teachings from them that are very much typical of Mahayana Sutras. Some early Mahayana Sutras are Ratnagunasamcayagatha and the Astasaharika.

Some scholars contend that the Mahayana sutras were mainly composed in the south of India, and that later the activity of writing additional scriptures was continued in the east and north of India.

Late Mahayana Buddhism

During the period of Late Mahayana Buddhism, four major types of thought developed: Madhyamaka, Yogacara, Tathagatagarbha, and Buddhist Logic as the last and most recent. In India, the two main philosophical schools of the Mahayana were the Madhyamaka and the later Yogacara. According to Dan Lusthaus, Madhyamaka and Yogacara have a great deal in common, and the commonality stems from early Buddhism. There were no great Indian teachers associated with tathagatagarbha thought.

Vajrayana (Esoteric Buddhism)

Scholarly research concerning Esoteric Buddhism is still in its early stages and has a number of problems which make research difficult:

1. Vajrayana Buddhism was influenced by Hinduism, and therefore the research has to include research on Hinduism as well.
2. The scriptures of Vajrayana have not yet been put in any kind of order.
3. Ritual has to be examined as well, not just doctrine.

The Early Development of Buddhism

Buddhism may have spread only slowly in India until the time of the Mauryan emperor Ashoka, who was a public supporter of the religion. The support of Ashoka and his descendants led to the construction of more stûpas (Buddhist religious memorials) and to efforts to spread Buddhism throughout the enlarged Maurya empire and even into neighboring lands—particularly to the Iranian-speaking regions of Afghanistan and Central Asia, beyond the Mauryas' northwest border, and to the island of Sri Lanka south of India. These two missions, in opposite directions, would ultimately lead, in the first case to the spread of Buddhism into China, and in the second case, to the emergence of Theravâda Buddhism and its spread from Sri Lanka to the coastal lands of Southeast Asia.

This period marks the first known spread of Buddhism beyond India. According to the edicts of Ashoka, emissaries were sent to various countries west of India in order to spread Buddhism (Dharma), particularly in eastern provinces of the neighboring Seleucid Empire, and even farther to Hellenistic kingdoms of the Mediterranean. This led, a century later, to the emergence of Greek-speaking Buddhist monarchs in the Indo-Greek Kingdom, and to the development of the Greco-Buddhist art of Gandhâra. During this period Buddhism was exposed to a variety of influences, from Persian and Greek civilization, and from changing trends in non-Buddhist Indian religions—themselves influenced by Buddhism. It is a matter of disagreement among scholars whether or not these emissaries were accompanied by Buddhist missionaries.

The Theravada school spread south from India in the 3rd century BC, to Sri Lanka and Thailand and Burma and later also Indonesia. The Dharmagupta school spread (also in 3rd century BC) north to Kashmir, Gandhara and Bactria (Afghanistan). In the 2nd century AD, Mahayana Sutras spread from that general area to China, and then to Korea and Japan, and were translated into Chinese. During the Indian period of Esoteric Buddhism (from 8th century onwards), Buddhism spread from India to Tibet and Mongolia.

Buddhism Today

By the late Middle Ages, Buddhism had become virtually extinct in India, and although it continued to exist in surrounding countries, its influence was no longer expanding. It is now again gaining strength in India and elsewhere. Estimates of the number of Buddhist followers by scholars range from 230 million to 500 million, with most around 350 million. Most scholars classify similar numbers of people under a category they call "Chinese folk" or "traditional" religion, an amalgam of various traditions that includes Buddhism.

Formal membership varies between communities, but basic lay adherence is often defined in terms of a traditional formula in which the practitioner takes refuge in The Three Jewels: the *Buddha*, the *Dharma* (the teachings of the Buddha), and the *Sangha* (the Buddhist community).

Estimates are uncertain for several reasons:

- difficulties in defining who counts as a Buddhist;
- syncretism among the Eastern religions. Buddhism is practiced by adherents alongside many other religious traditions- including Taoism, Confucianism, Shinto, traditional religions, shamanism, and animism- throughout East and Southeast Asia.
- difficulties in estimating the number of Buddhists

who do not have congregational memberships and often do not participate in public ceremonies;

- official policies on religion in several historically Buddhist countries that make accurate assessments of religious adherence more difficult; most notably China, Vietnam and North Korea. In many current and former Communist governments in Asia, government policies may discourage adherents from reporting their religious identity, or may encourage official counts to underestimate religious adherence.

According to one analysis, Buddhism is the fourth-largest religion in the world behind Christianity, Islam and Hinduism. The monks' order (Sangha), which began during the lifetime of the Buddha, is among the oldest organizations on earth.

- Theravâda Buddhism, using Pâli as its scriptural language, is the dominant form of Buddhism in Cambodia, Laos, Thailand, Sri Lanka, and Burma. The Dalit Buddhist movement in India (inspired by B. R. Ambedkar) also practices Theravada. Approximately 124 million adherents.
- East Asian forms of Mahayana Buddhism that use scriptures in Chinese are dominant in most of China, Japan, Korea, Taiwan, Singapore and Vietnam as well as within Chinese and Japanese communities within Indochina, Southeast Asia and the West. Approximately 185 million adherents.
- Tibetan Buddhism is found in Tibet, Bhutan, Mongolia, surrounding areas in India, China, Nepal, and the Russian Federation. Approximately 20 million adherents.

Most Buddhist groups in the West are at least nominally affiliated with one of these three traditions.

At the present time, the teachings of all three branches of Buddhism have spread throughout the world, and Buddhist texts are increasingly translated into local languages. While, in the West, Buddhism is often seen as exotic and progressive, in the East, Buddhism is regarded as familiar and traditional. Buddhists in Asia are frequently well organized and well funded. In a number of countries, it is recognized as an official religion and receives state support. In the West, Buddhism is recognized as one of the growing spiritual influences. Modern influences increasingly lead to new forms of Buddhism that significantly depart from traditional beliefs and practices.

Schools and Traditions

Buddhists generally classify themselves as either Theravada or Mahayana. This classification is also used by some scholars and is the one ordinarily used in the English language. An alternative scheme used by some scholars divides Buddhism into the following three traditions or geographical or cultural areas: Theravada, East Asian Buddhism and Tibetan Buddhism.

Some scholars use other schemes. Buddhists themselves have a variety of other schemes. Hinayana (literally "lesser vehicle") is used by Mahayana followers to name the family of early philosophical schools and traditions from which contemporary Theravada emerged, but as this term is rooted in the Mahayana viewpoint and can be considered derogatory, a variety of other terms are increasingly used instead, including Œrâvakayâna, Nikaya Buddhism, early Buddhist schools, sectarian Buddhism, conservative Buddhism, mainstream Buddhism and non-Mahayana Buddhism.

Not all traditions of Buddhism share the same

philosophical outlook, or treat the same concepts as central. Each tradition, however, does have its own core concepts, and some comparisons can be drawn between them.

Mahayana Buddhism shows a great deal of doctrinal variation and development over time, and even more variation in terms of practice. While there is much agreement on general principles, there is disagreement over which texts are more authoritative.

Despite differences among the Theravada and Mahayana schools there are, for example according to one Buddhist ecumenical organization, several concepts common to both major Buddhist branches:

- Both accept the Buddha as their teacher.
- Both accept the Middle way, Dependent origination, the Four Noble Truths, the Noble Eightfold Path and the Three marks of existence, in theory, though in practice these have little or no importance in some traditions.
- Both accept that members of the laity and of the sangha can pursue the path toward enlightenment (bodhi).
- Both consider buddhahood to be the highest attainment; however Theravadins consider the nirvana (nibbana to the Theravadins) attained by arahants as identical to that attained by the Buddha himself, as there is only one type of nirvana. According to Theravadins, a buddha is someone who has discovered the path all by himself and taught it to others.

Theravada School

Theravâda ("Doctrine of the Elders", or "Ancient

Doctrine") is the oldest surviving Buddhist school. It is relatively conservative, and *generally* closest to early Buddhism. This school is derived from the Vibhajjavâda grouping which emerged amongst the older Sthavira group at the time of the Third Buddhist Council (c. 250 BCE). This school gradually declined on the Indian subcontinent, but its branch in Sri Lanka and South East Asia continues to survive.

The Theravada school bases its practice and doctrine exclusively on the Pâli Canon and its commentaries. After being orally transmitted for a few centuries, its scriptures, the Pali Canon, were finally committed to writing in the last century BCE, in Sri Lanka, at what the Theravada usually reckon as the fourth council. It is also one of the first Buddhist schools to commit the complete set of its canon into writing. The Sutta collections and Vinaya texts of the Pâli Canon (and the corresponding texts in other versions of the Tripitaka), are generally considered by modern scholars to be the earliest Buddhist literature, and they are accepted as authentic in every branch of Buddhism.

Theravâda is primarily practiced today in Sri Lanka, Burma, Laos, Thailand, Cambodia as well as small portions of China, Vietnam, Malaysia and Bangladesh. It has a growing presence in Europe and America.

Mahayana School

Mahayana Buddhism flourished in India from the fifth century AD onwards, during the dynasty of the Guptas. Mahâyâna centres of learning were established, the most important one being the Nâlandâ University in north-eastern India.

Mahayana schools recognize all or part of the Mahayana Sutras. Some of these sutras became for Mahayanists a manifestation of the Buddha himself, and faith in and veneration of those texts are stated in some sutras (e.g. the Lotus Sutra and the Mahaparinirvana Sutra) to lay the foundations for the later attainment of Buddhahood itself.

Native Mahayana Buddhism is practiced today in China, Japan, Korea, Singapore, parts of Russia and most of Vietnam (also commonly referred to as "Eastern Buddhism"). The Buddhism practiced in Tibet, the Himalayan regions, and Mongolia is also Mahayana in origin, but will be discussed below under the heading of Vajrayana (also commonly referred to as "Northern Buddhism". There are a variety of strands in Eastern Buddhism, of which "the Pure Land school of Mahayana is the most widely practised today.". In most of this area however, they are fused into a single unified form of Buddhism. In Japan in particular, they form separate denominations with the five major ones being: Nichiren, peculiar to Japan; Pure Land; Shingon, a form of Vajrayana; Tendai; and Chan/Zen. In Korea, nearly all Buddhists belong to the Chogye school, which is officially Son (Zen), but with substantial elements from other traditions.

Vajrayana School

The Vajrayana school of Buddhism spread to China, Mongolia, and Tibet. In Tibet, Vajrayana has always been a main component of Tibetan Buddhism, while in China it formed a separate sect. However, Vajrayana Buddhism became extinct in China but survived in elements of Japan's Shingon and Tendai sects.

There are differing views as to just when Vajrayâna and its tantric practice started. In the Tibetan tradition, it is claimed that the historical Úâkyamuni Buddha taught tantra, but as these are esoteric teachings, they were passed on orally first and only written down long after the Buddha's other teachings. Nâlandâ University became a center for the development of Vajrayâna theory and continued as the source of leading-edge Vajrayâna practices up through the 11th century. These practices, scriptures and theories were transmitted to China, Tibet, Indochina and Southeast Asia. China generally received Indian transmission up to the 11th century including tantric practice, while a vast amount of what is considered to be Tibetan Buddhism (Vajrayâna) stems from the late (9th–12th century) Nâlandâ tradition.

In one of the first major contemporary academic treatises on the subject, Fairfield University professor Ronald M. Davidson argues that the rise of Vajrayana was in part a reaction to the changing political climate in India at the time. With the fall of the Gupta dynasty, in an increasingly fractious political environment, institutional Buddhism had difficulty attracting patronage, and the folk movement led by siddhas became more prominent. After perhaps two hundred years, it had begun to get integrated into the monastic establishment.

Vajrayana combined and developed a variety of elements, a number of which had already existed for centuries. In addition to the Mahâyâna scriptures, Vajrayâna Buddhists recognise a large body of Buddhist Tantras, some of which are also included in Chinese and Japanese collections of Buddhist literature, and versions of a few even in the Pali Canon.

Buddhist Texts

Buddhist scriptures and other texts exist in great variety. Different schools of Buddhism place varying levels of value on learning the various texts. Some schools venerate certain texts as religious objects in themselves, while others take a more scholastic approach. Buddhist scriptures are written in these languages: Pâli, Tibetan, Mongolian, Chinese, along with some texts that still exist in Sanskrit and Buddhist Hybrid Sanskrit.

Unlike many religions, Buddhism has no single central text that is universally referred to by all traditions. However, some scholars have referred to the Vinaya Pitaka and the first four Nikayas of the Sutta Pitaka as the common core of all Buddhist traditions. However, this could be considered misleading, as Mahâyâna considers these merely a preliminary, and not a core, teaching, the Tibetan Buddhists have not even translated most of the âgamas, though theoretically they recognize them, and they play no part in the religious life of either clergy or laity in China and Japan. Other scholars say there is no universally accepted common core. The size and complexity of the Buddhist canons have been seen by some (including Buddhist social reformer Babasaheb Ambedkar) as presenting barriers to the wider understanding of Buddhist philosophy.

The followers of Theravâda Buddhism take the scriptures known as the Pâli Canon as definitive and authoritative, while the followers of Mahâyâna Buddhism base their faith and philosophy primarily on the Mahâyâna sûtras and their own *vinaya*. The Pâli sutras, along with other, closely related scriptures, are known to the other schools as the *âgamas*.

Over the years, various attempts have been made to synthesize a single Buddhist text that can encompass all of the major principles of Buddhism. In the Theravada tradition, condensed 'study texts' were created that combined popular or influential scriptures into single volumes that could be studied by novice monks. Later in Sri Lanka, the Dhammapada was championed as a unifying scripture.

Dwight Goddard collected a sample of Buddhist scriptures, with the emphasis on Zen, along with other classics of Eastern philosophy, such as the Tao Te Ching, into his 'Buddhist Bible' in the 1920s. More recently, Dr. Babasaheb Ambedkar attempted to create a single, combined document of Buddhist principles in "The Buddha and His Dhamma". Other such efforts have persisted to present day, but currently there is no single text that represents all Buddhist traditions.

Pâli Tipitaka

The Pâli Tipitaka, which means "three baskets", refers to the *Vinaya Pitaka*, the *Sutta Pitaka*, and the *Abhidhamma Pitaka*. The *Vinaya Pitaka* contains disciplinary rules for the Buddhist monks and nuns, as well as explanations of why and how these rules were instituted, supporting material, and doctrinal clarification. The *Sutta Pitaka* contains discourses ascribed to Gautama Buddha. The *Abhidhamma Pitaka* contains material often described as systematic expositions of the Gautama Buddha's teachings.

The Pâli Tipitaka is the only early Tipitaka (Sanskrit: *Tripimaka*) to survive intact in its original language, but a number of early schools had their own recensions of the Tipitaka featuring much of the same material. We have portions of the Tipitakas of the Sârvâstivâda, Dharmaguptaka, Sammitya, MahâsaEghika, Kâúyapîya, and Mahîúâsaka schools, most of which survive in Chinese translation only. According to some sources, some early schools of Buddhism had five or seven pitakas.

According to the scriptures, soon after the death of the Buddha, the first Buddhist council was held; a monk named Mahâkâúyapa (Pâli: Mahâkassapa) presided. The goal of the council was to record the Buddha's teachings. Upâli recited the *vinaya*. Ânanda, the Buddha's personal attendant, was called upon to recite the dhamma. These became the basis of the Tripitaka. However, this record was initially transmitted orally in form of chanting, and was committed to text in the last century BCE. Both the sûtras and the *vinaya* of every Buddhist school contain a wide variety of elements including discourses on the Dharma, commentaries on other teachings, cosmological and cosmogonical texts, stories of the Gautama Buddha's previous lives, and various other subjects.

Much of the material in the Canon is not specifically "Theravadin", but is instead the collection of teachings that this school preserved from the early, non-sectarian body of teachings. According to Peter Harvey, it contains material which is at odds with later Theravadin orthodoxy. He states: "The Theravadins, then, may have *added* texts to the Canon for some time, but they do not appear to have tampered with what they already had from an earlier period."

Mahayana Sutras

The Mahayana sutras are a very broad genre of Buddhist scriptures that the Mahayana Buddhist tradition holds are original teachings of the Buddha. The adherents of Mahayana accept both the early teachings (including in this the Sarvastivada Abhidharma, which was criticized by Nagarjuna and is in fact opposed to early Buddhist thought) and the Mahayana sutras as authentic teachings of Gautama Buddha, and claim they were designed for different types of persons and different levels of spiritual understanding.

The Mahayana sutras often claim to articulate the Buddha's deeper, more advanced doctrines, reserved for those who follow the bodhisattva path. That path is explained as being built upon the motivation to liberate all living beings from unhappiness. Hence the name *Mahâyâna* (lit., *the Great Vehicle*).

According to Mahayana tradition, the Mahayana sutras were transmitted in secret, came from other Buddhas or Bodhisattvas, or were preserved in non-human worlds because human beings at the time couldn't understand them:

> Some of our sources maintain the authenticity of certain other texts not found in the canons of these schools (the early schools). These texts are those held genuine by the later school, not one of the eighteen, which arrogated to itself the title of Mahayana, 'Great Vehicle'. According to the Mahayana historians these texts were admittedly unknown to the early schools of Buddhists. However, they had all been promulgated by the Buddha. [The Buddha's] followers on earth, the sravakas ('pupils'), had not been sufficiently advanced to understand them, and hence were not given them to remember, but they were taught to various supernatural beings and then preserved in such places as the Dragon World.
>
> —*Indian Buddhism*

Approximately six hundred Mahayana sutras have survived in Sanskrit or in Chinese or Tibetan translations. In addition, East Asian Buddhism recognizes some sutras regarded by scholars to be of Chinese rather than Indian origin.

Generally, scholars conclude that the Mahayana scriptures were composed from the first century CE onwards: "Large numbers of Mahayana sutras were being composed in the period between the beginning of the common era and the fifth century." five centuries after the historical Gautama Buddha, with some of them having their roots in other scriptures, composed in the first century BCE. It was not until after the fifth century CE that the Mahayana sutras started to influence the behavior of mainstream Buddhists in India: "But outside of texts, at least in India, at exactly the same period, very different—in fact seemingly older—ideas and aspirations appear to be motivating actual behavior, and old and established Hinnayana groups appear to be the only ones that are patronized and supported." These texts were apparently not universally accepted among Indian Buddhists when they appeared; the pejorative label 'Hinayana' was applied by Mahayana supporters to those who rejected the Mahayana sutras.

Only the Theravada school does not include the Mahayana scriptures in its canon. As the modern Theravada school is descended from a branch of Buddhism that diverged and established itself in Sri Lanka prior to the emergence of the Mahayana texts, debate exists as to whether the Theravada were historically included in the 'hinayana' designation; in the modern era, this label is seen as in any case derogatory, and generally avoided.

REFERENCES

1. Armstrong, Karen (2001). *Buddha*. Penguin Books. p. 187.
2. Bechert, Heinz & Richard Gombrich (ed.) (1984). *The World of Buddhism*, Thames & Hudson.
3. Buswell, Robert E. (ed.) (2003). *Encyclopedia of Buddhism*. MacMillan Reference Books.
4. Coogan, Michael D. (ed.) (2003). *The Illustrated Guide to World Religions*. Oxford University Press.
5. Davidson, Ronald M. (2003). *Indian Esoteric Buddhism: A Social History of the Tantric Movement*. New York: Columbia University Press.
6. de Give, Bernard (2006). *Les rapports de l'Inde et de l'Occident des origines au règne d'Asoka*. Les Indes savants.

7. Donath, Dorothy C. (1971). *Buddhism for the West: Theravâda, Mahâyâna and Vajrayâna; a comprehensive review of Buddhist history, philosophy, and teachings from the time of the Buddha to the present day*. Julian Press.
8. Embree, Ainslie T. (ed.), Stephen N. Hay (ed.), Wm. Theodore de Bary (ed.), A.L. Bashram, R.N. Dandekar, Peter Hardy, J.B. Harrison, V. Raghavan, Royal Weiler, and Andrew Yarrow (1958; 2nd ed. 1988). *Sources of Indian Tradition: From the Beginning to 1800* (vol. 1). NY: Columbia U. Press.
9. Gethin, Rupert (1998). *Foundations of Buddhism*. Oxford University Press.
10. Gombrich, Richard F. (1988; 6th reprint, 2002). *Theravâda Buddhism: A Social History from Ancient Benares to Modern Colombo* (London: Routledge).
11. Harvey, Peter (1990). *An Introduction to Buddhism: Teachings, History and Practices*. Cambridge University Press.
12. Gunaratana, Bhante Henepoia (2002). *Mindfulness in Plain English*. Wisdom Publications. ISBN 0-86171-321-4. Also available on this websites: saigon.com urbandharma.org vipassana.com
13. Gyatso, Geshe Kelsang. *Introduction to Buddhism*: An Explanation of the Buddhist Way of Life, Tharpa Publications (2nd. ed., 2001, US ed. 2008)
14. Morgan, Kenneth W. (ed), *The Path of the Buddha: Buddhism Interpreted by Buddhists*, Ronald Press, New York, 1956; reprinted by Motilal Banarsidass, Delhi; distributed by Wisdom Books
15. Nattier, Jan (2003). *A Few Good Men: The Bodhisattva Path according to The Inquiry of Ugra (Ugrapariprccha)*. University of Hawai'i Press.
16. Robinson, Richard H. and Willard L. Johnson (1970; 3rd ed., 1982). *The Buddhist Religion: A Historical Introduction* (Belmont, CA: Wadsworth Publishing).
17. Sinha, H.P. (1993). *Bhâratîya Darshan kî rûprekhâ (Features of Indian Philosophy)*. Motilal Banarasidas Publ..
18. Thanissaro Bhikkhu (2001). *Refuge: An Introduction to the Buddha, Dhamma, & Sangha (3rd ed., rev.)*.

19. Thich Nhat Hanh (1974), *The Heart of the Buddha's Teaching*, Broadway Books

20. Thurman, Robert A. F. (translator) (1976). *Holy Teaching of Vimalakirti: Mahayana Scripture*. Pennsylvania State University Press.

2

Buddhism Through Ages

Here we intend to present the journey of Buddhism since birth of Lord Buddha, the proponent of Buddhism to the present day.

Here it is remarkable that some sources give the date of the Buddha's birth as 563 BCE and others as 624 BCE; Theravada Buddhist countries tend to use the latter figure. This displaces all the dates in the following table about 61 years further back.

Similarly, there is controversy about the base date of the Buddhist Era, with 544 BC and 483 BC being advanced as the date of the *parinibbana* of the Buddha.

THE CHRONOLOGY

Before Christian Era

- **563 BCE:** Siddhârtha Gautama, Buddha-to-be, is born in Lumbini into a leading royal family in the republic of the Shakyas, which is now part of Nepal.
- **534 BCE:** Prince Siddhartha goes outside the palace for the first time and sees The Four Sights: an old man, an ill man, a dead man, and a holy man. He is shocked by the first three—he did not know what

age, disease, and death were—but is inspired by the holy man to give up his wealth. He leaves his house and lives with three ascetics. However, he wants more than to starve himself, so he becomes a religious teacher.

- **528 BCE:** Siddhartha attains Enlightenment in Buddha Gaya (modern-day Bodhgaya), then travels to a deer park in Sarnath (near Varanasi), India, and begins expounding the Dharma.
- **528 BCE** According to legend, Trapusha and Bhallika, two trader-brothers from Okkala (modern-day Yangon), offer the Gautama's first meal as the enlightened Buddha. The Buddha gives eight strands of his hair to the two brothers; the strands are brought back to Burma and enshrined in the Shwedagon Pagoda. Thus, according to myth, this is the year when the Shwedagon Pagoda was built.
- **c. 490–410 BCE:** Life of the Buddha, according to recent research.
- **c. 483 BCE:** Gautama Buddha dies ('attains *parinibbana*') at Kusinara (now called Kushinagar), India. Three months following his death, the First Buddhist Council is convened.
- **383 BCE:** The Second Buddhist Council is convened by King Kalasoka and held at Vaisali.
- **c. 250 BCE:** Third Buddhist Council, convened by Ashoka the Great and chaired by Moggaliputta Tissa, compiles the *Kathavatthu* to refute the heretical views and theories held by some Buddhist sects. Ashoka issues a number of edicts (Edicts of Ashoka) about the kingdom in support of Buddhism.
- **c. 250 BCE:** Emperor Ashoka the Great sends various

Buddhist missionaries to faraway countries, as far as China and the Mon & Malay kingdoms in the east and the Hellenistic kingdoms in the west, in order to make Buddhism known to them.

- **c. 250 BCE:** First fully developed examples of Kharosòtòhî script date from this period (the Ashokan inscriptions at Shâhbâzgaròhî and Mânsehrâ, a northwestern Indian subcontinent).
- **200s BCE:** Indian traders regularly visit ports in Arabia, explaining the prevalence of place names in the region with Indian or Buddhist origin; e.g., *bahar* (from the Sanskrit *vihara*, a Buddhist monastery). Ashokan emissary monks bring Buddhism to Suwannaphum, the location of which is disputed. The *Dipavamsa* and the Mon believe it was a Mon seafaring settlement in present-day Burma.
- **c. 220 BCE:** Theravada Buddhism is officially introduced to Sri Lanka by the Venerable Mahinda, son of the emperor Ashoka of India during the reign of King Devanampiya Tissa.
- **185 BCE:** Brahmin general Pusyamitra Sunga overthrows the Mauryan dynasty and establishes the Sunga dynasty, apparently starting a wave of persecution against Buddhism.
- **180 BCE:** Greco-Bactrian King Demetrius invades India as far as Pataliputra and establishes the Indo-Greek kingdom (180–10 BCE), under which Buddhism flourishes.
- **c. 150 BCE:** Indo-Greek king Menander I converts to Buddhism under the sage Nâgasena, according to the account of the Milinda Panha.

- **120 BCE:** The Chinese Emperor Han Wudi (156–87 BCE) receives two golden statues of the Buddha, according to inscriptions in the Mogao Caves, Dunhuang.
- **1st century BCE:** The Indo-Greek governor Theodorus enshrines relics of the Buddha, dedicating them to the deified "Lord Shakyamuni."
- **29 BCE:** According to the Sinhalese chronicles, the Pali Canon is written down in the reign of King VammagamiGi (29–17 BCE)
- **2 BCE:** The Hou Hanshu records the visit in 2 BCE of Yuezhi envoys to the Chinese capital, who give oral teachings on Buddhist sutras.

AD

- **65:** Liu Ying's sponsorship of Buddhism is the first documented case of Buddhist practices in China.
- **67:** Buddhism comes to China with the two monks Moton and Chufarlan.
- **68:** Buddhism is officially established in China with the founding of the White Horse Temple.
- **78:** Ban Chao, a Chinese General, subdues the Buddhist Kingdom of Khotan.
- **78–101:** According to Mahayana tradition, the Fourth Buddhist council takes place under Kushana king Kanishka's reign, near Jalandar, India.
- **116 CE:** The Kushans, under Kanishka, establish a kingdom centered on Kashgar, also taking control of Khotan and Yarkand—previously Chinese dependencies in the Tarim Basin, modern Xinjiang.
- **148:** An Shigao, a Parthian prince and Buddhist

monk, arrives in China and proceeds to make the first translations of Theravada texts into Chinese.

- **178:** The Kushan monk Lokaksema travels to the Chinese capital of Loyang and becomes the first known translator of Mahayana texts into Chinese.
- **100s/200s:** Indian and Central Asian Buddhists travel to Vietnam.
- **200s:** Use of Kharosòtòhî script in Gandhara stops.
- **200s & 300s:** Kharoshthhî script is used in the southern Silk Road cities of Khotan and Niya.
- **296:** The earliest surviving Chinese Buddhist scripture dates from this year (*Zhu Fo Yao Ji Jing*, discovered in Dalian, late 2005).
- **300s:** Two Chinese monks take scriptures to the Korean kingdom of Goguryeo and establish papermaking in Korea.
- **320-467:** The University at Nalanda grows to support 3,000–10,000 monks.
- **399-414:** Fa Xian travels from China to India, then returns to translate Buddhist works into Chinese.
- **400s:** The kingdom of Funan (centered in modern Cambodia) begins to advocate Buddhism in a departure from Hinduism. Earliest evidence of Buddhism in Myanmar (Pali inscriptions). Earliest evidence of Buddhism in Indonesian (statues). Earliest reinterpretations of Pali texts. The stupa at Dambulla (Sri Lanka) is constructed.
- **402:** At the request of Yao Xing, Kumarajiva travels to Changan and translates many Buddhist texts into Chinese.

- **403:** In China, Hui Yuan argues that Buddhist monks should be exempt from bowing to the emperor.
- **405:** Yao Xing honours Kumarajiva.
- **425:** Buddhism reaches Sumatra.
- **464:** Buddhabhadra reaches China to preach Buddhism.
- **495:** The Shaolin temple is built in the name of Buddhabhadra, by edict of emperor Wei Xiao Wen.
- **485:** Five monks from Gandhara travel to the country of Fusang (Japan, or possibly the American continent), where they introduce Buddhism.
- **500s:** Zen adherents enter Vietnam from China. Jataka stories are translated into Persian by order of the Zoroastrian king, Khosrau I of Persia.
- **527:** Bodhidharma settles into the Shaolin monastery in Henan province of China.
- **552:** Buddhism is introduced to Japan via Baekje (Korea), according to Nihonshoki; some scholars place this event in 538.
- **Early 600s:** Jingwan begins carving sutras onto stone at Fangshan, Yuzhou, 75 km southwest of modern-day Beijing.
- **607:** A Japanese imperial envoy is dispatched to Sui, China to obtain copies of sutras.
- **600s:** Xuan Zang travels to India, noting the persecution of Buddhists by Sasanka (king of Gouda, a state in northwest Bengal) before returning to Chang An in China to translate Buddhist scriptures. End of sporadic Buddhist rule in the Sindh. King Songtsen Gampo of Tibet sends messengers to India

to get Buddhist texts. Latest recorded use of the Kharoshthhî script amongst Buddhist communities around Kucha.

- **671:** Chinese Buddhist pilgrim Yi Jing visits Palembang, capital of the partly Buddhist kingdom of Srivijaya on the island of Sumatra, Indonesia, and reports over 1000 Buddhist monks in residence. Uisang returns to Korea after studying Chinese Huayan Buddhism and founds the Hwaeom school.
- **736:** Huayan is transmitted to Japan via Korea, when Rôben invites the Korean Hwaeom monk Simsang to lecture, and formally founds Japan's Kegon tradition in the Tôdaiji temple.
- **743–754:** The Chinese monk Jianzhen attempts to reach Japan eleven times, succeeding in 754 to establish the Japanese Ritsu school, which specialises in the *vinaya* (monastic rules).
- **700s:** Buddhist Jataka stories are translated in to Syriac and Arabic as Kalilag and Damnag. An account of Buddha's life is translated into Greek by John of Damascus and widely circulated to Christians as the story of Barlaam and Josaphat. By the 1300s, this story of Josaphat becomes so popular that he is made a Catholic saint.
- **700s:** Under the reign of King Trisong Deutsen, Padmasambhava travels from Afghanistan to establish tantric Buddhism in Tibet (later known as the Nyingma school of Tibetan Buddhism), replacing Bonpo as the kingdom's main religion. Buddhism quickly spreads to Sikkim and Bhutan also.
- **c. 760:** Construction is begun on Borobodur, the famous Indonesian Buddhist structure, probably as

a non-Buddhist shrine. It is completed as a Buddhist monument in 830, after about 50 years of work.

- **804:** Under the reign of Emperor Kammu of Japan, a fleet of four ships sets sail for mainland China. Of the two ships that arrive, one carries the monk Kûkai—recently ordained by the Japanese government as a Bhiksu—who absorbs Vajrayana teachings in Chang'an and returns to Japan to found the Japanese Shingon school. The other ship carries the monk Saichô, who returns to Japan to found the Japanese Tendai school, partly based upon the Chinese Tiantai tradition.
- **838–847:** Ennin, a priest of the Tendai school, travels in China for nine years. He reaches both the famous Buddhist mountain of Wutaishan and the Chinese capital, Chang'an, keeping a detailed diary that is a primary source for this period of Chinese history, including the Buddhist persecution.
- **841–846:** Emperor Wuzong of the Tang Dynasty (given name: Li Yan) reigns in China; he is one of three Chinese emperors to prohibit Buddhism. From 843-845, Wuzong carries out the Great Anti-Buddhist Persecution, permanently weakening the institutional structure of Buddhism in China.
- **9th-century Tibet:** Decline of Buddhism; persecution by King Langdarma.
- **900s:** Buddhist temple construction commences at Bagan, Myanmar (Burma). In Tibet, a strong Buddhist revival is begun. The Caodong school of Zen is founded by Dongshan Liangjie and his disciples in southern China.
- **971:** Chinese Song Dynasty commissions Chengdu

woodcarvers to carve the entire Buddhist canon for printing. Work is completed in 983; 130,000 blocks are produced, in total.

- **991:** A printed copy of the Song Dynasty Buddhist canon arrives in Korea, impressing the government.
- **1000s:** Marpa, Konchog Gyalpo, Atisha, and others introduce the Sarma lineages into Tibet.
- **1009:** Vietnam's Ly Dynasty begins, which is partly brought about by an alliance with the Buddhist monkhood. Ly emperors patronize Mahayana Buddhism, in addition to traditional spirits.
- **1010:** Korea begins carving its own woodblock print edition of the Buddhist canon. No completion date is known; the canon is continuously expanded, with the arrival of new texts from China.
- **1017:** In Southeast Asia, and especially in Sri Lanka, the Bhikkhuni (Buddhist nuns) Order dies out due to invasions. The bhikkhu line in Sri Lanka is later revived with bhikkhus from Burma.
- **1025:** Srivijaya, a Buddhist kingdom based in Sumatra, is raided by the Chola empire of southern India; it survives, but declines in importance. Shortly after the raid, the centre of the kingdom moves northward from Palembang to Jambi-Melayu.
- **1044–1077:** In Burma, Pagan's first king Anoratha reigns. He converts the country to Theravada Buddhism with the aid of monks and books from Sri Lanka. He is said to have been converted to Theravada Buddhism by a Mon monk, though other beliefs persist.
- **1057:** Anawrahta of Myanmar captures Thaton in

northern Thailand, strengthening Theravada Buddhism in the country.

- **1063:** A copy of the Khitans' printed canon arrives in Korea from mainland China.
- **1070:** Bhikkhus from Pagan arrive in Polonnaruwa, Sri Lanka to reinstate the Theravada ordination line
- **1084–1113:** In Myanmar, Pagan's second king, Kyanzittha (son of Anawrahta), reigns. He completes the building of the Shwezigon Pagoda, a shrine for relics of the Buddha, including a tooth brought from Sri Lanka. Various inscriptions refer to him as an incarnation of Vishnu, a chakravartin, a bodhisattva, and dharmaraja.
- **1100s:** Sanskrit is subsequently written in Devanagari.
- **1100–1125:** Huizong reigns during the Chinese Song Dynasty and outlaws Buddhism to promote the Dao. He is one of three Chinese emperors to have prohibited Buddhism.
- **1113:** Alaungsithu reigns in Pagan, Myanmar until his son Narathu smothers him to death and assumes the throne.
- **1133–1212:** Hônen establishes Pure Land Buddhism as an independent sect in Japan.
- **1164:** Polonnaruwa, Sri Lanka destroyed by foreign invasion. With the guidance of two forest monks - Ven. Mahakassapa and Ven. Sariputta, Parakramabahu I reunites all bhikkhus in Sri Lanka into the Mahavihara sect
- **1181:** The self-styled bodhisattva Jayavarman VII,

a devout follower of Mahayana Buddhism (though he also patronised Hinduism), assumes control of the Khmer kingdom. He constructs the Bayon, the most prominent Buddhist structure in the Angkor temple complex. This sets the stage for the later conversion of the Khmer people to Theravada Buddhism.

- **1190:** In Myanmar, Anawrahta's lineage regains control with the assistance of Sri Lanka. Pagan has been in anarchy. The new regime reforms Burmese Buddhism on Sri Lankan Theravada models.
- **1236:** Bhikkhus from Kañchipuram, India, arrive in Sri Lanka to revive the Theravada ordination line.
- **Late 1100s:** The great Buddhist educational centre at Nalanda, India, (the origin of Buddhism) where various subjects were taught subjects such as Buddhism, Logic, Philosophy, Law, Medicine, Grammar, Yoga, Mathematics, Alchemy, and Astrology, is sacked, looted and burnt by islamic invaders. Nalanda is supported by kings of several dynasties and serves as a great international centre of learning.
- **1200s:** Theravada overtakes Mahayana—previously practised alongside Hinduism—as the dominant form of Buddhism in Cambodia; Sri Lanka is an influence in this change. In Persia, the historian Rashid-al-Din Hamadani records some eleven Buddhist texts circulating in Arabic translation, amongst which the Sukhavati-vyuha and Karanda-vyuha Sutras are recognizable. Portions of the Samyutta and Anguttara-Nikayas, along with parts of the Maitreya-vyakarana, are identified in this collection.

- **1222:** Birth of Nichiren Daishonin (1222–1282), the Japanese founder of Nichiren Buddhism.
- **c. 1238:** The Thai Kingdom of Sukhothai is established, with Theravada Buddhism as the state religion.
- **1227:** Dogen Zenji takes the Caodong school of Zen from China to Japan as the Soto sect.
- **1244:** Eiheiji Soto Zen Temple and Monastery are established by Dogen Zenji.
- **1277:** Burma's Pagan empire begins to disintegrate after being defeated by Kublai Khan at the Battle of Ngasaunggyan, at Yunnan, near the Chinese border.
- **1285:** Arghun makes the Il-Khanate a Buddhist state.
- **1287:** The Theravada kingdom at Pagan, Myanmar falls to the Mongols and is overshadowed by the Shan capital at Ava.
- **c. 1279–1298:** Sukhothai's third and most famous ruler, Ramkhamhaeng (Rama the Bold), reigns and makes vassals of Laos, much of modern Thailand, Pegu (Burma), and parts of the Malay Peninsula, thus giving rise to Sukhothai artistic tradition. After Ramkhamhaeng's death, Sukhothai loses control of its territories as its vassals become independent.
- **1295:** Mongol leader Ghazan Khan is converted to Islam, ending a line of Tantric Buddhist leaders.
- **1305–1316:** Buddhists in Persia attempt to convert Uldjaitu Khan.
- **1321:** Sojiji Soto Zen Temple and Monastery established by Keizan Zenji.

- **1351:** In Thailand, U Thong. possibly the son of a Chinese merchant family, establishes Ayutthaya as his capital and takes the name of Ramathibodi.
- **1391–1474:** Gyalwa Gendun Drubpa, first Dalai Lama of Tibet.
- **1405–1431:** The Chinese eunuch admiral Zheng He makes seven voyages in this period, through southeast Asia, India, the Persian Gulf, East Africa, and Egypt. At the time, Buddhism is well-established in China, so visited peoples may have had exposure to Chinese Buddhism.
- **1578:** Altan Khan of the Tümed gives the title of Dalai Lama to Sonam Gyatso (later known as the third Dalai Lama).
- **1600s & 1700s:** When Vietnam divides during this period, the Nguyen rulers of the south choose to support Mahayana Buddhism as an integrative ideology for the ethnically plural society of their kingdom, which is also populated by Chams and other minorities.
- **1614:** The Toyotomi family rebuilds a great image of Buddha at the Temple of Hôkôji in Kyôtô.
- **1615:** The Oirat Mongols convert to the Geluk school of Tibetan Buddhism.
- **1635:** In Zanabazar, the first Jebtsundamba Khutughtu is born as a great-grandson of Abadai Khan of the Khalkha.
- **1642:** Güüshi Khan of the Khoshuud donates the sovereignty of Tibet to the fifth Dalai Lama.
- **1766–67:** In Thailand, many Buddhist texts are destroyed as the Burmese invade Ayutthaya.

- **1800s:** In Thailand, King Mongkut—himself a former monk—conducts a campaign to reform and modernise the monkhood, a movement that has continued in the present century under the inspiration of several great ascetic monks from the northeast part of the country.
- **1802–20:** Nguyen Anh comes to the throne of the first united Vietnam; he succeeds by quelling the Tayson rebellion in south Vietnam with help from Rama I in Bangkok, then takes over the north from the remaining Trinh. After coming to power, he creates a Confucianist orthodox state and is eager to limit the competing influence of Buddhism. He forbids adult men to attend Buddhist ceremonies.
- **1820–41:** Minh Mang reigns in Vietnam, further restricting Buddhism. He insists that all monks be assigned to cloisters and carry identification documents. He also places new restrictions on printed material and begins the persecution of Catholic missionaries and converts that his successors (not without provocation) continue.
- **c. 1860:** In Sri Lanka, against all expectations, the monastic and lay communities bring about a major revival in Buddhism, a movement that goes hand in hand with growing nationalism; the revival follows a period of persecution by foreign powers. Since then, Buddhism has flourished, and Sri Lankan monks and expatriate lay people have been prominent in spreading Theravada Buddhism in Asia, the West, and even in Africa.
- **1879:** A council is convened under the patronage of King Mindon Min of Burma to re-edit the Pali canon. The king has the texts engraved on 729

stones, which are then set upright on the grounds of a monastery near Mandalay.

- **1882:** Jade Buddha Temple is founded in Shanghai, China, with two Jade Buddha statues imported from Burma.
- **1893:** The World Parliament of Religions meets in Chicago, Illinois; Anagarika Dharmapala and Soyen Shaku attend.
- **1896:** Using Fa Xian's records, Nepalese archaeologists rediscover the great stone pillar of Ashoka at Lumbini.
- **1899:** Gordon Douglas is ordained in Myanmar; he is the first Westerner to be ordained in the Theravada tradition.
- **1922:** Zenshuji Soto Mission is founded as the first Soto Zen temple in North America.
- **1930:** Soka Gakkai is founded in Japan.
- **1949:** Mahabodhi Temple in Bodh Gaya is returned to partial Buddhist control.
- **1950:** World Fellowship of Buddhists is founded in Colombo, Sri Lanka.
- **1954:** The Sixth Buddhist Council is held in Yangon, Myanmar, organized by U Nu. It ends in time for the 2500th anniversary of the passing of the Buddha.
- **1956:** Indian untouchable leader B.R. Ambedkar converts to Buddhism, with more than 350,000 followers—beginning the modern Neo-Buddhist movement.
- **1956:** The Zen Studies Society is founded in New York to support the work of D.T. Suzuki.
- **1957:** Caves near the summit of Pai-tai mountain,

Fangshan district, 75km southwest of Beijing, are reopened, revealing thousands of Buddhist sutras that had been carved onto stone since the 7th century. Seven sets of rubbings are made, and the stones are numbered, in work that continues until 1959.

- **1959:** Together with some 100,000 Tibetans, the 14th Dalai Lama flees the Chinese occupation of Tibet and establishes an exile community in India. The Chinese invaders completely destroy all but a handful of monasteries and severely persecute Buddhist practitioners.
- **1962:** The Dharma Realm Buddhist Association is founded by Tripitaka Master Shramana Hsuan Hua, who later founds the City of Ten Thousand Buddhas and ordains the first five fully-ordained American Buddhist monks and nuns.
- **1962:** The San Francisco Zen Center is founded by Shunryu Suzuki.
- **1963:** Thích Qu£ng Đéc immolates himself to protest the oppression of the Buddhist religion by Ngo Dinh Diem.
- **1965:** The Burmese government arrests over 700 monks in Hmawbi, near Rangoon, for refusing to accept government rule.
- **1966:** The World Buddhist Sangha Council is convened by Theravadins in Sri Lanka with the hope of bridging differences and working together. The first convention is attended by leading monks from many countries and sects, Mahayana as well as Theravada. Nine *Basic Points Unifying the Theravada and Mahayana* are written by Ven. Walpola Rahula are approved unanimously.

- **1968:** The Shurangama Sutra and Shurangama Mantra are lectured for the first time in the West (San Francisco) by Tripitaka Master Shramana Hsuan Hua during 90 day retreat. The first five American Bhikshus and Bhikshunis are ordained in the Chinese tradition including the oldest still-in-robes American Bhikshuni nun Heng Chr.
- **1970s:** Indonesian Archaeological Service and UNESCO restore Borobodur.
- **1974:** Wat Pah Nanachat, the first monastery dedicated to providing training and support for western Buddhist monks, is founded in Thailand by Venerable Ajahn Chah. The monks trained here would later establish branch monasteries throughout the world.
- **1974:** The Naropa Institute (now Naropa University) is founded in Boulder, Colorado.
- **1974:** In Burma, during demonstrations at U Thant's funeral, 600 monks are arrested and several are bayoneted by government forces.
- **1975:** Lao Communist rulers attempt to change attitudes to religion—in particular, calling on monks to work, not beg. This causes many to return to lay life, but Buddhism remains popular.
- **1975:** The Insight Meditation Society is established in Barre, Massachusetts.
- **1975–79:** Cambodian Communists under Pol Pot try to completely destroy Buddhism, and very nearly succeed. By the time of the Vietnamese invasion of Cambodia in 1978, nearly every monk and religious intellectual has been either murdered or driven into

exile, and nearly every temple and Buddhist library has been destroyed.

- **1976:** Bhikshus Rev. Heng Sure and Rev. Martin Verhoeven, the American Buddhist Monk disciples of Ven. Tripitaka Master Hsuan Hua, for the sake of world peace, undertook an over six hundred mile three steps one bow pilgrimage from Los Angeles area to City of Ten Thousand Buddhas in Mendocino area, repeatedly taking three steps and one bow to cover the entire journey. In the entire 2.5 years taken to make the pilgrimage, Shramana Heng Sure observed a practice of total silence.
- **1976:** Following a demonstration in Burma, the government seeks to discredit the critical monk La Ba by claiming that he is a cannibal and a murderer.
- **1978:** In Burma, more monks and novices are arrested, disrobed, and imprisoned by the government. Monasteries are closed and property seized. The critical monk U Nayaka is arrested and dies, the government claiming it is suicide.
- **1980:** The Burmese military government asserts authority over the sangha, and violence against monks continues through the decade.
- **1983:** The Shanghai Institute of Buddhism is established at Jade Buddha Temple, under the Shanghai Buddhist Association.
- **1988:** During the 1988 uprising, SPDC troops gun down monks. After the uprising, U Nyanissara, a senior monk, records a tape that discusses democracy in Buddhist precepts; the tape is banned.
- **1990, August 27:** Over 7000 monks meet in Mandalay, in Burma, to call for a boycott of the

military. They refuse to accept alms from military families or perform services for them. The military government seizes monasteries and arrests hundreds of monks, including senior monks U Sumangala and U Yewata. The monks face long-term imprisonment, and all boycotting monks are disrobed; some monks are tortured during interrogation.

- **1992:** The Buddha Statue in Hyderabad, India is installed, a work of former Chief Minister of Andhra Pradesh, Late Sri N.T. Rama Rao. The 16-meter tall, 350-ton monolithic colossus rises high from the placid waters of picturesque Husain Sagar Lake. It is made of white granite, finely sculptured and stands majestically amidst the shimmering waters of the lake. It is later consecrated by Dalai Lama.
- **1996, India:** The Bhikkhuni (Buddhist nuns) Order and lineage is revived in Sarnath, India through the efforts of Sakyadhita, an International Buddhist Women Association. The revival is done with some resistance from some of the more literal interpreters of the Buddhist Vinaya (monastic code) and lauded by others in the community.
- **1998, January 25:** Liberation Tigers of Tamil Eelam (LTTE) terrorists commit a deadly suicide attack on Sri Lanka's most sacred Buddhist site and a UNESCO World Heritage centre: the Temple of the Tooth, where Buddha's tooth relic is enshrined. Eight civilians are killed and 25 others are injured and significant damage is done to the temple structure, which was first constructed in 1592 AD.
- **2001, May:** Two of the world's tallest ancient Buddha statues, the Buddhas of Bamyan, are completely destroyed by the Taliban in Bamyan, Afghanistan.

- **2004, April:** In Sri Lanka, Buddhist monks acting as candidates for the Jaathika Hela Urumaya party win nine seats in elections.
- **2006, April 13 to 16:** First World Buddhist Forum held in People's Republic of China.
- **2006, November:** In the United States, two Buddhists are elected for the first time to the 110th Congress.
- **2007 (September):** Thousands of Burmese Buddhist monks and nuns protest against the military regime; the military regime responds with a bloody crackdown. Thousands are arrested, and hundreds flee to Thailand and India; the death toll is in the hundreds.
- **2007, October 17:** The U.S. Congress presents the 14th Dalai Lama with the U.S. Congressional Gold Medal and meets in public with President George W. Bush.
- **2008 (March):** Tibetan monks protest in Lhasa, and many Tibetans join in calling for the end of Chinese rule. Many Chinese businesses are attacked and burned. The Chinese respond by sending in troops and ordering a strict lockdown of the capital city of Lhasa. Many Tibetans are killed, with the death toll maybe over a hundred. Outraged, thousands of exiled Tibetans around the world protest.
- **2009, March 28 to April 1:** Second World Buddhist Forum held in China.

[*Source:* Timeline of Buddhism, Wikipedia]

3

Gautama Buddha: A Life Sketch

Lord Buddha was the founder of ancient religion Buddhism. According to Hindu canons he is considered as the last but one incarnation of Lord Vishnu. But many scholars refute this While studying Buddhism, it is important to know about the life of Lord Buddha.

Here in this chapter, we will present a vivid account of the life of lord Buddha. The information furnished herein is based on researches of many Buddhist scholars

Siddhârtha Gautama was a spiritual teacher from the north eastern region of South Asia who founded Buddhism. In most Buddhist traditions, he is regarded as the Supreme *Buddha* (Sammâsambuddha) of our age, "Buddha" meaning "awakened one" or "the enlightened one."

The time of his birth and death are uncertain: most early 20th-century historians dated his lifetime as c. 563 BCE to 483 BCE; more recently, however, at a specialist symposium on this question, the majority of those scholars who presented definite opinions gave dates within 20 years either side of 400 BCE for the Buddha's death, with others supporting earlier or later dates.

Gautama, also known as *Sâkyamuni* or *Shakyamuni,*

is the key figure in Buddhism, and accounts of his life, discourses, and monastic rules are believed by Buddhists to have been summarized after his death and memorized by his followers. Various collections of teachings attributed to Gautama were passed down by oral tradition, and first committed to writing about 400 years later.

It is pertinent to note here that the primary sources of information regarding Siddhârtha Gautama's life are the Buddhist texts. According to these, the Buddha and his monks spent four months each year discussing and rehearsing his teachings, and after his death his monks set about preserving them.

A council was held shortly after his death, and another was held a century later. At these councils the monks attempted to establish and authenticate the extant accounts of the life and teachings of the Buddha following systematic rules. They divided the teachings into distinct but overlapping bodies of material, and assigned specific monks to preserve each one. In some cases, essential aspects of teachings attributed to the Buddha were incorporated into stories and chants in an effort to preserve them accurately. From then on, the teachings were transmitted orally. From internal evidence it seems clear that the oldest texts crystallized into their current form by the time of the second council or shortly after it. The scriptures were not written down until three or four hundred years after the Buddha's death.

By this point, the monks had added or altered some material themselves, in particular magnifying the figure of the Buddha. The ancient Indians were generally not concerned with chronologies, being more focused on philosophy. The Buddhist texts reflect this tendency, providing a clearer picture of what Shakyamuni may have taught than of the dates of the events in his life. These texts contain descriptions of the culture and daily life of ancient India which can be corroborated from the Jain scriptures, and make the Buddha's time the earliest period in Indian history for which significant accounts exist.

According to Michael Carrithers, there are good reasons to doubt the traditional account, though, according to Carrithers, the outline of "birth, maturity, renunciation, search, awakening and liberation, teaching, death" must be true.

As a popular belief Siddhartha was born in Lumbini and raised in the small kingdom or principality of Kapilvastu, both of which are in modern day Nepal. At the time of the Buddha's birth, the area was at or beyond the boundary of Vedic civilization, the dominant culture of northern India at the time; it is even possible that his mother tongue was not an Indo-Aryan language. The early texts suggest that Gautama was not familiar with the dominant religious teachings of his time until he left on his religious search, which was motivated by an existential concern with the human condition.

At the time, a multitude of small city-states existed in Ancient India, called Janapadas. Republics and chiefdoms with diffused political power and limited social stratification, were not uncommon amongst them, and were referred to as gana-sanghas. The Buddha's community does not seem to have had a caste system. It was not a monarchy, and seems to have been structured either as an oligarchy, or as a form of republic.

The more egalitarian gana-sangha form of government, as a political alternative to the strongly hierarchical kingdoms, may have influenced the development of the Shramana type Jain and Buddhist sanghas, where monarchies tended toward Vedic Brahmanism.

According to the traditional biography, the Buddha's father was King Suddhodana, the leader of Shakya clan, whose capital was Kapilavastu, and who were later annexed by the growing Kingdom of Kosala during the Buddha's lifetime; Gautama was the family name. His mother, Queen Maha Maya (Mâyâdevî) and Suddhodana's wife, was a Koliyan princess. On the night Siddhartha was conceived, Queen Maya dreamt that a white elephant with six white tusks entered her right side, and ten months later Siddhartha was born.

As was the Shakya tradition, when his mother Queen Maya became pregnant, she left Kapilvastu for her father's kingdom to give birth. However, she gave birth on the way, at Lumbini, in a garden beneath a sal tree.

Remarkable the day of the Buddha's birth is widely celebrated in Theravada countries as Vesak. Various sources hold that the Buddha's mother died at his birth, a few days or seven days later. The infant was given the name Siddhartha (Pâli: Siddhatta), meaning "he who achieves his aim". During the birth celebrations, the hermit seer Asita journeyed from his mountain abode and announced that the child would either become a great king (chakravartin) or a great holy man. This occurred after Siddhartha placed his feet in Asita's hair and Asita examined the birthmarks. Suddhodana held a naming ceremony on the fifth day, and invited eight brahmin scholars to read the future. All gave a dual prediction that the baby would either become a great king or a great holy man. Kaundinya (Kondanna), the youngest, and later to be the first arahant other than the Buddha, was the only one who unequivocally predicted that Siddhartha would become a Buddha. While later tradition and legend characterized Œuddhodana as a hereditary monarch, the descendant of the Solar Dynasty of Ikcvâku (Okkâka), many scholars believe that Œuddhodana was the elected chief of a tribal confederacy.

Siddhartha, said to have been destined to a luxurious life as a prince, had three palaces (for seasonal occupation) especially built for him. His father, King Shuddhodana, wishing for Siddhartha to be a great king, shielded his son from religious teachings or knowledge of human suffering. Siddhartha was brought up by his mother's younger sister, Maha Pajapati. As the boy reached the age of 16, his father arranged his marriage to Yasodharâ, a cousin of the same age. According to the traditional account, in time, she gave birth to a son, Rahula. Siddhartha spent 29 years as a Prince in Kapilavastu. Although his father ensured that Siddhartha was provided with everything he could want or need, Siddhartha felt that material wealth was not the ultimate goal of life.

At the age of 29, Siddhartha left his palace in order to meet his subjects. Despite his father's effort to remove the sick, aged and suffering from the public view, Siddhartha was said to have seen an old man. Disturbed by this, when told that all people would eventually grow old by his charioteer Channa, the prince went on further trips where he encountered, variously, a diseased man, a decaying corpse, and an ascetic.

Deeply depressed by these sights, he sought to overcome old age, illness, and death by living the life of an ascetic. Siddhartha escaped his palace, accompanied by Channa aboard his horse Kanthaka, leaving behind this royal life to become a mendicant. It is said that, "the horse's hooves were muffled by the gods" to prevent guards from knowing of the Bodhisatta's departure. This event is traditionally called "The Great Departure".

Siddhartha initially went to Rajagaha and began his ascetic life by begging for alms in the street. Having been recognised by the men of King Bimbisara, Bimbisara offered him the throne after hearing of Siddhartha's quest. Siddhartha rejected the offer, but promised to visit his kingdom of Magadha first, upon attaining enlightenment. Siddhartha left Rajagaha and practised under two hermit teachers. After mastering the teachings of Alara Kalama, Siddhartha was asked by Kalama to succeed him, but moved on after being unsatisfied with his practices. He then became a student of Udaka Ramaputta, but although he achieved high levels of meditative consciousness and was asked to succeed Ramaputta, he was still not satisfied with his path, and moved on. Siddhartha and a group of five companions led by Kaundinya then set out to take their austerities even further.

They tried to find enlightenment through near total deprivation of worldly goods, including food, practising self-mortification. After nearly starving himself to death by restricting his food intake to around a leaf or nut per day, he collapsed in a river while bathing and almost drowned. Siddhartha began to reconsider his path. Then, he remembered a moment in childhood in which he had been watching his father start the season's plowing, and he had fallen into a naturally concentrated and focused state that was blissful and refreshing, the jhâna.

Enlightenment

After asceticism and concentrating on meditation and Anapana-sati (awareness of breathing in and out),

Siddhartha is said to have discovered what Buddhists call the Middle Way—a path of moderation away from the extremes of self-indulgence and self-mortification. He accepted a little milk and rice pudding from a village girl named Sujata, who wrongly believed him to be the spirit that had granted her a wish, such was his emaciated appearance.

Then, sitting under a pipal tree, now known as the Bodhi tree in Bodh Gaya, India, he vowed never to arise until he had found the Truth. Kaundinya and the other four companions, believing that he had abandoned his search and become undisciplined, left. After 49 days meditating, at the age of 35, he attained Enlightenment; according to some traditions, this occurred approximately in the fifth lunar month, and according to others in the twelfth. Gautama, from then on, was known as the *Buddha* or "Awakened One." Buddha is also sometimes translated as "The Enlightened One." Often, he is referred to in Buddhism as Shakyamuni Buddha or "The Awakened One of the Shakya Clan." At this point, he is believed to have realized complete awakening and insight into the nature and cause of human suffering which was ignorance, along with steps necessary to eliminate it. This was then categorized into 'Four Noble Truths'; the state of supreme liberation—possible for any being—was called Nirvana.

He then allegedly came to possess the Ten Characteristics, which are said to belong to every Buddha. According to one of the stories in the *Âyâcana Sutta* (Samyutta Nikaya VI.1), a scripture found in the Pâli and other canons, immediately after his Enlightenment, the Buddha was wondering whether or not he should teach the *Dharma* to human beings. He was concerned that, as human beings were overpowered by greed, hatred and delusion, they would not be able to see the true *dharma*, which was subtle, deep and hard to understand.

However, Brahmâ Sahampati, interceded and asked that he teach the *dharma* to the world, as "there will be those who will understand the *Dharma*". With his great compassion to all beings in the universe, the Buddha agreed to become a teacher.

After becoming enlightened, two merchants whom the Buddha met, named Tapussa and Bhallika became the first lay disciples. They are given some hairs from the Buddha's head, which are believed to now be enshrined in the Shwe Dagon Temple in Rangoon, Burma. The Buddha intended to visit Asita, and his former teachers, Alara Kalama and Uddaka Ramaputta to explain his findings, but they had already died. The Buddha thus journeyed to Deer Park near VrGas+ (Benares) in northern India, he set in motion thc Wheel of Dharma by delivering his first sermon to the group of five companions with whom he had previously sought enlightenment.

They, together with the Buddha, formed the first saEgha, the company of Buddhist monks, and hence, the first formation of Triple Gem (Buddha, Dharma and Sangha) was completed, with Kaundinya becoming the first stream-enterer. All five soon become arahants, and with the conversion of Yasa and fifty four of his friends, the number of arahants swelled to 60 within the first two months.

The conversion of the three Kassapa brothers and their 200, 300 and 500 disciples swelled the sangha over 1000, and they were dispatched to explain the dharma to the populace. It is unknown what the Buddha's mother tongue was, and no conclusive documentation has been made at this point. It is likely that he preached and his teachings were originally preserved in a variety of closely related Middle Indo-Aryan dialects, of which Pali may be a standardization.

For the remaining 45 years of his life, the Buddha is said to have traveled in the Gangetic Plain, in what is now Uttar Pradesh, Bihar and southern Nepal, teaching his doctrine and discipline to an extremely diverse range of people— from nobles to outcaste street sweepers, mass murderers such as Angulimala and cannibals such as Alavaka. This extended to many adherents of rival philosophies and religions. The Buddha founded the community of Buddhist monks and nuns (the *Sangha*) to continue the dispensation after his *Parinirvâna* (Pâli: Parinibbâna) or "complete Nirvâna", and made thousands of converts. His religion was open to all races and classes and had no caste structure.

He was also subject to attack from opposition religious groups, including attempted murders and framings. The sangha travelled from place to place in India, expounding the dharma. This occurred throughout the year, except during the four months of the vassana rainy season. Due to the heavy amount of flooding, travelling was difficult, and ascetics of all religions in that time did not travel, since it was more difficult to do so without stepping on submerged animal life, unwittingly killing them.

During this period, the sangha would retreat to a monastery, public park or a forest and people would come to them. The first vassana was spent at Varanasi when the sangha was first formed. After this, he travelled to Rajagaha, the capital of Magadha to visit King Bimbisara, in accordance with his promise after enlightenment. It was during this visit that Sariputta and Mahamoggallana were converted by Assaji, one of the first five disciples; they were to become the Buddha's two foremost disciples. The Buddha then spent the next three seasons at Veluvana Bamboo Grove monastery in Rajagaha, the capital of Magadha.

The monastery, which was of a moderate distance from the city centre was donated by Bimbisara. Upon hearing of the enlightenment, Suddhodana dispatched royal delegations to ask the Buddha to return to Kapilavastu. Nine delegations were sent in all, but the delegates joined the sangha and became arahants. Neglecting worldly matters, they did not convey their message. The tenth delegation, led by Kaludayi, a childhood friend, resulted in the message being successfully conveyed as well as becoming an arahant.

Since it was not the vassana, the Buddha agreed, and two years after his enlightenment, took a two month journey to Kapilavastu by foot, preaching the dharma along the way. Upon his return, the royal palace had prepared the midday meal, but since no specific invitation had come, the sangha went for an alms round in Kapilavastu. Hearing this, Suddhodana hastened to approach the Buddha, stating "Ours is the warrior lineage of Mahamassata, and not a single warrior has gone seeking alms", to which the Buddha replied. That is not the custom of your royal lineage. But it is the custom of my Buddha lineage. Several thousands of Buddhas have gone by seeking alms.

Suddhodana invited the sangha back to the royal palace for the meal, followed by a dharma talk, after which he became a sotapanna. During the visit, many members of the royal family joined the sangha. His cousins Ananda and Anuruddha were to become two of his five chief disciples. His son Rahula also joined the sangha at the age of seven, and was one of the ten chief disciples.

His half-brother Nanda also joined the sangha and became an arahant. Another cousin Devadatta also became a monk although he later became an enemy and tried to kill the Buddha on multiple occasions. Of his disciples, Sariputta, Mahamoggallana, Mahakasyapa, Ananda and Anuruddha comprised the five chief disciples. His ten foremost disciples were completed by the quintet of Upali, Subhoti, Rahula, Mahakaccana and Punna.

Remarkably, the fifth vassana, the Buddha was staying at Mahavana near Vesali. Hearing of the impending death of Suddhodana, the Buddha went to his father and preached the dharma, and Suddhodana became an arahant prior to death. The death and cremation led to the creation of the order of nuns. Buddhist texts record that he was reluctant to ordain women as nuns. His foster mother Maha Pajapati approached him asking to join the sangha, but the Buddha refused, and began the journey from Kapilavastu back to Rajagaha. Maha Pajapati was so intent on renouncing the world that she led a group of royal Sakyan and Koliyan ladies, following the sangha to Rajagaha. The Buddha eventually accepted them five years after the formation of the Sangha on the grounds that their capacity for enlightenment was equal to that of men, but he gave them certain additional rules (Vinaya) to follow.

This occurred after Ananda interceded on their behalf. Yasodhara also became a nun, with both becoming arahants. During his ministry, Devadatta (who was not an arahant) frequently tried to undermine the Buddha. At one point Devadatta asked the Buddha to stand aside to let him lead the sangha.

The Buddha declined, and stated that Devadatta's actions did not reflect on the Triple Gem, but on him alone. Devadatta conspired with Prince Ajatasattu, son of

Bimbisara, so that they would kill and usurp the Buddha and Bimbisara respectively. Devadatta attempted three times to kill the Buddha. The first attempt involved the hiring of a group of archers, whom upon meeting the Buddha became disciples.

A second attempt followed when Devadatta attempted to roll a large boulder down a hill. It hit another rock and splintered, only grazing the Buddha in the foot. A final attempt by plying an elephant with alcohol and setting it loose again failed. Failing this, Devadatta attempted to cause a schism in the sangha, by proposing extra restrictions on the vinaya. When the Buddha declined, Devadatta started a breakaway order, criticising the Buddha's laxity. At first, he managed to convert some of the bhikkhus, but Sariputta and Mahamoggallana expounded the dharma to them and succeeded in winning them back. When the Buddha reached the age of 55, he made Ananda his chief attendant.

According to the *Mahaparinibbana Sutta* of the Pali canon, at the age of 80, the Buddha announced that he would soon reach Parinirvana or the final deathless state abandoning the earthly body. After this, the Buddha ate his last meal, which he had received as an offering from a blacksmith named Cunda. Falling violently ill, Buddha instructed his attendant Ânanda to convince Cunda that the meal eaten at his place had nothing to do with his passing and that his meal would be a source of the greatest merit as it provided the last meal for a Buddha. Mettanando and von Hinüber argue that the Buddha died of mesenteric infarction, a symptom of old age, rather than food poisoning.

The precise contents of the Buddha's final meal are not clear, due to variant scriptural traditions and ambiguity over the translation of certain significant terms; the

Theravada tradition generally believes that the Buddha was offered some kind of pork, while the Mahayana tradition believes that the Buddha consumed some sort of truffle or other mushroom. The Mahayana Vimalakirti Sutra claims, in Chapter 3, that the Buddha doesn't really become ill or old but purposely presents such an appearance only to teach those born into samsara about the impermanence and pain of defiled worlds and to encourage them to strive for Nirvana.

> "Reverend Ánanda, the Tathágatas have the body of the Dharma—not a body that is sustained by material food. The Tathágatas have a transcendental body that has transcended all mundane qualities. There is no injury to the body of a Tathágata, as it is rid of all defilements. The body of a Tathágata is uncompounded and free of all formative activity. Reverend Ánanda, to believe there can be illness in such a body is irrational and unseemly!' Nevertheless, since the Buddha has appeared during the time of the five corruptions, he disciplines living beings by acting lowly and humble."

Ananda protested Buddha's decision to enter Parinirvana in the abandoned jungles of Kusinâra (present-day Kushinagar, India) of the Malla kingdom. Buddha, however, reminded Ananda how Kushinara was a land once ruled by a righteous wheel-turning king that resounded with joy:

> 44. Kusavati, Ananda, resounded unceasingly day and night with ten sounds—the trumpeting of elephants, the neighing of horses, the rattling of chariots, the beating of drums and tabours, music and song, cheers, the clapping of hands, and cries of "Eat, drink, and be merry!"

Buddha then asked all the attendant Bhikshus to clarify any doubts or questions they had. They had none. He then finally entered Parinirvana. The Buddha's final words were, "All composite things pass away. Strive for your own liberation with diligence."

The Buddha's body was cremated and the relics were placed in monuments or stupas, some of which are believed to have survived until the present. For example, The Temple of the Tooth or "Dalada Maligawa" in Sri Lanka is the place where the relic of the right tooth of Buddha is kept at present.

At his death, the Buddha told his disciples to follow no leader, but to follow his teachings (dharma). However, at the First Buddhist Council, Mahakasyapa was held by the sangha as their leader, with the two chief disciples Mahamoggallana and Sariputta having died before the Buddha.

Personality

Buddha is perhaps one of the few sages for whom we have mention of his rather impressive physical characteristics. A kshatriya by birth, he had military training in his upbringing, and by Shakyan tradition was required to pass tests to demonstrate his worthiness as a warrior in order to marry. He had a strong enough body to be noticed by one of the kings and was asked to join his army as a general. He is also believed by Buddhists to have "the 32 Signs of the Great Man". The Brahmin Sonadanda described him as "handsome, good-looking, and pleasing to the eye, with a most beautiful complexion. He has a godlike form and countenance, he is by no means unattractive."(D,I:115).

"It is wonderful, truly marvellous, how serene is the good Gotama's appearance, how clear and radiant his complexion, just as the golden jujube in autumn is clear and radiant, just as a palm-tree fruit just loosened from the stalk is clear and radiant, just as an adornment of red gold wrought in a crucible by a skilled goldsmith, deftly beaten and laid on a yellow-cloth shines, blazes and glitters, even so, the good Gotama's senses are calmed, his complexion is clear and radiant." (A,I:181)

A disciple named Vakkali, who later became an Arahant, was so obsessed by Buddha's physical presence that Buddha had to tell him to stop and reminded Vakkali to know Buddha through the Dhamma and not physical appearances.

Although the Buddha was not represented in human form until around the 1st century CE (see Buddhist art), the physical characteristics of fully-enlightened Buddhas are described by the Buddha in the Digha Nikaya's *Lakkhana Sutta* (D,I:142). In addition, the Buddha's physical appearance is described by Yasodhara to their son Rahula upon the Buddha's first post-Enlightenment return to his former princely palace in the non-canonical Pali devotional hymn, *Narasîha Gâthâ* ("The Lion of Men").

Some scholars believe that some portions of the Pali Canon and the Agamas could contain the actual substance of the historical teachings (and possibly even the words) of the Buddha. This is not the case for the later Mahayana sutras. The scriptural works of Early Buddhism precede the Mahayana works chronologically, and are treated by many Western scholars as the main credible source for information regarding the actual historical teachings of Gautama Buddha.

According to tradition, the Buddha emphasized ethics and correct understanding. He questioned the average person's notions of divinity and salvation. He stated that there is no intermediary between mankind and the divine; distant gods are subjected to karma themselves in decaying heavens; and the Buddha is solely a guide and teacher for the sentient beings who must tread the path of Nirvna (Nibbâna) themselves to attain the spiritual awakening called *bodhi* and see truth and reality as it is.

REFERENCES

1. Cousins, L.S. (1996), "The dating of the historical Buddha: a review article", *Journal of the Royal Asiatic Society* **(3)6(1)**: 57–63.
2. Mettanando Bhikkhu and Oskar von Hinueber, "The Cause of the Buddha's Death"; Vol. XXVI of the Journal of the Pali Text Society, 2000.
3. Michael Carrithers, *The Buddha,* 1983, pages 13, 14. Found in *Founders of Faith,* Oxford University Press, 1986.
4. Narada (1992). *A Manual of Buddhism.* Buddha Educational Foundation. p. 9–12.
5. Richard Gombrich, *Theravada Buddhism: A Social History from Ancient Benares to Modern Colombo.* Routledge and Kegan Paul, 1988, p. 49.
6. Romila Thapar, *The Penguin History of Early India: From Origins to AD 1300.* Penguin Books, 2002, p. 137.
7. Sue Hamilton, *Early Buddhism: A New Approach: The I of the Beholder.* Routledge 2000, p. 47.
8. Turpie, D. 2001. Wesak And The Re-Creation of Buddhist Tradition. Master's Thesis. Montreal, Quebec: McGill University. (p. 3). Available from: Mcgill.ca, Accessed 17 November 2006.
9. Ven. Elgiriye Indaratana Maha Thera, *Vandana: The Album of Pali Devotional Chanting and Hymns*, 2002, pp. 49-52.
10. Walshe, Maurice *The Long Discourses of the Buddha: A Translation of the Digha Nikaya*, 1995, Boston: Wisdom Publications.

4

Buddhism in Historical Perspective

The History of Buddhism spans the 5th century BCE to the present, starting with the birth of Siddhartha Gautama (Lord Buddha) in Lumbini, Nepal. This makes it one of the oldest religions practiced today. Starting in the north eastern region of the Indian Subcontinent, the religion evolved as it spread through Central Asia, East Asia, and Southeast Asia. At one time or another it affected most of the Asian continent. The history of Buddhism is also characterized by the development of numerous movements and schisms among them the Theravâda, Mahâyâna and Vajrayâna traditions, with contrasting periods of expansion and retreat.

Siddhârtha Gautama was the historical founder of Buddhism. He was born as a Kshatriya prince in Lumbini, Nepal in 623 BCE. His particular family of Sakya Kshatriyas were of Brahmin 'lineage' as per their family name "Gautama". 19th century scholars like Dr. Eitel connected it to the Brahmin Rishi Gautama. In many Buddhist texts Buddha is said to be a descendant of the Brahmin Sage Angirasa.

For example, "*In the Pâli Mahavagga "Angirasa" occurs as a name of Buddha Gautama who evidently belonged to the Angirasa tribe...*". Scholar Edward J. Thomas too connected Buddha with sages Gautama and Angirasa.

After asceticism and meditation, Siddhartha Gautama discovered the Buddhist Middle Way (Madhyam Marga)—a path of moderation away from the extremes of self-indulgence and self-mortification.

Siddhartha Gautama attained enlightenment sitting under a pipal tree, now known as the Bodhi tree in Bodh Gaya, India. Gautama, from then on, was known as *"The Perfectly Self-Awakened One,"* the Samyaksambuddha.

Buddha found patronage in the ruler of Magadha, emperor Bimbisâra. The emperor accepted Buddhism as his personal faith and allowed the establishment of many Buddhist *vihàras*. This eventually led to the renaming of the entire region as Bihar.

At the Deer Park near Varanasi in northern India, Buddha set in motion the Wheel of Dharma by delivering his first sermon to a group of five companions with whom he had previously sought enlightenment. Together with the Buddha they formed the first Sangha, the company of Buddhist monks, and hence, the first formation of the Triple Gem (Buddha, Dharma and Sangha) was completed.

For the remaining years of his life, the Buddha is said to have traveled in the Gangetic Plain of Northeastern India and other regions.

Buddha attained *parinirvâna* in the abandoned jungles of Kushinâra.

Just before Buddha died, he reportedly told his followers that thereafter the Dharma (doctrine, teaching) would be their leader. The early arhants considered Gautama's words the primary source of Dharma and Vinaya (rules of discipline and community living), and took great pains to formulate and transmit his teachings accurately. Nonetheless, no ungarnished collection of his sayings has survived. The versions of the canon (accepted scripture) preserved in [Pâli Canon], Sanskrit, Chinese, and Tibetan are sectarian variants of a corpus that grew and crystallized during three centuries of oral transmission.

Facets of Early Buddhism

Early Buddhism remained centered around the Ganges valley, spreading gradually from its ancient heartland. The canoṇical sources record two councils, where the moṇastic Sangha established the textual collections based on the Buddha's teachings and settled certain disciplinary problems within the community.

First Buddhist Council (5th c. BCE)

The first Buddhist council was held soon just after Buddha died, and presided over by Venerable Mahâkâshyapa, one of His most senior disciples, at Râjagriha (today's Rajgir) during the 5th century under the noble support of king Ajâthashatru. The objective of the council was to record all of Buddha's teachings into the doctrinal teachings (sutra) and Abhidhamma and to codify the monastic rules (vinaya). Ânanda, one of the Buddha's main disciples and his cousin, was called upon to recite the discourses and Abhidhamma of the Buddha, and Upali, another disciple, recited the rules of the vinaya. These became the basis of the Tripiṃaka (Three Baskets), which is preserved only in Pali.

Second Buddhist Council (4th c. BCE)

The second Buddhist council was held at Vaisali following a dispute that had arisen in the Sangha over a relaxation by some monks of various points of discipline. Eventually it was decided to hold a second council at which the original Vinaya texts that had been preserved at the first Council were cited to show that these relaxations went against the recorded teachings of the Buddha.

Ashokan Proselytism (c. 261 BCE)

The Mauryan Emperor Ashoka the Great (273–232 BCE) converted to Buddhism after his bloody conquest of the territory of Kalinga (modern Orissa) in eastern India during the Kalinga War. Regretting the horrors brought about by the conflict (or using Buddhism as a cover to protect his empire), the king decided to renounce violence (as non-violence prevents revolts, etc.). He propagated the faith by building stupas and pillars urging, amongst other things, respect of all animal life and enjoining people to follow the Dharma. Perhaps the finest example of these is the Great Stupa in Sanchi, (near Bhopal).

It was constructed in the third century BCE and later enlarged. Its carved gates, called Tohans, are considered among the finest examples of Buddhist art in India. He also built roads, hospitals, resthouses, universities and irrigation systems around the country. He treated his subjects as equals regardless of their religion, politics or caste.

It is pertinent to note that Ashokan period marks the first spread of Buddhism beyond India to other countries. According to the plates and pillars left by Ashoka (the edicts of Ashoka), emissaries were sent to various countries in order to spread Buddhism, as far south as Sri Lanka and as far west as the Greek kingdoms, in particular the neighboring Greco-Bactrian Kingdom, and possibly even farther to the Mediterranean.

Third Buddhist Council (c.250 BCE)

King Ashoka convened the third Buddhist council around 250 BCE at Pataliputra (today's Patna). It was held by the monk Moggaliputtatissa. The objective of the council was to purify the Sangha, particularly from non-Buddhist ascetics who had been attracted by the royal patronage. Following the council, Buddhist missionaries were dispatched throughout the known world.

Hellenistic World

Some of the edicts of Ashoka describe the efforts made by him to propagate the Buddhist faith throughout the Hellenistic world, which at that time formed an uninterrupted continuum from the borders of India to Greece. The edicts indicate a clear understanding of the political organization in Hellenistic territories: the names and locations of the main Greek monarchs of the time are identified, and they are claimed as recipients of Buddhist proselytism: Antiochus II Theos of the Seleucid Kingdom (261–246 BCE), Ptolemy II Philadelphos of Egypt (285–247 BCE), Antigonus Gonatas of Macedonia (276–239 BCE), Magas (288–258 BCE) in Cyrenaica (modern Libya), and Alexander II (272–255 BCE) in Epirus (modern Northwestern Greece).

The conquest by Dharma has been won here, on the borders, and even six hundred yojanas (5,400–9,600 km) away, where the Greek king Antiochos rules, beyond there where the four kings named Ptolemy, Antigonos, Magas and Alexander rule, likewise in the south among the Cholas, the Pandyas, and as far as Tamraparni (Sri Lanka)." (*Edicts of Ashoka,* 13th Rock Edict, S. Dhammika).

Furthermore, according to Pâli sources, some of Ashoka's emissaries were Greek Buddhist monks, indicating close religious exchanges between the two cultures:

> "When the thera (elder) Moggaliputta, the illuminator of the religion of the Conqueror (Ashoka), had brought the (third) council to an end (...) he sent forth theras, one here and one there: (...) and to Aparantaka (the "Western countries" corresponding to Gujarat and Sindh) he sent the Greek (Yona) named Dhammarakkhita". (Mahavamsa XII).

The fact that some of Ashoka's emissaries were Greek agrees with Dr. Ranajit Pal's observation that Ashoka was the same as the Indo-Greek King Diodotus-I. Ashoka also issued edicts in the Greek language as well as in Aramaic. One of them, found in Kandahar, advocates the adoption of "piety" (using the Greek term *eusebeia* for Dharma) to the Greek community:

> "Ten years (of reign) having been completed, King Piodasses (Ashoka) made known (the doctrine of) piety to men; and from this moment he has made men more pious, and everything thrives throughout the whole world." (Trans. from the Greek original by G.P. Carratelli)

Remarkably, it is not clear how much these interactions may have been influential, but some authors have commented that some level of syncretism between Hellenist thought and Buddhism may have started in Hellenic lands at that time. They have pointed to the presence of Buddhist communities in the Hellenistic world around that period, in particular in Alexandria (mentioned by Clement of Alexandria), and to the pre-Christian monastic order of the Therapeutae (possibly a deformation of the Pâli word "Theravâda"), who may have "almost entirely drawn (its) inspiration from the teaching and practices of Buddhist asceticism" and may even have been descendants of Ashoka's emissaries to the West.

The philosopher Hegesias of Cyrene, from the city of Cyrene where Magas of Cyrene ruled, is sometimes thought to have been influenced by the teachings of Ashoka's Buddhist missionnaries.

Buddhist gravestones from the Ptolemaic period have also been found in Alexandria, decorated with depictions of the Dharma wheel. The presence of Buddhists in Alexandria has even drawn the conclusion: "It was later in this very place that some of the most active centers of Christianity were established".

In the 2nd century CE, the Christian dogmatist, Clement of Alexandria recognized Bactrian Buddhists (*œramanas*) and Indian *gymnosophists* for their influence on Greek thought:

> "Thus philosophy, a thing of the highest utility, flourished in antiquity among the barbarians, shedding its light over the nations. And afterwards it came to Greece. First in its ranks were the prophets of the Egyptians; and the Chaldeans among the Assyrians; and the Druids among the Gauls; and the *shramanas* among the Bactrians; and the philosophers of the Celts; and the Magi of the Persians, who foretold the Saviour's birth, and came into the land of Judea guided by a star. The Indian gymnosophists are also in the number, and the other barbarian philosophers. And of these there are two classes, some of them called *shramanas* and others *Brahmins*. Clement of Alexandria *"The Stromata, or Miscellanies,"* Book I, Chapter XV.

Expansion to Sri Lanka and Burma

Sri Lanka was proselytized by Ashoka's son Mahinda and six companions during the 2nd century BCE. They converted the king Devanampiya Tissa and many of the nobility. In addition, Ashoka's daughter, SaEghamitta also established the bhikkhunî (order for nuns) in SriLanka, also bringing with her a sapling of the sacred bodhi tree that was subsequently planted in Anuradhapura. This is when the Mahâvihâra monastery, a center of Sinhalese orthodoxy, was built. The Pâli canon was written down in Sri Lanka during the reign of king Vattagamani (29–17 BCE), and the Theravâda tradition flourished there. Later some great commentators worked there, such as Buddhaghoca (4th–5th century) and Dhammapâla (5th–6th century), and they systemised the traditional commentaries that had been handed down.

Although Mahâyâna Buddhism gained some influence in Sri Lanka at that time, the Theravâda ultimately prevailed and Sri Lanka turned out to be the last stronghold of it. From there it would expand again to South-East Asia from the 11th century.

In the areas east of the Indian subcontinent (modern Burma and Thailand), Indian culture strongly influenced the Mons. The Mons are said to have been converted to Buddhism from the 3rd century BCE under the proselytizing of the Indian Emperor Ashoka, before the fission between Mahâyâna and Hinayâna Buddhism. Early Mon Buddhist temples, such as Peikthano in central Burma, have been dated to between the 1st and the 5th century CE.

The Buddhist art of the Mons was especially influenced by the Indian art of the Gupta and post-Gupta periods, and their mannerist style spread widely in South-East Asia following the expansion of the Mon kingdom between the 5th and 8th centuries. The Theravâda faith expanded in the northern parts of Southeast Asia under Mon influence, until it was progressively displaced by Mahâyâna Buddhism from around the 6th century CE.

According to the *Aúokâvadâna* (2nd century CE), Ashoka sent a missionary to the north, through the Himalayas, to Khotan in the Tarim Basin, then the land of the Tocharians, speakers of an Indo-European language.

Sunga Era

The Sunga dynasty (185–73 BCE) was established in 185 BCE, about 50 years after Ashoka's death. After assassinating King Brihadrata (last of the Mauryan rulers), military commander-in-chief Pusyamitra Sunga took the throne. Buddhist religious scriptures such as the Aúokâvadâna allege that Pusyamitra (an orthodox Brahmin) was hostile towards Buddhists and persecuted the Buddhist faith. Buddhists wrote that he "destroyed monasteries and killed Monks": 84,000 Buddhist stupas which had been built by Ashoka were destroyed (Romila. Thapar), and 100 gold coins were offered for the head of each Buddhist monk. In addition, Buddhist sources allege that a large number of Buddhist monasteries (*vihâras*) were converted to Hindu temples, in such places as Nalanda, Bodhgaya, Sarnath, or Mathura.

Following Ashoka's sponsorship of Buddhism, it is possible that Buddhist institutions fell on harder times under the Sungas but no evidence of active persecution has been noted. Etienne Lamotte observes: *"To judge from the documents, Pushyamitra must be acquitted through lack of proof."* Another eminent historian, Romila Thapar points to archaeological evidence that "suggests the contrary" to the claim that Pusyamitra was a fanatical anti-Buddhist and never actually destroyed 84000 stupas as claimed by Buddhist works. Thapar stresses that Buddhist accounts are probably hyperbolic renditions of Pusyamitra's attack of the Mauryas, and merely reflect the frustration of the Buddhist religious figures in the face of the decline in the importance of their religion under the Sungas. During the period, Buddhist monks deserted the Ganges valley, following either the northern road (*uttarapatha*) or the southern road (*dakshinapatha*). Conversely, Buddhist artistic creation stopped in the old Magadha area, to reposition itself either in the northwest area of Gandhâra and Mathura or in the southeast around Amaravati. Some artistic activity also occurred in central India, as in Bhârhut, to which the Sungas may or may not have contributed.

Greco-Buddhist Interaction

In Bactria (today's northern Afghanistan), the areas west of the Indian subcontinent, neighboring Greek kingdoms had been in place since the time of the conquests of Alexander the Great around 326 BCE: first the Seleucids from around 323 BCE, then the Greco-Bactrian kingdom from around 250 BCE.

Greco-Bactrian king Demetrius I invaded India in 180 BCE as far as Pâtaliputra, establishing an Indo-Greek kingdom that was to last in various parts of northern India until the end of the 1st century BCE. Buddhism flourished under the Indo-Greek kings, and it has been suggested that their invasion of India was intended to show their support for the Mauryan empire and to protect the Buddhist faith from the alleged religious persecutions of the Sungas (185–73 BCE).

It is remarkable that one of the most famous Indo-Greek kings is Menander (reigned c. 160–135 BCE). He apparently converted to Buddhism and is presented in the Mahâyâna tradition as one of the great benefactors of the faith, on a par with king Aúoka or the later Kushan king Kanishka. Menander's coins bear the mention of the "saviour king" in Greek, and sometimes designs of the eight-spoked wheel. Direct cultural exchange is also suggested by the dialogue of the Milinda Pañha between Menander and the monk Nâgasena around 160 BCE. Upon his death, the honor of sharing his remains was claimed by the cities under his rule, and they were enshrined in stupas, in a parallel with the historic Buddha. Several of Menander's Indo-Greek successors inscribed the mention "Follower of the Dharma" in the Kharocmhî script on their coins, and depicted themselves or their divinities forming the *vitarka* mudrâ. The interaction between Greek and Buddhist cultures may have had some influence on the evolution of Mahâyâna, as the faith developed its sophisticated philosophical approach and a man-god treatment of the Buddha somewhat reminiscent of Hellenic gods.

It is also around that time that the first anthropomorphic representations of the Buddha are found, often in realistic Greco-Buddhist style: "One might regard the classical influence as including the general idea of representing a man-god in this purely human form, which was of course well familiar in the West, and it is very likely that the example of westerner's treatment of their gods was indeed an important factor in the innovation."

In Central Asia

A Buddhist gold coin from India was found in northern Afghanistan at the archaeological site of Tillia Tepe, and dated to the 1st century CE. On the reverse, it depicts a lion with a nandipada, with the Kharosthi legend "Sih[o] vigatabhay[o]" ("The lion who dispelled fear"). On the obverse, an almost naked man only wearing an Hellenistic chlamys and a petasus hat (an iconography similar to that of Hermes/ Mercury) rolls a Buddhist wheel. The legend in Kharosthi reads "Dharmacakrapravata[ko]" ("The one who turned the Wheel of the Law"). It has been suggested that this may be an early representation of the Buddha.

Rise of Mahâyâna

The rise of Mahâyâna Buddhism from the 1st century

BCE was accompanied by complex political changes in northwestern India. The Indo-Greek kingdoms were gradually overwhelmed, and their culture assimilated by the Indo-Scythians, and then the Yuezhi, who founded the Kushan Empire from around 12 BCE.

Notably, Kushans were supportive of Buddhism, and a fourth Buddhist council was convened by the Kushan emperor Kanicka, around 100 CE at Jalandhar or in Kashmir, and is usually associated with the formal rise of Mahâyâna Buddhism and its secession from Theravâda Buddhism. Theravâda Buddhism does not recognize the authenticity of this council, and it is sometimes called the "council of heretical monks".

Remarkably, the new form of Buddhism was characterized by an almost god-like treatment of the Buddha, by the idea that all beings have a Buddha-nature and should aspire to Buddhahood, and by a syncretism due to the various cultural influences within northwestern India and the Kushan Empire.

The Two Fourth Councils

The Fourth Council is said to have been convened during the reign of the Kushan emperor Kanishka around 100 CE at Jalandhar or in Kashmir. Theravâda Buddhism had its own Fourth Council in Sri Lanka about 200 years earlier in which the Pâli canon was written down *in toto* for the first time. Therefore there were two Fourth Councils: one in Sri Lanka (Theravâda), and one in Kashmir (Sarvâstivâdin).

It is said that for the Fourth Council of Kashmir, Kanishka gathered 500 monks headed by Vasumitra, partly, it seems, to compile extensive commentaries on the Abhidharma, although it is possible that some editorial work was carried out upon the existing canon itself. Allegedly during the council there were altogether three hundred thousand verses and over nine million statements compiled, and it took twelve years to complete. The main fruit of this council was the compilation of the vast commentary known as the Mahâ-Vibhâshâ ("Great Exegesis"), an extensive compendium and reference work on a portion of the Sarvâstivâdin Abhidharma. Scholars believe that it was also around this time that a significant change was made in the language of the Sarvâstivâdin canon, by converting an earlier Prakrit version into Sanskrit.

Although this change was probably effected without significant loss of integrity to the canon, this event was of particular significance since Sanskrit was the sacred language of Brahmanism in India, and was also being used by other thinkers, regardless of their specific religious or philosophical allegiance, thus enabling a far wider audience to gain access to Buddhist ideas and practices.

For this reason there was a growing tendency among Buddhist scholars in India thereafter to write their commentaries and treatises in Sanskrit. Many of the early schools, however, such as Theravâda, never switched to Sanskrit, partly because Buddha explicitly forbade translation of his discourses into what was an elitist religious language (as Latin was in medieval Europe). He wanted his monks to use a local language instead - a language which could be understood by all. Over time however, the language of the Theravâdin scriptures (Pâli) became a scholarly or elitist language as well.

Mahâyâna Expansion

From that point on, and in the space of a few centuries, Mahâyâna was to flourish and spread in the East from

India to South-East Asia, and towards the north to Central Asia, China, Korea, and finally to Japan in 538 CE and Tibet in the 7th century.

Buddhism in India

After the end of the Kushans, Buddhism flourished in India during the dynasty of the Guptas (4th-6th century). Mahâyâna centers of learning were established, especially at Nâlandâ in north-eastern India, which was to become the largest and most influential Buddhist university for many centuries, with famous teachers such as Nâgârjuna. The influence of the Gupta style of Buddhist art spread along with the faith from south-east Asia to China. Indian Buddhism had weakened in the 6th century following the White Hun invasions and Mihirkulas persecution.

Remarkably, Xuanzang reported in his travels across India during the 7th century of Buddhism being popular in Andhra, Dhanyakataka, and Dravida, which area today roughly corresponds to the modern day Indian states of Andhra Pradesh and Tamil Nadu. While reporting many deserted stupas in the area around modern day Nepal and the persecution of Buddhists by Ssanka in the Kingdom of Gouda in modern day West Bengal, Xuanzang complimented the patronage of Harcavardana during the same period.

After the Harcavardana kingdom, the rise of many small kingdoms that led to the rise of the Rajputs across the gangetic plains and marked the end of Buddhist ruling clans along with a sharp decline in royal patronage until a revival under the Pâla Empire in the Bengal region. Here Mahâyâna Buddhism flourished and spread to Tibet, Bhutan and Sikkim between the 7th and the 12th centuries before the Pâlas collapsed under the assault of the Hindu

Sena dynasty. The Pâlas created many temples and a distinctive school of Buddhist art.

Xuanzang noted in his travels that in various regions Buddhism was giving way to Jainism and Hinduism. By the 10th century Buddhism had experienced a sharp decline beyond the Pâla realms in Bengal under a resurgent Hinduism and the incorporation in Vaishnavite Hinduism of Buddha as the 9th incarnation of Vishnu. A milestone in the decline of Indian Buddhism in the North occurred in 1193 when Turkic Islamic raiders under Muhammad Khilji burnt Nâlandâ.

By the end of the 12th century, following the Islamic conquest of the Buddhist strongholds in Bihar and the loss of political support coupled with social and caste pressures, the practice of Buddhism retreated to the Himalayan foothills in the North and Sri Lanka in the south. Additionally, the influence of Buddhism also waned due to Hinduism's revival movements such as Advaita, the rise of the bhakti movement and the missionary work of Sufis.

In Central Asia

Central Asia had been influenced by Buddhism probably almost since the time of the Buddha. According to a legend preserved in Pâli, the language of the Theravâdin canon, two merchant brothers from Bactria named Tapassu and Bhallika visited the Buddha and became his disciples. They then returned to Bactria and built temples to the Buddha. Central Asia long played the role of a meeting place between China, India and Persia. During the 2nd century BCE, the expansion of the Former Han to the west brought them into contact with the Hellenistic civilizations of Asia, especially the Greco-Bactrian Kingdoms. Thereafter, the expansion of Buddhism to the north led to the formation of Buddhist communities and even Buddhist kingdoms in the oases of Central Asia. Some Silk Road cities consisted almost entirely of Buddhist stupas and monasteries, and it seems that one of their main objectives was to welcome and service travelers between east and west. The Theravâdin traditions first spread among the Turkic tribes before combining with the Mahâyâna forms during the 2nd and 3rd centuries BCE to cover modern-day Pakistan, Kashmir, Afghanistan, eastern and coastal Iran, Uzbekistan, Turkmenistan and Tajikistan. These were the ancient states of Gandhâra, Bactria, Parthia and Sogdia from where it spread to China.

Among the first of these Turkic tribes to adopt Buddhism was the Turki-Shahi as early as the 3rd century BCE. It was not, however, the exclusive faith of this region. There were also Zoroastrians, Hindus, Nestorian Christians, Jews, Manichaeans, and followers of shamanism, Tengrism, and other indigenous, nonorganized systems of belief. Various Nikâya schools persisted in Central Asia and China until around the 7th century CE. Mahâyâna started to become dominant during the period, but since the faith had not developed a Nikaya approach, Sarvâstivâdins and Dharmaguptakas remained the Vinayas of choice in Central Asian monasteries.

Various Buddhist kingdoms rose and prospered in both the Central Asian region and downwards into the Indian sub-continent such as the Kushan Empire prior to the White Hun invasion in the 5th century where under the King Mihirkula they were heavily persecuted.

It is pertinent to note that Buddhism in Central Asia started to decline with the expansion of Islam and the destruction of many stupas in war from the 7th century. The Muslims accorded them the status of dhimmis as "people of the Book", such as Christianity or Judaism and Al-Biruni wrote of Buddha as prophet "burxan". Buddhism saw a surge during the reign of Mongols following the invasion of Genghis Khan and the establishment of the Il Khanate and the Chagatai Khanate who brought their Buddhist influence with them during the 13th century, however within 100 years the Mongols who remained in that region would convert to Islam and spread Islam across all the regions of central Asia. Only the eastern Mongols and the Mongols of the Yuan dynasty would keep Vajrayâna Buddhism.

Buddhism in Parthia

Buddhism expanded westward into Arsacid Parthia, at least to the area of Merv, in ancient Margiana, today's territory of Turkmenistan. Soviet archeological teams have excavated in Giaur Kala near Merv a Buddhist chapel, a gigantic Buddha statue and a monastery. Parthians were directly involved in the propagation of Buddhism: An Shigao (c. 148 CE), a Parthian prince, went to China, and is the first known translator of Buddhist scriptures into Chinese.

In Tarim Basin

The eastern part of central Asia (Chinese Turkestan, Tarim Basin, Xinjiang) has revealed extremely rich Buddhist works of art (wall paintings and reliefs in numerous caves, portable paintings on canvas, sculpture, ritual objects), displaying multiple influences from Indian and Hellenistic cultures. Serindian art is highly reminiscent of the Gandhâran style, and scriptures in the Gandhâri script Kharocmhî have been found. Central Asians seem to have played a key role in the transmission of Buddhism to the East. The first translators of Buddhists scriptures into Chinese were Parthian (Ch: Anxi) like An Shigao (c. 148

CE) or An Hsuan, Kushan of Yuezhi ethnicity like Lokaksema (c. 178 CE), Zhi Qian and Zhi Yao or Sogdians like Kang Sengkai.

Thirty-seven early translators of Buddhist texts are known, and the majority of them have been identified as Central Asians. Central Asian and East Asian Buddhist monks appear to have maintained strong exchanges until around the 10th century, as shown by frescoes from the Tarim Basin.

These influences were rapidly absorbed however by the vigorous Chinese culture, and a strongly Chinese particularism develops from that point.

Buddhism in China

Buddhism probably arrived in China around the 1st century CE from Central Asia, although there are some traditions about a monk visiting China during Ashoka's reign. Until the 8th century it became an extremely active center of Buddhism. The year 67 CE saw Buddhism's official introduction to China with the coming of the two monks Moton and Chufarlan. In 68 CE, under imperial patronage, they established the White Horse Temple, which still exists today, close to the imperial capital at Luoyang. By the end of the second century, a prosperous community had settled at Pengcheng (modern Xuzhou, Jiangsu). The first known Mahâyâna scriptural texts are translations into Chinese by the Kushan monk Lokakcema in Luoyang, between 178 and 189 CE.

Some of the earliest known Buddhist artifacts found in China are small statues on "money trees", dated circa 200 CE, in typical Gandhâran drawing style: "That the imported images accompanying the newly arrived doctrine came from Gandhâra is strongly suggested by such early Gandhâra characteristics on this "money tree" Buddha as the high ucnica, vertical arrangement of the hair, moustache, symmetrically looped robe and parallel incisions for the folds of the arms."

Buddhism flourished during the beginning of the Tang Dynasty (618–907). The dynasty was initially characterized by a strong openness to foreign influences and renewed exchanges with Indian culture due to the numerous travels of Chinese Buddhist monks to India from the 4th to the 11th century.

The Tang capital of Chang'an (today's Xi'an) became an important center for Buddhist thought. From there Buddhism spread to Korea, and Japanese embassies of Kentoshi helped gain footholds in Japan. However foreign influences came to be negatively perceived towards the end of the Tang Dynasty. In the year 845, the Tang emperor Wuzong outlawed all "foreign" religions including Christian Nestorianism, Zoroastrianism, and Buddhism in order to support the indigenous Taoism.

Throughout his territory, he confiscated Buddhist possessions, destroyed monasteries and temples, and executed Buddhist monks, ending Buddhism's cultural and intellectual dominance. However, about a hundred years after the Great Anti-Buddhist Persecution, Buddhism revived during the Song Dynasty (1127–1279). Pure Land and Chan Buddhism, however, continued to prosper for some centuries, the latter giving rise to Japanese Zen. In China, Chan flourished particularly under the Song dynasty (1127–1279), when its monasteries were great centers of culture and learning.

Remarkably, today China boasts one of the richest collections of Buddhist arts and heritages in the world.

UNESCO World Heritage Sites such as the Mogao Caves near Dunhuang in Gansu province, the Longmen Grottoes near Luoyang in Henan province, the Yungang Grottoes near Datong in Shanxi province, and the Dazu Rock Carvings near Chongqing are among the most important and renowned Buddhist sculptural sites. The Leshan Giant Buddha, carved out of a hillside in the 8th century during the Tang Dynasty and looking down on the confluence of three rivers, is still the largest stone Buddha statue in the world.

Buddhism in Korea

Buddhism was introduced around 372 CE, when Chinese ambassadors visited the Korean kingdom of Goguryeo, bringing scriptures and images. Buddhism prospered in Korea - in particular Seon (Zen) Buddhism from the 7th century onward. However, with the beginning of the Confucean Yi Dynasty of the Joseon period in 1392, a strong discrimination took place against Buddhism until it was almost completely eradicated, except for a remaining Seon movement.

Buddhism in Japan

It is remarkable that Buddhism of Japan was introduced from Three Kingdoms of Korea in the sixth century. The Chinese priest Ganjin offered the system of Vinaya to the Buddhism of Japan in 754. As a result, the Buddhism of Japan has developed rapidly. Saichô and Kûkai succeeded to a legitimate Buddhism from China in the ninth century. Being geographically at the end of the Silk Road, Japan was able to preserve many aspects of Buddhism at the very time it was disappearing in India, and being suppressed in Central Asia and China.

From 710 CE numerous temples and monasteries were

built in the capital city of Nara, such as the five-story pagoda and Golden Hall of the Hôryû-ji, or the Kôfuku-ji temple. Countless paintings and sculptures were made, often under governmental sponsorship.

The creations of Japanese Buddhist art were especially rich between the 8th and 13th century during the periods of Nara, Heian and Kamakura. From the 12th and 13th centuries, a further development was Zen art, following the introduction of the faith by Dogen and Eisai upon their return from China. Zen art is mainly characterized by original paintings (such as sumi-e and the Enso) and poetry (especially haikus), striving to express the true essence of the world through impressionistic and unadorned "non-dualistic" representations.

The search for enlightenment "in the moment" also led to the development of other important derivative arts such as the Chanoyu tea ceremony or the Ikebana art of flower arrangement. This evolution went as far as considering almost any human activity as an art with a strong spiritual and aesthetic content, first and foremost in those activities related to combat techniques (martial arts). Buddhism remains very active in Japan to this day. Around 80,000 Buddhist temples are preserved and regularly restored.

In Tibet

It is pertinent to note that Buddhism arrived late in Tibet - the 7th century CE. The form that predominated, via the south of Tibet, was a blend of *mahâyâna* and *vajrayâna* from the universities of the Pâla empire of north India. Sarvâstivâdin influence came from the south west (Kashmir) and the north west (Khotan). Although these practitioners did not succeed in maintaining a presence in Tibet, their texts found their way into the Tibetan Buddhist canon, providing the Tibetans with almost all of their primary sources about the Foundation Vehicle. A subsect of this school, Mûlasarvâstivâda was the source of the Tibetan Vinaya.

Chan Buddhism was introduced via east Tibet from China and left its impression, but was rendered of lesser importance by early political events. From the outset Buddhism was opposed by the native shamanistic Bon religion, which had the support of the aristocracy, but with royal patronage it thrived to a peak under King Rälpachän (817-836). Terminology in translation was standardised around 825, enabling a translation methodology that was highly literal. Despite a reversal in Buddhist influence which began under King Langdarma (836-842), the following centuries saw a colossal effort in collecting available Indian sources, many of which are now extant only in Tibetan translation.

Tibetan Buddhism exerted a strong influence from the 11th century CE among the peoples of Central Asia, especially in Mongolia and Manchuria. It was adopted as an official state religion by the Mongol Yuan dynasty and the Manchu Qing dynasty that ruled China.

Southeast Asia

During the 1st century CE, the trade on the overland Silk Road tended to be restricted by the rise in the Middle-East of the Parthian empire, an unvanquished enemy of Rome, just as Romans were becoming extremely wealthy and their demand for Asian luxury was rising. This demand revived the sea connections between the Mediterranean and China, with India as the intermediary of choice. From that time, through trade connection, commercial settlements, and even political interventions, India started to strongly influence Southeast Asian countries.

Trade routes linked India with southern Burma, central and southern Siam, lower Cambodia and southern Vietnam, and numerous urbanized coastal settlements were established there. For more than a thousand years, Indian influence was therefore the major factor that brought a certain level of cultural unity to the various countries of the region. The Pâli and Sanskrit languages and the Indian script, together with Theravâda and Mahâyâna Buddhism, Brahmanism, and Hinduism, were transmitted from direct contact and through sacred texts and Indian literature such as the *Râmâyana* and the *Mahâbhârata.*

Remarkably, from the 5th to the 13th century, South-East Asia had very powerful empires and became extremely active in Buddhist architectural and artistic creation. The main Buddhist influence now came directly by sea from the Indian subcontinent, so that these empires essentially followed the Mahâyâna faith. The Sri Vijaya Empire to the south and the Khmer Empire to the north competed for influence, and their art expressed the rich Mahâyâna pantheon of the bodhisattvas.

Khmer Empire

Later, from the 9th to the 13th centuries, the Mahâyâna Buddhist and Hindu Khmer Empire dominated much of the South-East Asian peninsula. Under the Khmer, more than 900 temples were built in Cambodia and in neighboring Thailand. Angkor was at the center of this development, with a temple complex and urban organization able to support around one million urban dwellers. One of the greatest Khmer kings, Jayavarman VII (1181–1219), built large Mahâyâna Buddhist structures at Bayon and Angkor Thom.

Srivijayan Empire

Srivijaya, a maritime empire centered at Palembang on the island of Sumatra in Indonesia, adopted Mahâyâna and Vajrayâna Buddhism under a line of rulers named the Sailendras. Yijing described Palembang as a great centre of Buddhist learning where the emperor supported over a thousand monks at his court. Atisha studied there before travelling to Tibet as a missionary. Srivijaya spread Buddhist art during its expansion in Southeast Asia. Numerous statues of bodhisattvas from this period are characterized by a very strong refinement and technical sophistication, and are found throughout the region.

Extremely rich architectural remains are visible at the temple of Borobudur the largest Buddhist structure in the world, built from around 780 CE in Java, which has 505 images of the seated Buddha. Srivijaya declined due to conflicts with the Chola rulers of India, before being destabilized by the Islamic expansion from the 13th century.

Vietnam

Following the destruction of Buddhism in mainland India during the 11th century, Mahâyâna Buddhism declined in southeast Asia, to be replaced by the introduction of Theravâda Buddhism from Sri Lanka.

Emergence of the Vajrayâna

It is remarkable here that Vajrayâna Buddhism, also called tantric Buddhism, first emerged in eastern India between the 5th and 7th centuries CE. It is sometimes considered a sub-school of Mahâyâna and sometimes a third major "vehicle" (*yâna*) of Buddhism in its own right. The Vajrayâna is an extension of Mahâyâna Buddhism in that it does not offer new philosophical perspectives, but rather introduces additional techniques (*upaya*, or 'skilful means'), including the use of visualizations and other yogic practices.

Many of the practices of tantric Buddhism are common with Hindu tantricism: the usage of mantras, yoga and the burning of sacrificial offerings. Early Vajrayâna practitioners were forest-dwelling mahasiddhas who lived on the margins of society, but by the 9th century Vajrayâna had won acceptance at major Mahâyâna monastic universities such as Nâlandâ and Vikramashîla.

Along with much of the rest of Indian Buddhism, the Vajrayâna was eclipsed in the wake of the late 12th century Muslim invasions. It has persisted in Tibet, where it was wholly transplanted from the 7th to 12th centuries, and on a limited basis in Japan as well where it evolved into Shingon Buddhism.

Theravâda Renaissance

From the 11th century, the destruction of Buddhism in the Indian mainland by Islamic invasions led to the decline of the Mahâyâna faith in South-East Asia. Continental routes through the Indian subcontinent being compromised, direct sea routes developed from the Middle-East through Sri Lanka to China, leading to the adoption of the Theravâda Buddhism of the Pâli canon, introduced to the region around the 11th century CE from Sri Lanka. King Anawrahta (1044–1077); the historical founder of the Burmese empire, unified the country and adopted the Theravâdin Buddhist faith. This initiated the creation of thousands of Buddhist temples at Pagan, the capital, between the 11th and 13th century

Around 2,000 of them are still standing. The power of the Burmese waned with the rise of the Thai, and with the seizure of the capital Pagan by the Mongols in 1287, but

Theravâda Buddhism remained the main Burmese faith to this day. The Theravâda faith was also adopted by the newly founded ethnic Thai kingdom of Sukhothai around 1260. Theravâda Buddhism was further reinforced during the Ayutthaya period (14th–18th century), becoming an integral part of Thai society.

Remarkably, in the continental areas, Theravâda Buddhism continued to expand into Laos and Cambodia in the 13th century. From the 14th century, however, on the coastal fringes and in the islands of south-east Asia, the influence of Islam proved stronger, expanding into Malaysia, Indonesia, and most of the islands as far as the southern Philippines. Nevertheless, since Soeharto's rise to power in 1966, there has been a remarkable renaissance of Buddhism in Indonesia.

This is partly due to the requirements of Soeharto's New Order for the people of Indonesia to adopt one of the five official religions: Islam, Protestantism, Catholicism, Hinduism or Buddhism. Today it is estimated there are some 10 millions Buddhists in Indonesia. A large part of them are people of Chinese ancestry.

Buddhism to the Western Hemisphere

It is pertinent to note here that after the Classical encounters between Buddhism and the West recorded in Greco-Buddhist art, information and legends about Buddhism seem to have reached the West sporadically. An account of Buddha's life was translated in to Greek by John of Damascus, and widely circulated to Christians as the story of Barlaam and Josaphat. By the 1300s this story of Josaphat had become so popular that he was made a Catholic saint. The next direct encounter between Europeans and Buddhism happened in Medieval times when the Franciscan friar

William of Rubruck was sent on an embassy to the Mongol court of Mongke by the French king Saint Louis in 1253. The contact happened in Cailac (today's Qayaliq in Kazakhstan), and William originally thought they were wayward Christians (Foltz, "Religions of the Silk Road").

During the period after Hulagu, the Mongol Ilkhans increasingly adopted Buddhism. Numerous Buddhist temples dotted the landscape of Persia and Iraq, none of which survived the 14th century. The Buddhist element of the Il-Khanate died with Arghun. The Kalmyk Khanate was founded in the 17th century with Tibetan Buddhism as its main religion, following the earlier migration of the Oirats from Dzungaria through Central Asia to the steppe around the mouth of the Volga River. During the course of the 18th century, they were absorbed by the Russian Empire.

At the end of the Napoleonic wars, Kalmyk cavalry units in Russian service entered Paris. Kalmykia is remarkable for being the only state in Europe where the dominant religion is Buddhism. Interest in Buddhism increased during the colonial era, when Western powers were in a position to witness the faith and its artistic manifestations in detail. The opening of Japan in 1853 created a considerable interest in the arts and culture of Japan, and provided access to one of the most thriving Buddhist cultures in the world.

Buddhism started to enjoy a strong interest from the general population in the West following the turbulence of the 20th century. In the wake of the 1959 Tibetan uprising, a Tibetan diaspora has made Tibetan Buddhism in particular more widely accessible to the rest of the world. It has since spread to many Western countries, where the tradition has gained popularity.

Among its prominent exponents is the 14th Dalai Lama of Tibet. The number of its adherents is estimated to be between ten and twenty million.

Buddhism has been displaying a strong power of attraction, due to its tolerance, its lack of deist authority and determinism, and its focus on understanding reality through self inquiry.

Buddhist way of life is of curious interest to many westerners. They are inclined to mysterious chanting and other Buddhist practices. Thus, to sum up, it can be surmised that as a religion Buddhism is still a live religion, gaining recognition in present day's materialistic societies.

In the next chapers we will discuss the main schools of Buddhism.

REFERENCES

1. Bhagwan Das, *"Revival of Buddhism in India and Role of Dr. Baba Saheb B.R. Ambedkar"* (Dalit Today Prakashan, 18/455, Indira Nagar, Lucknow, U.P., India, 1998).
2. *Damien Keown Dictionary of Buddhism* (Oxford University Press, 2003).
3. John Boardman, *The Diffusion of Classical Art in Antiquity* (Princeton University Press, 1994)
4. "Living Zen" by Robert Linssen (Grove Press, New York, 1958).
5. *"National Museum Arts asiatiques- Guimet"* (Editions de la Reunion des Musées Nationaux, Paris, 2001).
6. Richard Foltz *Religions of the Silk Road* by (St. Martin's Griffin, New York, 1999).
7. Sir Charles Eliot, *"Hinduism and Buddhism: An Historical Sketch."*
8. "The Crossroads of Asia. Transformation in Image and symbol", 1992.
9. *"The Times Atlas of Archeology"* (Times Books Limited, London, 1991).

10. Thomas McEvilley, *"The Shape of Ancient Thought. Comparative studies in Greek and Indian Philosophies"* (Allworth Press, New York, 2002).

5

Mahayana School

The historical source of the name "Mahâyâna" is polemical, having its origin in a debate about what the real teachings of the Buddha are. As such, its use in any context except as that pertaining to a living tradition is controversial amongst Theravadin practitioners and some scholars. The earliest known mention of "Mahâyâna" occurs in the *Lotus Sûtra* between the first century BCE and the first century CE. However, some scholars such as Seishi Karashima suggest the term first used in an earlier Gandhari Prakrit version of the *Lotus Sûtra* was not "*mahâyâna*" but the Prakrit word "*mahâjâna*" in the sense of "*mahâjñâna*" (great knowing). At a later stage when the early Prakrit word was converted into Sanskrit, this "*mahâjâna*", being phonetically ambivalent, was mistakenly converted into "*mahâyâna*", possibly by contamination arising through proximity to the famous *Parable of the Burning House* which talks of carts.

In fact, Mahayana ('Great Vehicle') is one of the two main existing branches of Buddhism and a term for classification of Buddhist philosophies and practice. It was founded in India.

The name "Mahâyâna" is used in three main senses:

1. As a living tradition, Mahâyâna is the larger of the

two major traditions of Buddhism existing today, the other being Theravâda. This classification is largely undisputed by all Buddhist schools.

2. According to the Mahâyâna method of classification of Buddhist philosophies, "Mahâyâna" refers to a level of spiritual motivation (also known as "Bodhisattvayâna"). According to this classification, the alternative approach is called "Hînayâna", or "Úravakayâna". It is also recognized by Theravâda Buddhism, but is not considered very relevant for practice.
3. According to the Vajrayâna scheme of classification of practice paths, Mahâyâna refers to one of the three routes to enlightenment, the other two being Hînayâna and Vajrayâna. This classification is the teachings of Vajrayâna Buddhism, and is not recognized by Mahâyâna and Theravâda Buddhism.

Although the Mahâyâna movement traces its origin to Gautama Buddha, scholars believe that it originated in India in the 1st century CE, or the 1st century BCE. Scholars hold that Mahâyâna only became a mainstream movement in India in the fifth century CE, since that is when Mahâyânist inscriptions started to appear in epigraphic records in India. Before the 11th century CE (while Mahâyâna was still present in India), the Mahâyâna sûtras were still in the process of being revised. Thus, several different versions may have survived of the same sûtra. These different versions are invaluable to scholars attempting to reconstruct the history of Mahâyâna.

Remarkably, in the course of its history, Mahâyâna spread throughout East Asia. The main countries in which it is practiced today are China, Japan, Korea, and Vietnam.

The main schools of Mahâyâna Buddhism today are Pure Land, Zen (Chan), Nichiren Buddhism, Shingon, Tibetan Buddhism and Tendai. The latter three schools have both Mahâyâna and Vajrayâna practice traditions.

Mahâyâna Buddhism in India can be divided into two periods: early Mahâyâna Buddhism and late Mahâyâna Buddhism.

The period of Early Mahâyâna Buddhism concerns the origins of Mahâyâna and the contents of early Mahâyâna sûtras.

The origins of Mahâyâna are still not completely understood. Although the Mahâyâna movement traces its origin to Gautama Buddha, scholars believe that it originated in south India in the 1st century CE, or the 1st century BCE. Other scholars point to evidence that Mahâyâna originated in north-west India in the 1st century CE.

Some scholars say that Mahâyâna could have initially developed in the south-east of India as a non-monastic tradition, and that later it underwent a process of monasticization and emerged in the north-west of India as a monastic movement. Mahâyâna was first propagated into China by Lokakcema, the first translator of Mahâyâna sûtras into Chinese during the second century CE. Three sources appear to have made significant contributions to the rise of Mahâyâna Buddhism:

1. The Early Buddhist Schools. Some important Mahâyâna texts such as the Prajñâpâramitâ often refer to doctrines associated with the Sarvâstivâda, which were mentioned or incorporated into Mahâyâna texts. In terms of content, however, the MahâsaEghika doctrine is closer to Mahâyâna

thought, particularly those of the sub-schools such as the Lokottaravâdins.

2. Biographical literature of the Buddha composed by people said to have belonged to "the vehicle that praised the Buddha". This literature (comprising the jâtakas, avadânas and other texts describing the life of Buddha) may have had its origins in the various early schools, but developed in ways that transcended the existing sectarian lines and contributed to the rise of Mahâyâna Buddhism.

   Buddhist poets wrote their work with purposes different from those of scholars who were concerned with doctrinal issues, and they used literary expressions which transcended doctrinal lines between the schools.

3. Stûpa worship. Stûpas — which were initially mere monuments to Gautama Buddha — increasingly became places of devotion and of spreading Buddhism to the masses, the majority of whom were illiterate laymen. On the inside wall of a stûpa, pictures were drawn or sculpted depicting the life of Buddha and his previous lives as a bodhisattva. This has given rise to devotion to the Buddha and the bodhisattvas, distinct from the purely monastic *sangha* of the Early Buddhist schools. However, this theory has been rejected by a number of scholars. Early Mahâyânists may well have used the stûpas that were not affiliated with the early Buddhist schools as a basis for proselytizing. The commonly expressed misconception that Mahâyâna started as a lay-inspired movement is based on a selective reading of a very tiny sample of extant Mahâyâna sûtra literature.

Currently scholars have moved away from this limited corpus of literature, and have started to open up early Mahâyâna literature which is very ascetic and expounds the ideal of the monk's life in the forest. A scholarly consensus about the origin of the Mahâyâna has not yet been reached, but it has been suggested that by the time Mahâyâna in India became mainstream in the 5th century CE, "it had become what it originally most strongly objected to: a fully landed, sedentary, lay-oriented monastic institution". Before that, the Mahâyâna movement may well have been either a marginalized ascetic group of monks living in the forest, or a group of conservatives embedded in mainstream, socially engaged early Buddhist monasteries. Most scholars conclude that Mahâyâna remained a marginal movement until the 5th century CE.

The earliest sûtras which show some Mahâyâna influence are the Proto-Mahâyâna sûtras such as the *Ajitasena Sûtra*. These sûtras contain a mixture of Mahâyâna and pre-Mahâyâna ideas, and occur in a world where monasticism is the norm, which is typical of the Pâli Suttas; there is none of the antagonism towards the *úrâvakas* or the notion of arahantship, which is typical of many later Mahâyâna sûtras such as the *Lotus Sûtra*, or *Vimalakîrti Nirdesha*.

However, the sûtra also has an arahant seeing all the Buddha fields, it is said that reciting the name of the sûtra will save beings from suffering and the hell realms, and a meditative practice is described which allows the practitioner to see with the eyes of a Buddha, and to receive teachings from Buddhas in ways that are very much typical of Mahâyâna sûtras. The earliest Mahâyâna sûtras proper were thc very first versions of the *Perfection of Wisdom* series and texts concerning Akcobhya Buddha, which were probably composed in the first century BCE in the south of

India. Some slightly later early Mahâyâna sûtras are the Chinese translations made by the Kushan monk Lokakcema in the Chinese capital of Luoyang between 178 and 189 CE.

Thus scholars generally think that the earliest Mahâyâna sûtras were mainly composed in the south of India, and later the activity of writing additional scriptures was continued in the north. However, the assumption that the presence of an evolving body of Mahâyâna scriptures implies the contemporaneous existence of Mahâyâna as a distinct religious movement may be a serious misstep.

The earliest stone inscription containing a recognizably Mahâyâna formulation and a mention of the Buddha Amitabha was found in the Indian subcontinent in Mathura, and dated to around 180 CE. Remains of a statue of a Buddha bear the Brahmi inscription:

> "Made in the year 28 of the reign of king Huvishka, ... for the Buddha Amitabha" (Mathura Museum).

However, this image was in itself extremely marginal and isolated in the overall context of Buddhism in India at the time, and had no lasting or long-term consequences. The epigraphical evidence for Mahâyâna in the period before the 5th century is very limited in comparison to the multiplicity of Mahâyâna writings transmitted from central Asia to China at that time.

During the period of late Mahâyâna Buddhism, four major types of thought developed: Madhyamaka, Yogâcâra, Tathâgatagarbha, and Buddhist Logic as the last and most recent. In India, the two main philosophical schools of the Mahâyâna were the Madhyamaka and the later Yogâcâra. Although Harvey claims that there were no great Indian teachers associated with *tathâgatagarbha* thought, others such as Williams point out the centrality of *Ratnagotravibhâga* (*Uttaratantra*) to the *tathâgatagarbha* tradition. However, he states: "One of the features of Tibetan Buddhism in contrast with that of East Asia is the strong tendency to approach the sutras indirectly through the medium of exegetical treatises if at all. The Ratnagotravibhâga has played a relatively small role in East Asian Buddhism, where the primacy has always been given to sutra study."

Remarkably, from the 5th century CE onwards, Mahâyâna was a strong movement in India, possibly owing to support by the Gupta dynasty. It spread from India to south-east Asia, and towards the north to central Asia and the far east. The influence of Mahâyâna in China seems to have been reached at an earlier time than in India, where Mahâyâna remained an obscure group until the 5th century. The late stage of Mahâyâna Buddhism in India is found largely in the Vajrayâna schools, which were replaced in India and central Asia after the early milliennium by Islam (Sufism etc) and Hinduism, and in south-east Asia by Theravâda Buddhism from Sri Lanka and Islam and continued to exist in certain regions of the Himalayas. The earlier stage forms such as Pure Land Buddhism are still popular in East Asia, where many new religious movements and syncretisms have also been formed with Mahâyâna elements.

Main Philosophy

It is pertinent to note that a few things can be said with certainty about Mahâyâna Buddhism, especially its early Indian form, other than that the Buddhism practiced in China, Vietnam, Korea, Tibet, and Japan is Mahâyâna Buddhism. Mahâyâna can be described as a loosely bound bundle of many teachings, which was thus able to contain the various contrasting ideas found between those differing teachings of whose elements it is comprised. Mahâyâna is a large religious and philosophical structure. It constitutes an inclusive faith characterized by the adoption of new Mahâyâna sûtras in addition to the earlier *Âgama* texts, and a shift in the basic purpose and concepts of Buddhism. Mahâyâna sees itself as penetrating further and more profoundly into the Buddha's Dharma.

There is a tendency in Mahâyâna sûtras to regard adherence to these sûtras as generating spiritual benefits greater than those which arise from being a follower of the non-Mahâyâna approaches to Dharma.

Thus the *Úrîmâlâ Sûtra* claims that the Buddha said that devotion to Mahâyâna is inherently superior in its virtues to the following of the *œravaka* or *pratyekabuddha* path. Mahâyâna Buddhist schools de-emphasize the ideal of the release from suffering and the attainment of *nirvâGa*, found in the early Buddhist schools. The fundamental principles of Mahâyâna doctrine were based on the possibility of universal liberation from suffering for all beings (hence the "great vehicle") and the existence of Buddhas and bodhisattvas embodying Buddha-nature.

Some Mahâyâna schools simplify the expression of faith by allowing salvation to be alternatively obtained through the grace of the Buddha Amitabha by having faith and devoting oneself to chanting to Amitabha. This devotional lifestyle of Buddhism is most strongly emphasized by the Pure Land schools and has greatly contributed to the success of Mahâyâna in East Asia, where spiritual elements traditionally relied upon chanting of a Buddha's name, of *mantras* or *dhâranîs*; reading of Mahâyâna sûtras and mysticism. In Chinese Buddhism, most monks, let alone lay people, practice Pure Land, some combining it with Chan (Zen). Most Mahâyâna schools believe in a pantheon of quasi-divine bodhisattvas that devote themselves to personal excellence, ultimate knowledge, and the salvation of humanity and all other sentient beings (animals, ghosts, demigods, etc.).

Zen Buddhism is a school of Mahâyâna which often de-emphasizes the pantheon of bodhisattvas and instead focuses on the meditative aspects of the religion. In Mahâyâna, the Buddha is seen as the ultimate, highest being, present in all times, in all beings, and in all places, and the bodhisattvas come to represent the universal ideal of altruistic excellence.

Main Characteristics

- Universalism, in that, in those schools of Mahâyâna that still have large followings, everyone will become a Buddha. (See, for example, the *Lotus Sûtra*);
- Bodhicitta as the main focus of realization. (See, for example, various *Prajñâpâramitâ sûtras*);
- Compassion through the transferral of merit;
- Transcendental immanence, in that the immortal Buddha principle is present within all beings. (See, for example, Buddha-nature and the *MahaparinirvâGa Sûtra*, *Angulimaliya Sutra*, *Úrîmâlâ Sûtra* and *Tathâgatagarbha Sûtra*.)

"Philosophical" Mahâyâna tends to focus on the first three characteristics (universalism, enlightened wisdom, compassion) and, in some schools, the Buddha-nature, without showing much interest in supernatural constructions, while "devotional" Mahâyâna focuses mainly on salvation towards other-worldly realms.

Universalism

Mahâyâna traditions generally consider that attainment of the level of an arhat is not final. This is based on a subtle doctrinal distinction between the Mahâyâna and some of the early Buddhist schools concerning the issues of *nirvana-with-remainder* and *nirvana-without-remainder*. The Mahâyâna position here is similar to that of the early school of the Mahâsanghika. Some of the early schools considered that nirvana-without-remainder always follows nirvana-with-remainder (buddhas first achieve enlightenment and then, at 'death', mahâparinirvâna) and that nirvana-without-remainder is final; whereas the Mahâyâna traditions consider that nirvana-without-remainder is always followed by nirvana-with-remainder – the state of attainment of the Hînayâna arhat is not final, and is eventually succeeded by the total awakening of buddhahood.

This distinction is most evident regarding doctrinal concerns about the capability of a Buddha after nirvana, which is identified by the early schools as being nirvana-without-remainder. Most importantly, amongst the early schools, a complete buddha is not able to directly point the way to nirvana after death. This is a major distinction between the early schools and some schools of the Mahâyâna, who conversely state that once a *sanyaksanbuddha* arises, he or she continues to directly and actively point the way to nirvana until there are no beings left in sansâra. Because the views of early schools and Mahâyâna differ in this respect, this is exactly why some Mahâyâna schools do not talk about a bodhisattva postponing nirvana, and exactly why the early schools do. However, some Mahâyâna schools do talk of a bodhisattva deliberately refraining from Buddhahood. For example, the early schools held that

Maitreya will not attain nirvana while Gautama Buddha's teachings still exist. In contrast, some Mahâyâna schools hold that Maitreya will be the next buddha manifest in this world and will introduce the Dharma when it no longer exists; he is not postponing his nirvana to do so, and when he dies (or enters *mahâparinirvâna*), he will likewise continue to teach the Dharma for all time. Moreover, some Mahâyâna schools argue that although it is true that, for this world-system, Maitreya will be the next buddha to manifest, there are an infinite number of world-systems, many of which have currently active buddhas or buddhas-to-be manifesting. Because the Mahâyâna traditions assert that eventually everyone will achieve total enlightenment, the Mahâyâna is labeled universalist, whereas the stance of the early scriptures is that attaining *nibbâna* depends on effort and is not pre-determined.

Bodhisattva

The later Mahâyâna school holds that pursuing only the release from suffering and attainment of nirvana (as held by pre-sectarian Buddhism and the early Buddhist schools) is too narrow an aspiration, because it lacks the motivation of actively resolving to liberate all other beings as well as oneself from *samsâra*.

Remarkably, the primary focus of some Mahâyâna schools is bodhicitta, the vow to strive for the awakened mind of buddhahood for the benefit of both oneself and all other sentient beings. As Ananda Coomaraswamy notes, "The most essential part of the Mahayana is its emphasis on the Bodhisattva ideal, which replaces the Arhatta, or ranks before it."

According to Mahâyâna teachings, being a high-level bodhisattva involves possessing a mind of great compassion conjoined with insight (*prajñâ*) realizing the reality of emptiness and/or the buddha essence of all beings. Mahâyâna teaches that the practitioner will realize Buddhahood, the final goal of full awakening: an omniscient, blissful mind completely free from suffering and its causes, with which one is able to work tirelessly for the benefit of all living beings. Six virtues or perfections (*pâramitâ*) are listed for the bodhisattva: generosity, morality, patience, energy, meditation, and wisdom.

Many "philosophical" schools and Mahâyâna sûtras have focused on the nature of enlightenment and nirvana itself, from the Madhyamaka and its rival Yogâcâra, to the Tathâgatagarbha teachings and Zen.

Compassion

Compassion (*karuna*) is the other key concept of Mahâyâna. It is important in all schools of Buddhism but is particularly emphasized in Mahâyâna as a prerequisite for bodhicitta. It is also linked to the idea that acquired merit can be transmitted to others. The bodhisattvas are the main actors of compassion, Avalokiteœvara (known in East Asia as Guan Yin) being foremost among them.

Although having reached enlightenment, bodhisattvas usually make a vow to postpone entering into nirvana until all other beings have also been saved. They devote themselves to helping others reach enlightenment. This teaching may be a skillful means one strives to liberate all beings only as long as one is under the delusion that there are any actual "beings" to save.

The Mahâyâna idea that liberation is universal also allows for one to focus less on the release of personal suffering and more on humanity's salvation and is consequently said to be more universally compassionate and caring for the welfare of others than other traditions of Buddhism.

A comparison between the Hînayâna and Mahâyâna approaches in Buddhist philosophy, made by the 10th century Tibetan author Jé Gampopa in *The Jewel Ornament of Liberation* follows:

> Clinging to the well-being of mere peace signifies the lower capacity [Hinayana] attitude wherein the longing to transcend suffering is focused on oneself alone. This precludes the cherishing of others and hence there is little development of altruism. [...] When loving kindness and compassion become part of one, there is so much care for other conscious beings that one could not bear to liberate oneself alone. [...] Master Manjuúrîkîrti has said: "A Mahâyâna follower should not be without loving kindness and compassion for even a single moment", and "It is not anger and hatred but loving kindness and compassion that vouchsafe the welfare of others".

Skillful means is found in the *Lotus Sûtra*, the earliest dated Mahâyâna sûtra and is accepted in all Mahâyâna schools of thought. It is any effective method which aids the attainment of awakening. It does not necessarily mean that some particular method is "untrue" but is simply any means or stratagem that is conducive to spiritual growth and which leads the various types of beings to awakening and nirvana. A skillful means could thus be certain motivational words for a particular listener or even the noble eightfold path itself.

Basic Buddhism (what Mahâyâna would term *úravakayâna* or *pratyekabuddhayâna*) is an expedient method for helping people begin the noble Buddhic path and advance quite far. But the path is not wholly traversed, according to some Mahâyâna schools, until the practitioner has striven for and attained Buddhahood for the liberation of all other sentient beings from suffering. In an ultimate sense, all verbalised Dharma is a "skillful means", since Dharma or Truth cannot really be expressed in words or concepts.

Anything that effectively points the way to liberation can be termed a "skillful means" - an effective method for awakening beings from the sleep of spiritual ignorance. Mahâyâna often adopts a pragmatic notion of truth: doctrines are "true" in the sense of being spiritually beneficial. Some scholars have stated that the exercise of skill to which it refers, the ability to adapt one's message to the audience, is of enormous importance in the Pâli Canon. In fact the Pâli term *upâya-kosalla* does occur in the Pâli Canon, in the *Sangiti Sutta* of the *Digha Nikaya*.

"Devotional" Mahâyâna developed a rich cosmography, with various Buddhas and bodhisattvas residing in paradise realms. The concept of the three bodies (*trikâya*) supports these constructions, making the Buddha himself a transcendental figure. Dr. Guang Xing describes the Mahâyâna Buddha as "an omnipotent divinity endowed with numerous supernatural attributes and qualities ...[He] is described almost as an omnipotent and almighty godhead." Under various conditions, the realms over which Buddha presides could be attained by devotees after their death so that when reborn they could strive towards buddhahood in the best possible conditions.

Depending on the sect, this salvation to "paradise" can be obtained by faith, imaging, or sometimes even by the simple invocation of the Buddha's name. This approach to salvation is at the origin of the mass appeal of devotional Buddhism, especially represented by the Pure Land. This rich cosmography also allowed Mahâyâna to be quite syncretic and accommodating of other faiths or deities. Various origins have been suggested to explain its emergence, such as "popular Hindu devotional cults (*bhakti*), and Persian and Greco-Roman theologies, which filtered into India from the northwest".

Buddha-Nature

The teaching of a "Buddha nature" or "Buddha principle" (*Buddha-dhâtu*), innate to and inseparable from each and every sentient being, is a doctrine which constitutes the "absolutely final culmination" of the Buddha's Dharma. It may be based on the "luminous mind" concept found in the Âgamas.

The essential idea, articulated in the Tathâgatagarbha sûtras, but not accepted by all Mahayanists, is that no being is without a concealed but indestructible interior link to the awakening of *bodhi* and that this link is an uncreated element (*dhâtu*) or principle deep inside each being which constitutes nothing less than the deathless, diamond-like "essence of the self". The *MahâparinirvâGa Sûtra* states: "The essence of the Self (*âtman*) is the subtle *tathâgatagarbha* ..." while the later *Lankâvatâra Sûtra* states that the *tathâgatagarbha* might be taken to be *âtman*, but it is not.

In the *tathâgatagarbha* class of sûtras, the word "*âtman*" is used in a way defined by and specific to these sûtras. According to some scholars, the Buddha nature (*tathâgatagarbha*) discussed in some Mahâyâna sûtras does not represent a substantial self (*âtman*); rather, it is a positive language and expression of emptiness (*úûnyatâ*) and represents the potentiality to realize Buddhahood through Buddhist practices.

It is the "true self" in representing the innate aspect of the individual which makes actualizing the ultimate personality possible. The actual "seeing and knowing" of this *Buddha-dhâtu* (co-terminous with the *Dharmakâya* or self of Buddha) is said to usher in nirvanic Liberation. This *Buddha-dhâtu* or *tathâgatagarbha* is stated to be found in every single person, ghost, god and sentient being. In the *tathâgatagarbha* sûtras, the Buddha is portrayed as describing the Buddha-dhatu as uncreated, deathless and ultimately beyond rational grasping or conceptualisation.

Yet it is this already real and present, hidden internal element of awakeness (*bodhi*) which, according to the *tathâgatagarbha* sûtras, prompts beings to seek liberation from worldly suffering and enables them to attain the spotless bliss which lies at the heart of their being. Once the veils of negative thoughts, feelings and unwholesome behaviour (the *kleœas*) have been eliminated from the mind and character, the indwelling Buddha Principle (*Buddha-dhâtu*: "Buddha Nature") is enabled to shine forth unimpededly and to transform the seer of it into a Buddha.

Prior to the period of these sûtras, Mahâyâna metaphysics had been dominated by teachings on emptiness in the form of Madhyamaka philosophy. The language used by this approach is primarily negative, and the *tathâgatagarbha* genre of sûtras can be seen as an attempt to state orthodox Buddhist teachings of dependent origination and on the mysterious reality of nirvana using positive language instead, to prevent people from being turned away from Buddhism by a false impression of nihilism. In these sûtras the perfection of the wisdom of not-self is stated to be the true self; the ultimate goal of the path is then characterized using a range of positive language that had been used in Indian philosophy previously by essentialist philosophers, but which was now transmuted into a new Buddhist vocabulary to describe a being who has successfully completed the Buddhist path. An exegetical treatise (i.e., interpretive text) on Buddha Nature is the *Uttaratantra*, which sees Buddha nature (*tathâgatagarbha*) not as that which is caused and conditioned but as that which is eternal, uncaused, unconditioned, and incapable of being destroyed, although temporarily concealed within worldly beings by adventitious defilements.

According to Buddhist scholar Dr. C. D. Sebastian, the *Uttaratantra's* reference to a transcendental Self (*âtma-pâramitâ*) should be understood as "the unique essence of the universe," thus the universal and immanent essence of Buddha nature is the same throughout time and space.

Main Scriptures

Like Theravâda, Mahâyâna Buddhism takes the basic teachings of the Buddha as recorded in early scriptures as the starting point of its teachings, such as those concerning karma and rebirth, the four noble truths, the middle way and the eightfold path. Whereas these basic teachings are preserved in the Pâli canon, transmitted by the Theravâdin tradition, Mahâyâna Buddhists use different recensions of these discourses in compilations known as the "*Âgamas*", and which largely overlap with the Pâli Canon in content. The surviving *Âgamas* in Chinese translation belong to at least two schools, while most of the *Âgamas* were never translated into Tibetan. In addition to accepting the scriptures of the various early Buddhist schools as valid, Mahâyâna Buddhism also maintains large additional collections of sûtras not found or recognized in Theravâda Buddhism.

In Mahâyâna Buddhism, these Mahayana sûtras have a greater importance than the *Âgamas*. Although these scriptures claim to be the factual words of the Buddha, scholars believe that they were written by monks who felt the need to restate and change the doctrines of early Buddhism. The first of the Mahâyâna-specific writings were written probably around the 1st century BCE or 1st century CE.

Some of the Mahâyâna sûtras, such as certain parts of the *Perfection of Wisdom* sûtras, are presented as actual sermons of the Buddha that had been hidden. By some accounts, these sermons were passed on by oral tradition, as with other sûtras; other accounts state that they were hidden and then revealed several centuries later by some mythological route. In addition to sûtras, some Mahâyâna texts are essentially commentaries. Among the earliest major Mahâyâna scriptures attested to historically are the *Perfection of Wisdom* (*Prajñâpâramitâ*) sûtras, the *Avatansaka Sûtra*, the *Lotus Sûtra*, the *Vimalakîrti Sûtra*, and the *Nirvâna Sûtra*.

Dating back at least to the *Sandhinirmocana Sûtra* is a classification of the exoteric corpus of Buddhism into three categories, based on ways of understanding the nature of reality, known as the "three turnings of the wheel of Dharma".

According to this view, there were three such "turnings":

1. In the first turning Úâkyamuni Buddha taught the four noble truths at VârâGasî in the 5th century BC, which led to the founding of Buddhism and the later of the early Buddhist schools. Details of the first turning are described in the Dhammacakkapavattana Sutta. The oldest scriptures do not mention any further turnings other than this first turning.

2. The Mahâyâna tradition claims there was a second turning in which the *Perfection of Wisdom* sûtras were taught at Vulture's Peak, which led to the Mahâyâna schools. Generally, scholars conclude that the Mahâyâna scriptures (including the *Perfection of Wisdom* sûtras) were composed from the first century CE onwards.
3. According to the Vajrayâna tradition, there was a third turning which took place at Dhanyakataka sixteen years after Buddha's enlightenment. Scholars have strongly denied that Vajrayâna teachings appeared at that time, and placed them at a much later time. The first tantric (Vajrayâna Buddhist) texts appeared in the 3rd century CE, and they continued to appear until the 12th century CE. The early Buddhist schools regard the second and third turnings as unauthentic and falsifications of the true teachings of the Buddha contained in the first turning. Mahâyâna tradition states that the first turning contains the basic doctrines aimed at the initial disciples (*úrâvakas*). Mahâyâna claims that the Madhyamaka teachings, the *Prajñâpâramitâ* sûtras and Yogâcâra doctrines are the most accurate view of reality.

Tibetan teachers, particularly of the Gelugpa school, regard the second turning as the highest teaching. The Tathâgatagarbha teachings are normally included in the third turning of the wheel. The Chinese tradition has a different scheme.

Scholars have noted that many key Mahâyâna ideas are closely connected to the earliest texts of Buddhism. The seminal work of Mahâyâna philosophy, Nâgârjuna's Mûlamadhyamakakârikâ, mentions the Canon's *Katyâyana*

Sûtra by name, and may be an extended commentary on that work (found in the *Âgamas*). Nâgârjuna systematized the Madhyamaka school of Mahâyâna philosophy.

He may have arrived at his positions from a desire to achieve a consistent exegesis of the Buddha's doctrine as recorded in the canon. In his eyes the Buddha was not merely a forerunner, but the very founder of the Madhyamaka system. Nâgârjuna also referred to a passage in the canon regarding "nirvanic consciousness" in two different works. Yogâcâra, the other prominent Mahâyâna school which exists in dialectic with the Madhyamaka school, gave a special significance to the canon's "Lesser Discourse on Emptiness".

A passage there (which the discourse itself emphasizes) is often quoted in later Yogâcâra texts as a true definition of emptiness. Both the Madhyamakas and the Yogâcârins saw themselves as preserving the Buddhist Middle Way between the extremes of nihilism (everything as unreal) and substantialism (substantial entities existing). The Yogâcârins criticized the Madhyamakas for tending towards nihilism, while the Madhyamakas criticized the Yogâcârins for tending towards substantialism.

Mahâyâna and Theravâda

Although the Theravâda school is usually described as belonging to Hînayâna, some authors have argued that it should not be considered such from the Mahâyâna perspective. Their view is based on a different understanding of the concept of Hînayâna. Rather than regarding the term as referring to any school of Buddhism that hasn't accepted the Mahâyâna canon and doctrines, such as those pertaining to the role of the boddhisatva, these authors argue that the classification of a school as "Hînayâna" should be crucially dependent on the adherence to a specific phenomenological position. They point out that unlike the now-extinct Sarvâstivâda school which was the primary object of Mahâyâna criticism, the Theravâda does not claim the existence of independent *dharmas*; in this it maintains the attitude of early Buddhism.

On the contrary, some contemporary Theravâdin figures have indicated a sympathetic stance toward the Mahâyâna philosophy found in the *Heart Sutra* and the *Fundamental Stanzas on the Middle Way* (*Mûlamadhyamakakârikâ*). The Mahâyânists were bothered by the substantialist thought of the Sarvâstivâdins and Sautrântikas, and in emphasizing the doctrine of emptiness, Kalupahana holds that they endeavored to preserve the early teaching. The Theravâdins too refuted the Sarvâstivâdins and Sautrântikas (and other schools) on the grounds that their theories were in conflict with the non-substantialism of the canon. The Theravâda arguments are preserved in the Kathâvatthu. Thus, according to this view, no form of real Hînayâna Buddhism survives today.

The *Basic Points Unifying the Theravâda and the Mahâyâna* is an important Buddhist ecumenical statement created in 1967 during the First Congress of the World Buddhist Sangha Council (WBSC), where its founder Secretary-General, the late Venerable Pandita Pimbure Sorata Thera, requested the Ven. Walpola Rahula to present a concise formula for the unification of all the different buddhist traditions. This text was then unanimously approved by the Council.

Text of the Original Document

1. The Buddha is our only Master (teacher and guide)

2. We take refuge in the Buddha, the Dharma and the SaEgha (the Three Jewels)
3. We do not believe that this world is created and ruled by a God.
4. We consider that the purpose of life is to develop compassion for all living beings without discrimination and to work for their good, happiness, and peace; and to develop wisdom (prajñâ) leading to the realization of Ultimate Truth
5. We accept the Four Noble Truths, namely dukkha, the arising of dukkha, the cessation of dukkha, and the path leading to the cessation of dukkha; and the law of cause and effect (pratîtyasamutpâda)
6. All conditioned things are impermanent (anitya) and dukkha, and that all conditioned and unconditioned things (dharma) are without self (anâtma).
7. We accept the thirty-seven qualities conducive to enlightenment (bodhipakcadharma) as different aspects of the Path taught by the Buddha leading to Enlightenment.
8. There are three ways of attaining bodhi or Enlightenment: namely as a disciple (úrâvaka), as a pratyekabuddha and as a samyaksambuddha (perfectly and fully enlightened Buddha). We accept it as the highest, noblest, and most heroic to follow the career of a Bodhisattva and to become a samyaksambuddha in order to save others.
9. We admit that in different countries there are differences regarding Buddhist beliefs and practices. These external forms and expressions should not be confused with the essential teachings of the Buddha.

Expansion of the Formula

Ven. Walpola Sri Rahula in 1981 offered an alternative to the Nine-point formula above restating it as follows:

- Whatever our sects, denominations or systems, as Buddhists we all accept the Buddha as our Master who gave us the Teaching.
- We all take refuge in the Triple Jewel: the Buddha, our Teacher; the Dhamma, his teaching; and the Sangha, the Community of holy ones. In other words, we take refuge in the Teacher, the Teaching and the Taught.
- Whether Theravâda or Mahâyâna, we do not believe that this world is created and ruled by a god at his will.
- Following the example of the Buddha, our Teacher, who is embodiment of Great Compassion (mahâkaruna) and Great Wisdom (mahâprajñâ), we consider that the purpose of life is to develop compassion for all living beings without discrimination and to work for their good, happiness and peace; and to develop wisdom leading to the realization of Ultimate Truth.
- We accept the Four Noble Truths taught by the Buddha, namely, Dukkha, the fact that our existence in this world is in predicament, is impermanent, imperfect, unsatisfactory, full of conflict; Samudaya, the fact that this state of affairs is due to our egoistic selfishness based on the false idea of self; Nirodha, the fact that there is definitely the possibility of deliverance, liberation, freedom from this predicament by the total eradication of the egoistic selfishness; and Magga, the fact that this liberation

can be achieved through the Middle Path which is eight-fold, leading to the perfection of ethical conduct (sila), mental discipline (samadhi) and wisdom (panna).

- We accept the universal law of cause and effect taught in the Pamiccasamuppada (Skt. pratîtyasamutpada; Conditioned Genesis or Dependent Origination), and accordingly we accept that everything is relative, interdependent and interrelated and nothing is absolute, permanent and everlasting in this universe.
- We understand, according to the teaching of the Buddha, that all conditioned things (samkhara) are impermanent (anicca) and imperfect and unsatisfactory (dukkha), and all conditioned and unconditioned things (dhamma) are without self (anatta).
- We accept the Thirty-seven Qualities conducive to Enlightenment (bodhipakkhiyadhamma) as different aspects of the Path taught by the Buddha leading to Enlightenment, namely:
  - o Four Forms of Presence of Mindfulness (Pali: satipatthana; Skt. smrtyupasthana);
  - o Four Right Efforts (Pali. sammappadhana; Skt. samyakpradhana);
  - o Four Bases of Supernatural Powers (Pali. iddhipada; Skt. rddhipada);
  - o Five Faculties (indriya: Pali. saddha, viriya, sati, samadhi, panna; Skt. sraddha, virya, smrti, samadhi, prajna);
  - o Five Powers (bala, same five qualities as above);

- o Seven Factors of Enlightenment (Pali. bojjhanga; Skt. bobhyanga);
- o Eight-fold Noble Path (Pali. ariyamagga; Skt. aryamarga).

- There are three ways of attaining Bodhi or Enlightenment according to the ability and capacity of each individual: namely, as a Sravaka (disciple), as a Pratyekabuddha (Individual Buddha) and as a Samyaksambuddha (Perfectly and Fully Enlightened Buddha). We accept it as the highest, noblest and most heroic to follow the career of a Boddhisattva and to become a Samyksambuddha in order to save others. But these three states are on the same Path, not on different paths. In fact, the Sandhinirmocana-sutra, a well-known important Mahayana sutra, clearly and emphatically says that those who follow the line of Úrâvakayâna (Vehicle of Disciples) or the line of Pratyekabuddha-yana (Vehicle of Individual Buddhas) or the line of Tathagatas (Mahayana) attain the supreme Nirvana by the same Path, and that for all of them there is only one Path of Purification (visuddhi-marga) and only one Purification (visuddhi) and no second one, and that they are not different paths and different purifications, and that Sravakayana and Mahayana constitute One Vehicle One Yana (ekayana) and not distinct and different vehicles or yanas.

REFERENCES

1. Beal, *Catena of Buddhist Scriptures from the Chinese*, (London, 1871).
2. D.T. Suzuki, in *The Monist*, volume xxiv, (Chicago, 1914). *The Monist* was edited by Paul Carus.

3. Kevin Lynch, *The Way of The Tiger: A Buddhist's Guide To Achieving Nirvana*, Yojimbo Temple, 2005.
4. Schopen, G. "The inscription on the Kusan image of Amitabha and the character of the early Mahayana in India", *Journal of the International Association of Buddhist Studies 10*, 1990.
5. "The Vision of the Buddha", Tom Lowenstein.

6

Theravada School of Buddhism

According to Buddhist scholar A.K. Warder, the Theravada "spread rapidly south from Avanti into Maharastra and Andhra and down to the Chola country (Kanchi), as well as Ceylon. For sometime they maintained themselves in Avanti as well as in their new territories, but gradually they tended to regroup themselves in the south, the Great Vihara (Mahavihara) in Anuradhapura, the capital of Ceylon, become the main centre of their tradition, Kanchi a secondary center and the northern regions apparently relinquished to other schools." There is little information about the later history of Theravada Buddhism in India, and it is not known when it disappeared in its country of origin.

Now we will discuss the theravada school of Buddhism. Theravada is the oldest surviving Buddhist school. It was founded in India. It is relatively conservative, and generally closest to early Buddhism, and for many centuries has been the predominant religion of Sri Lanka (about 70% of the population) and most of continental Southeast Asia (Cambodia, Laos, Burma, Thailand).

Theravada is also practiced by minorities in parts of southwest China (by the Shan and Tai ethnic groups),

Vietnam (by the Khmer Krom), Bangladesh (by the ethnic groups of Baruas, Chakma, and Magh), Malaysia and Indonesia, while recently gaining popularity in Singapore and the Western World. Today Theravada Buddhists number over 100 million worldwide, and in recent decades Theravada has begun to take root in the West and in the Buddhist revival in India.

The Theravâda school is ultimately derived from the Vibhajjavâda (or "doctrine of analysis") grouping which was a continuation of the older Sthavira (or "teaching of the Elders") group at the time of the Third Buddhist Council around 250 BC, during the reign of Emperor Asoka in India. Vibhajjavadins saw themselves as the continuation of orthodox Sthaviras and after the Third Council continued to refer to their school as the Sthaviras/Theras ('The Elders'), their doctrines were probably similar to the older Sthaviras but were not completely identical. After the Third Council geographical distance led to the Vibhajjavâdins gradually evolving into four groups: the Mahîúâsaka, Kâúyapîya, Dharmaguptaka and the Tâmraparnîya. The Theravada is descended from the Tâmraparnîya, which means "the Sri Lankan lineage". Some sources claim that only the Theravada actually evolved directly from the Vibhajjavâdins.

The name of Tamraparniya was given to the Sri Lankan lineage in India but there is no indication that this referred to any change in doctrine or scripture from the Vibhajjavadins, since the name points only to geographical location. The Theravadan accounts of its own origins mention that it received the teachings that were agreed upon during the Third Buddhist Council, and these teachings were known as the Vibhajjavada. In the 7th century, Chinese pilgrims Xuanzang and Yi Jing refer to the Buddhist school in Sri Lanka as 'Sthavira'. In ancient India, those schools that used Sanskrit as their religious language referred to this school as the *Sthaviras*, but those that use Pali as their religious language referred to this school as the *Theras*. Both Sthaviras and Theras both literally mean "the Elders". The school has been using the name *Theravada* for itself in a written form since at least the 4th century, when the term appears in the *Dipavamsa*.

The Theravada school had also reached Burma around the time it arrived in Sri Lanka and something of a synergy gradually developed. Around the end of the 10th century, for example, war in Sri Lanka had extinguished the Theravadan ordination lineage, and a contingent of Burmese monks had to be imported to rekindle it. Burmese and Sri Lankan Theravada reinforced each other sufficiently, so that by the time Buddhism died out in India in the 11th century, it had established a stable home in these countries. Gradually Theravada spread to Thailand, Laos, and Cambodia. Although the Theravada tradition was always reputed to be one of the more conservative schools, like the other Nikaya Buddhist schools in India at one point it included Mahâyâna practioners ("Mahâyâna-Theravâda" or "Mahâyâna-Sthaviravâda"), according to reports of Chinese pilgrims such as Xuanzang. Royal houses in Sri Lanka and Southeast Asia associated themselves closely with Buddhism. States in those areas strictly enforced orthodoxy, and ensured that Theravada remained traditionalist. This contrasts with the relationship of Buddhism to states throughout most of Buddhism's history in India.

According to Sinhalese tradition, Buddhism was first brought to Sri Lanka by Mahinda, who is believed to have been the son of the Mauryan emperor Asoka, in the third century BCE, as a part of the missionary activities of the Asokan era. In Sri Lanka, Mahinda established the

Mahavihara Monastery of Anuradhapura. Later it became divided into three subgroups, known after their monastic centers as the Mahavihara, the Abhayagiri Vihara, and the Jetavanavihara. In 1164, with the guidance of two monks from a forest branch of the Mahavihara, the Sri Lankan King reunited all bhikkhus in Sri Lanka into the orthodox Mahavihara school. A few years after the arrival of Sthavira Mahinda, Sanghamitta, who is also believed to be the daughter of Emperor Asoka, came to Sri Lanka. She started the first nun order in Sri Lanka, but the nun order died out in Sri Lanka in the 11th century and in Burma in the 13th. In 429 CE, by request of China's emperor, nuns from Anuradhapura were sent to China to establish the Nun Order. The order was then spread to Korea. In 1996, 11 selected Sri Lankan nuns were ordained fully as Bhikkhunis by a team of Theravada monks in concert with a team of Korean Nuns in India.

There is disagreement among Theravada vinaya authorities as to whether such ordinations are valid. In the last few years the head of the Dambulla chapter of the Siyam Nikaya in Sri Lanka has carried out ordination ceremonies for hundreds of nuns. This has been criticized by some other leading figures in the Siyam Nikaya and Amarapura Nikaya, and the governing council of Burmese Buddhism has declared that there can be no valid ordination of nuns in modern times, though some Burmese monks disagree with this. According to Mahavamsa the Sri Lanka chronical, after the conclusion of the Third Buddhist Council, a missionary was also sent to Suvannabhumi where two monks Sona and Uttara, are said to have proceeded. Scholar opinions differ as to where exactly this land of Suvannabhumi is located, but Suvannabhumi is believed to be located somewhere in the area which now includes lower Burma, Thailand, Malay Peninsula and Sumatra Island.

The Mon and Pyu were among the earliest people to inhabit Burma. Recent archaeological research at a Pyu settlement in the Samon Valley (around 100 km south-east of Bagan) has shown that they had trade links with India from 500-400 BC and with China around 200 BC. Chinese sources which have been dated to around 240 A.D. mention a Buddhist kingdom by the name of Lin-Yang, which some scholars have identified as the ancient Pyu kingdom of Beikthano 300 km north of Yangon.

The Burmese slowly became Theravadan when they came into contact with the Pyu and Mon civilization. The Thais also slowly became Theravadan as they came into contact with the Mon civilization. Despite its success in Southeast Asia, Theravada Buddhism in China has generally been limited to areas bordering Theravada countries.

Recent Developments

Coming to present age. The following modern trends or movements have been observed in theravada.

1. *Modernism:* attempts to adapt to the modern world and adopt some of its ideas; includes among other things:
   (a) green movement
   (b) syncretism with other Buddhist traditions
   (c) universal inclusivity.
2. *Reformism:* attempts to restore a supposed earlier, ideal state of Buddhism; includes in particular the adoption of Western scholars' theories of original

Buddhism (in recent times the "Western scholarly interpretation of Buddhism" is the official Buddhism prevailing in Sri Lanka and Thailand.)

3. *Neotraditionalism:* includes among other things
   (a) revival of ritualism
   (b) remythologization
4. *Ultimatism:* tendency to concentrate on advanced teachings such as the Four Noble Truths at the expense of more elementary ones
5. revival of the Theravada bhikkhuni lineage
6. revival of samatha meditation
7. insight meditation
8. social action
9. devotional religiosity
10. reaction to Buddhist nationalism
11. renewal of forest monks.

Buddhist revivalism has also reacted against changes in Buddhism caused by colonialist regimes. Western colonialists and Christian missionaries deliberately imposed a particular type of Christian monasticism on Buddhist clergy in Sri Lanka and colonies in Southeast Asia, restricting monks' activities to individual purification and temple ministries.

Prior to British colonial control, monks in both Sri Lanka and Burma had been responsible for the education of the children of lay people, and had produced large bodies of literature. After the British takeover, Buddhist temples were strictly administered and were only permitted to use their funds on strictly religious activities. Christian ministers were given control of the education system and their pay became state funding for missions. Foreign, especially British rule had an enervating effect on the sangha.

According to Walpola Rahula, Christian missionaries displaced and appropriated the educational, social, and welfare activities of the monks, and inculcated a permanent shift in views regarding the proper position of monks in society through their institutional influence upon the elite. Many monks in post-colonial times have been dedicated to undoing this paradigm shift. Movements intending to restore Buddhism's place in society have developed in both Sri Lanka and Myanmar.

Philosophy

Notably, Theravada promotes the concept of Vibhajjavada (Pali), literally "Teaching of Analysis." This doctrine says that insight must come from the aspirant's experience, critical investigation, and reasoning instead of by blind faith; however, the scriptures of the Theravadan tradition also emphasize heeding the advice of the wise, considering such advice and evaluation of one's own experiences to be the two tests by which practices should be judged. In Theravada, the cause of human existence and suffering (*dukkha*) is identified as craving (*tanha*), which carries with it the defilements (*kilesas*). Those defilements that bind human to the cycle of rebirth are classified into a set of ten "Fetters", while those defilements that impede concentration (*samadhi*) are presented in a fivefold set called the "Five Hindrances".

The level of defilement can be coarse, medium, and subtle. It is a phenomenon that frequently arises, remains temporarily and then vanishes. Theravadans believe defilements are not only harmful to oneself, but also harmful to others. They are the driving force behind all inhumanities a human being can commit. Theravadans believe these defilements are habits born of ignorance (*avijja*) that afflict the minds of all unenlightened beings, who cling to them and their influence in their ignorance of the truth.

But in reality, those mental defilements are nothing more than taints that have afflicted the mind, creating suffering and stress. Unenlightened beings cling to the body, under the assumption that it represents a Self, whereas in reality the body is an impermanent phenomenon formed from the four basic elements.

Often characterized by earth, water, fire and air, in the early Buddhist texts these are defined to be abstractions representing the sensorial qualities solidity, fluidity, temperature, and mobility, respectively. The mental defilements' frequent instigation and manipulation of the mind is believed to have prevented the mind from seeing the true nature of reality.

Unskillful behavior in turn can strengthen the defilements, but following the Noble Eightfold Path can weaken or eradicate them. Unenlightened beings are also believed to experience the world through their imperfect six sense doors (eye, ear, nose, tongue, tactile sense, and mind) and use the mind, clouded by defilements, to form their own interpretation, perception and conclusion. In such a condition the perception or conclusion made will be based on that being's own illusion of reality.

In the state of *jhana* (deep concentration), the five physical sense doors will fade, the mental defilements will be suppressed, and wholesome mental traits will become strengthened. The mind can then be used to investigate and gain insight into the true nature of reality. There are three stages of defilements. During the stage of passivity the defilements lies dormant at the base of the mental continuum as latent tendencies (*anusaya*), but through the impact of sensory stimulus it will manifest (*pariyutthana*) itself to the surface of consciousness in the form of unwholesome thoughts, emotions, and volitions.

If they gather additional strength, the defilement will reach the dangerous stage of transgression (*vitikkama*), which will then involve physical or vocal actions. In order to be free from suffering and stress, Theravadans believe that the defilements need to be permanently uprooted. Initially they are restrained through mindfulness to prevent them from taking over mental and bodily action.

They are then uprooted through internal investigation, analysis, experience and understanding of their true nature by using *jhana*. This process needs to be repeated for each and every defilement. The practice will then lead the meditator to realize the Four Noble Truths, Enlightenment, and Nirvana. Nirvana is the ultimate goal of Theravadans, and is said to be a state of perfect bliss wherein the person is liberated from the repeated cycle of birth, illness, aging and death. Theravadans believe that every individual is personally responsible for their own self-awakening and liberation, as they are the ones that were responsible for their own actions and consequences. Simply learning or believing in the true nature of reality as expounded by the Buddha is not enough, the awakening can only be achieved through direct experience and personal realization.

An individual will have to follow and practice the Noble Eightfold Path as taught by the Buddha to discover the reality for themselves. In Theravada belief, Buddhas, gods or deities are incapable of giving a human being the awakening or lifting them from the state of repeated cycle of birth, illness, aging and death (*samsara*).

For Theravadans, Buddha is only a Teacher of the Noble Eightfold Path, while gods or deities are still subject to anger, jealousy, hatred, vengeance, craving, greed, delusion, and death. It is believed that some people who practice with earnestness and zeal can attain Nirvana within a single lifetime, as did many of the first few generations of Buddha's disciples. For others, the process may take multiple lifetimes, with the individual reaching higher and higher states of realization. One who has attained Nirvana is called an *Arahant.*

Since Lord Buddha is believed to have possessed the ultimate knowledge on guiding a person through the process of enlightenment, Theravadans believe that disciples of a Buddha attain enlightenment the most quickly. According to the early scriptures, the Nirvana attained by *Arahants* is identical to that attained by the Buddha himself, as there is only one type of Nirvana. Buddha was superior to *Arahants* because the Buddha had discovered the path all by himself, and has taught it to others (i,e., metaphorically turning the wheel of Dhamma). *Arahants*, on the other hand, attained Nirvana due in part to the Buddha's teachings.

Theravadans revere the Buddha as a single supremely gifted person but do recognize the existence of other such Buddhas in the distant past and future. Maitreya (Pali: Metteyya), for example, is mentioned very briefly in the Pali Canon as a Buddha who will come in the distant future. Traditionally Theravadans can either have the conviction (or "faith") in the Buddha's teaching and practice the minor precepts in the hope of gaining some minor benefits or they can investigate and verify by direct experience the truth of the Buddha's teaching by practicing the *jhana* which is part of the Noble Eightfold Path for their own Enlightenment.

First and foremost, the Theravada philosophy is a continuous analytical process of life, not a mere set of ethics and rituals.

The ultimate theory of Theravada uses the Four Noble Truths, also known as the Four Sublime Truths. In the simplest form these can be described as the problem, the cause, the solution and the pathway to solution (implementation).

A formal description of the Four Noble Truths follows:

1. Dukkha (suffering): This can be somewhat broadly classified into three categories. Inherent suffering, or the suffering one undergoes in all the worldly activities, what one suffers in day-to-day life: birth, aging, diseases, death, sadness, etc. In short, all that one feels from separating from "loving" attachments and/or associating with "hating" attachments is encompassed into the term.

The second class of suffering, called *Suffering due to Change*, implies that things suffer due to attaching themselves to a momentary state which is held to be "good"; when that state is changed, things are subjected to suffering. The third, termed *Sankhara Dukkha*, is the most subtle. Beings suffer simply by not realizing that they are mere aggregates with no definite, unchanging identity.

2. Dukkha Samudaya (cause of suffering): Craving, which leads to Attachment and Bondage, is the cause of suffering. Formally, this is termed *Tanha*. It can be classified into three instinctive drives. *Kama Tanha* is the Craving for any pleasurable sense object (which involves sight, sound, touch, taste, smell and mental perceptives). *Bhava*

Tanha is the Craving for attachment to an ongoing process, which appears in various forms, including the longing for existence. *Vibhava Tanha* is the Craving for detachment from a process, which includes non-existence and causes the longing for self-annihilation.

3. Dukkha Nirodha (cessation of suffering): One cannot possibly adjust the whole world to one's taste in order to eliminate suffering and hope that it will remain so forever. This would violate the chief principle of Change. Instead, one adjusts one's own mind through detachment so that the Change, of whatever nature, has no effect on one's peace of mind. Briefly stated, the third Noble Truth implies that elimination of the cause (craving) eliminates the result (suffering). This is inferred in the scriptural quote by The Buddha, 'Whatever may result from a cause, shall be eliminated by the elimination of the cause'.

4. Dukkha Nirodha Gamini Patipada (pathway to freedom from suffering): This is the Noble Eightfold Pathway towards freedom or Nirvana. The path can roughly be rendered into English as right view, right intention, right speech, right actions, right livelihood, right effort, right mindfulness and right concentration.

Salient Features

These are the three characteristics of all conditioned phenomena in Theravada thought.

1. Anicca (impermanence): Change is. All conditioned phenomena are subject to change, including physical characteristics, qualities, assumptions, theories, knowledge, etc.

Nothing is permanent, because, for something to be permanent, there has to be an unchanging cause behind it. Since all causes are recursively bound together, there can be no ultimate unchanging cause.

2. Dukkha (suffering): Craving causes suffering, since what is craved is transitory, changing, and perishing. The craving for impermanent things causes disappointment and sorrow. There is a tendency to label practically everything in the world, as either "good", "comfortable" or "satisfying", as opposed to "bad", "uncomfortable", and "unsatisfying". Because we label things in terms of like and dislike, we create suffering for ourselves. If one succeeds in giving up the tendency to label things and free himself from the instincts that drive him towards attaining what he himself labels collectively as "liking", he attains the ultimate freedom. The problem, the cause, the solution and the implementation, all of these are within oneself, not outside.

3. Anatta (not-self): The concept of *Anatta* can be explained as the lack of a fixed, unchanging identity; there is no permanent, essential Self. A living being is a composite of the five aggregates (*khandhas*), which is the physical forms (*rupa*), feelings or sensations (*vedana*), perception (*sanna*), mental formations (*sankhara*), and consciousness (*vinnana*), none of which can be identified as one's Self. From the moment of conception, all entities (including all living beings) are subject to a process of continuous change.

A practitioner should, on the other hand, develop and refine his or her mind to a state so as to see through this phenomenon.

Noble Disciplines

The pathway towards Nirvana, or the Noble Eightfold Pathway is sometimes stated in a more concise manner, known as the Three Noble Disciplines. These are known as discipline (*sîla*), training of mind (*samâdhi*) and wisdom (*paññâ*).

Meditation

Meditation means the positive reinforcement of one's mind. Broadly categorized into Samatha and Vipassana, Meditation is the key tool implemented in attaining jnana. Samatha literally means "to make skillful", and has other renderings also, among which are "tranquilizing, calming", "visualizing", and "achieving". Vipassana means "insight", or "abstract understanding". In this context, Samatha Meditation makes a person skillful in concentration of mind. Once the mind is sufficiently concentrated, Vipassana allows one to see through the veil of ignorance.

In the Pali Canon discourses, the Buddha frequently instructs his disciples to practice samadhi (concentration) in order to establish and develop jhana (full concentration). Jhana is the instrument used by the Buddha himself to penetrate the true nature of phenomena (through investigation and direct experience) and to reach Enlightenment.

Right Concentration (*samma-samadhi*) is one of the elements in the Noble Eightfold Path. Samadhi can be developed from mindfulness with breathing (*anapanasati*), from visual objects (*kasina*), and repetition of phrases. The traditional list contains 40 objects of meditation (*kammammhâna*) to be used for Samatha Meditation. Every object has a specific goal; for example, meditation on the parts of the body (*kayanupassana* or *kayagathasathi*) will result in a lessening of attachment to our own bodies and those of others, resulting in a reduction of sensual desires.

Mettâ (loving kindness) generates the feelings of goodwill

and happiness toward ourselves and other beings; metta practice serves as an antidote to ill-will, wrath and fear.

Levels of Attainment

Through practice, (Theravadan) practitioners can achieve four stages of enlightenment:

1. Stream-Enterers: Those who have destroyed the first three fetters (false view of *Self*, doubt, and clinging to rites and rituals) will be safe from falling into the states of misery (they will not be born as an animal, preta (ghost, or hell being). At most they will have to be reborn only seven more times before attaining Nirvana.

2. Once-Returners: Those who have destroyed the first three fetters and have lessened the fetters of lust and hatred will attain Nirvana after being born once more in the world.

3. Non-Returners: Those who have destroyed the five lower fetters, which bind beings to the world of the senses. Non-returners will never again return to the human world and after they die, they will be born in the high heavenly worlds, there to attain Nirvana. Attaining the state of non-returner is portrayed in the early texts as the ideal goal for laity.

4. Arahants: Those who have reached Enlightenment, realized Nirvana, and have reached the quality of deathlessness are free from all the fermentations of defilement. Their ignorance, craving and attachments have ended. Attaining the state of arahant is portrayed in the early texts as the ideal goal for monastics.

Main Scriptures

The Theravada school upholds the Pali Canon or Tipitaka

as the most authoritative collection of texts on the teachings of Gautama Buddha. The Sutta and Vinaya portion of the Tipitaka shows considerable overlap in content to the Agamas, the parallel collections used by non-Theravada schools in India which are preserved in Chinese and partially in Sanskrit, Prakrit, and Tibetan, and the various non-Theravada Vinayas. On this basis, both these sets of texts are generally believed to be the oldest and most authoritative texts on Buddhism by scholars. It is also believed that much of the Pali Canon, which is still used by Theravâda communities, was transmitted to Sri Lanka during the reign of Asoka.

After being orally transmitted (as was the custom in those days for religious texts) for some centuries, were finally committed to writing in the last century BCE, at what the Theravada usually reckons as the fourth council, in Sri Lanka. Theravada is one of the first Buddhist schools to commit the whole complete set of its Buddhist canon into writing. Much of the material in the Canon is not specifically "Theravadan", but is instead the collection of teachings that this school preserved from the early, non-sectarian body of teachings. According to Peter Harvey:

The Theravadans, then, may have *added* texts to the Canon for some time, but they do not appear to have tampered with what they already had from an earlier period. The Pali Tipitaka consists of three parts: the Vinaya Pitaka, Sutta Pitaka and Abhidhamma Pitaka. Of these, the Abhidhamma Pitaka is believed to be a later addition to the first two pitakas, which, in the opinion of many scholars, were the only two pitakas at the time of the First Buddhist Council.

The Pali Abhidhamma was not recognized outside the Theravada school. In the 4th or 5th century Buddhaghosa

Thera wrote the first Pali commentaries to much of the Tipitaka (which were based on much older manuscripts, mostly in old Sinhalese), and after him many other monks wrote various commentaries, which have become part of the Theravada heritage. These texts, however, do not enjoy the same authority as the Tipitaka does. The Tipitaka is composed of 45 volumes in the Thai edition, 40 in the Burmese and 58 in the Sinhalese, and a full set of the Tipitaka is usually kept in its own (medium-sized) cupboard.

The commentaries, together with the Abhidhamma, define the specific Theravada heritage. Related versions of the Sutta Pitaka and Vinaya Pitaka were common to all the early Buddhist schools, and therefore do not define only Theravada, but also the other early Buddhist schools, and perhaps the teaching of Gautama Buddha himself. Theravada Buddhists consider much of what is found in the Chinese and Tibetan scriptural collections to be apocryphal, meaning that they are not authentic words of the Buddha.

Traditionally, Theravada Buddhism has observed a distinction between the practices suitable for a lay person and the practices undertaken by ordained monks (in ancient times, there was a separate body of practices for nuns). While the possibility of significant attainment by laymen is not entirely disregarded by the Theravada, it occupies a position of significantly less prominence than in the Mahayana and Vajrayana traditions.

This distinction - as well as the distinction between those practices advocated by the Pali Canon, and the folk religious elements embraced by many monks - have motivated some scholars to consider Theravada Buddhism to be composed of multiple separate traditions, overlapping though still distinct.

Most prominently, the anthropologist Melford Spiro in his work *Buddhism and Society* separated Burmese Theravada into three groups: *Apotropaic Buddhism* (concerned with providing protection from evil spirits), *Kammatic Buddhism* (concerned with making merit for a future birth), and *Nibbanic Buddhism* (concerned with attaining the liberation of Nirvana, as described in the Tipitaka).

He stresses that all three are firmly rooted in the Pali Canon. These categories are not accepted by all scholars, and are usually considered non-exclusive by those who employ them.

The role of lay people has traditionally been primarily occupied with activities that are commonly termed *merit making* (falling under Spiro's category of kammatic Buddhism). Merit making activities include offering food and other basic necessities to monks, making donations to temples and monasteries, burning incense or lighting candles before images of the Buddha, and chanting protective or merit-making verses from the Pali Canon.

Some lay practitioners have always chosen to take a more active role in religious affairs, while still maintaining their lay status. Dedicated lay men and women sometimes act as trustees or custodians for their temples, taking part in the financial planning and management of the temple. Others may volunteer significant time in tending to the mundane needs of local monks (by cooking, cleaning, maintaining temple facilities, etc.).

Lay activities have traditionally not extended to study of the Pali scriptures, nor the practice of meditation, though in the 20th Century these areas have become more accessible to the lay community, especially in Thailand. A number of senior monastics in the Thai Forest Tradition, including Ajahn Buddhadasa, Luang Ta Maha Bua, Ajahn Plien Panyapatipo, Ajahn Pasanno, and Ajahn Jayasaro, have begun teaching meditation retreats outside of the monastery for lay disciples.

In the UK, Ajahn Chah a disciple of Ajahn Mun, set up a monastic lineage at Chithurst in West Sussex, "Cittaviveka", with his disciple Ajahn Sumedho, then "Amaravati" in Hertfordshire was founded which has a retreat center for lay retreats. Ajahn Sumedho extended this to Harnham in Northumberland as Aruna Ratanagiri under the present guidance of Ajahn Munindo, another disciple of Ajahn Chah.

Nirvana, the highest goal of Theravada Buddhism, is attained through study and the practice of morality, meditation and wisdom (sila, samadhi, panna). The goal of Nirvana (and its associated techniques) have traditionally been seen as the domain of the fully ordained monastic, whereas many of the same techniques can be used by laypeople to generate happiness in their lives, without focusing on Nirvana. Monastic roles in the Theravada can be broadly described as being split between the role of the (often urban) scholar monk and the (often rural or forest) meditation monk.

Both types of monks serve their communities as spiritual teachers and officiants by presiding over spiritual ceremonies and providing instruction in basic Buddhist morality and teachings. Scholar monks undertake the path of studying and preserving the Pali literature of the Theravada. They may devote little time to the practice of meditation, but may attain great respect and renown by becoming masters of a particular section of the Pali Canon or its commentaries.

Masters of the Abhidhamma, called Abhidhammika, are particularly respected in the scholastic tradition.

Meditation monks, often called forest monks because of their association with certain wilderness-dwelling traditions, are considered to be specialists in meditation. While some forest monks may undertake significant study of the Pali Canon, in general meditation monks are expected to learn primarily from their meditation experiences and personal teachers, and may not know more of the Tipitaka than is necessary to participate in liturgical life and to provide a foundation for fundamental Buddhist teachings. More so than the scholastic tradition, the meditation tradition is associated with the attainment of certain supernatural powers described in both Pali sources and folk tradition. These powers include the attainment of Nirvana, mind-reading, supernatural power over material objects and their own material bodies, seeing and conversing with gods and beings living in hell, and remembering their past lives.

Ordination

The minimum age for ordaining as a Buddhist monk is 20 years, reckoned from conception. However, boys under that age are allowed to ordain as novices (samanera), performing a ceremony such as *Shinbyu* in Burma. Novices shave their heads, wear the yellow robes, and observe ten basic precepts. Although no specific minimum age for novices is mentioned in the scriptures, traditionally boys as young as seven are accepted. This tradition follows the story of the Lord Buddha's son, Rahula, who was allowed to become a novice at the age of seven. Monks follow 227 rules of discipline, while nuns follow 311 rules.

In most Theravada countries, it is a common practice for young men to ordain as monks for a fixed period of time.

In Thailand and Burma, young men typically ordain for the 3 month Rain Retreat (vassa), though shorter or longer periods of ordination are not rare. Traditionally, temporary ordination was even more flexible among Laotians. Once they had undergone their initial ordination as young men, Laotian men were permitted to temporarily ordain again at any time, though married men were expected to seek their wife's permission.

Throughout Southeast Asia, there is little stigma attached to leaving the monastic life. Monks regularly leave the robes after acquiring an education, or when compelled by family obligations or ill health. Ordaining as a monk, even for a short period, is seen as having many virtues. In many Southeast Asian cultures, it is seen as a means for a young man to "repay" his parents for their work and effort in raising him, because the merit from his ordination accrues to them as well. Thai men who have ordained as a monk may be seen as more fit husbands by Thai women, who refer to men who have served as monks with a colloquial term meaning "cooked" to indicate that they are more mature and ready for marriage.

Particularly in rural areas, temporary ordination of boys and young men traditionally gave peasant boys an opportunity to gain an education in temple schools without committing to a permanent monastic life. In Sri Lanka, temporary ordination is not practiced, and a monk leaving the order is frowned upon. The continuing influence of the caste system in Sri Lanka may play a role in the taboo against temporary ordination and leaving the monkhood.

Though Sri Lankan monastic nikayas are often organized along caste lines, men who ordain as monks temporarily pass outside of the conventional caste system, and as such during their time as monks may act (or be treated) in a way that would not be in line with the expected duties and privileges of their caste.

Monastic Practices

Basically, the practices usually vary in different sub-schools and monasteries within Theravada. But in the most orthodox forest monastery, the monk usually models his practice and lifestyle on that of the Buddha and his first generation of disciples by living close to nature in forest, mountains and caves. Forest monasteries still keep alive the ancient traditions through following the Buddhist monastic code of discipline in all its detail and developing meditation in secluded forests.

In a typical daily routine at the monastery during the 3 month vassa period, the monk will wake up before dawn and will begin the day with group chanting and meditation. At dawn the monks will go out to surrounding villages bare-footed on alms-round and will have the only meal of the day before noon by eating from the bowl by hand.

Most of the time is spent on Dhamma study and meditation. Sometimes the abbot or a senior monk will give a Dhamma talk to the visitors. Laity who stay at the monastery will have to abide by the traditional eight Buddhist precepts. After the end of the Vassa period, many of the monks will go out far away from the monastery to find a remote place (usually in the forest) where they can hang their umbrella tents and where it is suitable for the work of self-development. When they go wandering, they walk barefoot, and go wherever they feel inclined. Only those requisites which are necessary will be carried along.

These generally consist of the bowl, the three robes, a bathing cloth, an umbrella tent, a mosquito net, a kettle of water, a water filter, razor, sandals, some small candles, and a candle lantern. The monks do not fix their times for walking and sitting meditation, for as soon as they are free they just start doing it; nor do they determine for how long they will go on to meditate.

Some of them sometimes walk from dusk to dawn whereas at other times they may walk from between two to seven hours. Some may decide to fast for days or stay at dangerous places where ferocious animals live in order to aid their meditation. Those monks who have been able to achieve a high level of attainment will be able to guide the junior monks and lay Buddhists toward the four degrees of spiritual attainment.

In Pali the word for a male lay devotee is Upasaka. Upasika is its female equivalent. One of the duties of the lay followers, as taught by the Buddha, is to look after the needs of the monk/nuns. They are to see that the monk/nuns do not suffer from lack of the four requisites: food, clothing, shelter and medicine. As neither monks nor nuns are allowed to have an occupation, they depend entirely on the laity for their sustenance. In return for this charity, they are expected to lead exemplary lives.

In Burma and Thailand, the monastery was and is still regarded as a seat of learning. In fact today about half of the primary schools in Thailand are located in monasteries. Religious rituals and ceremonies held in a monastery are always accompanied by social activities. In times of crisis, it is to the monks that people bring their problems for counsel.

Traditionally, a ranking monk will deliver a sermon four times a month: when the moon waxes and wanes and the day before the new and full moons. The laity also have a chance to learn meditation from the monks during these times.

It is also possible for a lay disciple to become enlightened. As Bhikkhu Bodhi notes, "The Suttas and commentaries do record a few cases of lay disciples attaining the final goal of Nirvana. However, such disciples either attain Arahantship on the brink of death or enter the monastic order soon after their attainment. They do not continue to dwell at home as Arahant householders, for dwelling at home is incompatible with the state of one who has severed all craving."

REFERENCES

1. Bob Hudson, *The Origins of Bagan*, Thesis for University of Sydney,2004, page 36.
2. Elizabeth Moore, "Interpreting Pyu material culture: Royal chronologies and finger-marked bricks," *Myanmar Historical Research Journal,* No(13) June 2004, pp.1-57, page 6 & 7. Available
3. Harvey, *Introduction to Buddhism*, Cambridge University Press, 1990, p. 3.
4. Hirakawa Akira (translated and edited by Paul Groner), *A History Of India Buddhism*, Motilal Banarsidass Publishers, Delhi, 1993.
5. Etienne Lamotte, *History Of Indian Buddhism,* Peeters Publishers: 1988.
6. A.K. Warder Indian Buddhism Motilal Banarsidass: 2000.
7. Connolly & Hamilton, *Indian Insights*, (ed.) Luzac, London, 1997, pages 187-9.
8. Mario D'Amato,"Mapping the Mahâyâna: Some Historical and Doctrinal Issues". *Religion Compass* 2008, Vol II, Issue 4. pg 550
9. Peter Harvey, *The Selfless Mind.* Curzon Press, 1995, p. 9.
10. Randall Collins, *The Sociology of Philosophies: A Global Theory of Intellectual Change.* Harvard University Press, 2000.

11. Shaw, Sarah. "Buddhist Meditation Practices in the West". Department of Continuing Education, Oxford University. pp. 8. http://www.vesakday.net/vesak50/article/pdf_file/13_Buddhist_%20Meditation_Practices_West.pdf. Retrieved 2009-03-27.

12. Smith, Hudson. Novak, Philip. Buddhism. New York: HarperCollins Publishers, 2003.

13. Stanley Jeyaraja Tambiah, *Buddhism Betrayed?* The University of Chicago Press, 1992, pp. 35-36.

7

Pure Land Buddhism School

"It is important to apply our knowledge internally. The Buddha attained enlightenment in this way. The pure lands are internal; the mental afflictions are internal. The crucial factor is to recognize the mental afflictions. Only by recognizing their nature can we attain Buddhahood."

—Gyatrul

It is remarkable that Pure Land Buddhism also referred to as Amidism in English, is a broad branch of Mahayana Buddhism and currently one of the most popular schools of Buddhism in East Asia, along with Zen (Chinese: Ch'an). In Chinese Buddhism, most monks practise it in combination with Chán or other practices. It is a devotional or "faith"-oriented branch of Buddhism focused on Amitâbha Buddha.

The term is used to describe both the Pure Land soteriology of Mahayana Buddhism, which may be better understood as Pure Land traditions, and the Pure Land sects that developed in Japan: Pure Land Buddhism became a distinct sect/school in the Japanese medieval period (13th century, Kamakura period); in other countries and times, it formed part of the basis of Mahayana Buddhist traditions. Pure Land oriented practices and concepts are found within basic Mahayana Buddhist cosmology, and form an important component of the Mahayana Buddhist traditions in China, Japan, Korea, Taiwan, Vietnam, and Tibet.

Chinese Chan and Tiantai schools, as well as the Japanese Shingon and Tendai sects have strong Pure Land components to their practice and belief. However, Pure Land Buddhism eventually became an independent school in its own right as can be seen in the Japanese Jôdo Shû and Jôdo Shinshû schools. In Japan there are several Pure Land sects, but throughout the history of Mahayana Buddhism there was never an independent Pure Land sect in other Mahayana countries. One basic Mahayana Pure Land concept is that Nirvana (liberation, awakening, salvation) has become increasingly difficult to attain, and that only through devotion to Amitâbha Buddha and looking towards Amida Buddha for guidance can one be reborn in the Pure Land, a perfect realm in which enlightenment is guaranteed. The Pure Land Path has been popular among both commoners and elite monastics as it provided a straightforward way of attaining awakening.

In medieval Japan it was especially popular among those on the outskirts of society, such as prostitutes and social outcasts who, though often denied salvation by the mainstream traditions, were able to find solace in the newly formed Pure Land sect. It should be borne in mind that in no way does Pure Land Buddhism contradict other Buddhist traditions, inasmuch as Amida is not to be thought of in any sense as a God or a deity. The concept of a supreme being, as a world creator and deciding the fate of beings is contrary to Buddhist teaching in all traditions.

Pure Land Buddhism is based on the Pure Land sutras, first brought to China as early as 148 AD, when the Parthian monk Ân Shìgâo began translating sutras into

Chinese at the White Horse Temple in the imperial capital of Luòyáng, during the Hàn dynasty.

The Kushan monk Lokakshema, who arrived in Luòyáng two decades after An Shìgao, is often attributed with the earliest translations of the core sutras of Pure Land Buddhism. These sutras describe Amitâbha and his Pure Land of Bliss, called Sukhâvatî.

Although Amitabha was mentioned or featured in a number of Buddhist sutras, the Larger Sutra of Immeasurable Life is often considered the most important and definitive. In this sutra, the Buddha describes to his assistant, Ânanda, how Amitabha, as an advanced monk named Dharmakara, made a great series of vows to save all sentient beings, and through his great merit, created a realm called the Land of Bliss (Sukhavati).

This paradise would later come to be known as the Pure Land in Chinese translation. Pure Land Buddhism played a small role in early Indian Buddhism, particularly the Mahayana branch, but first became prominent with the founding of a monastery upon the top of Mount Lushan by Hui-yuan in 402.

It quickly spread throughout China and was systematised by a series of elite monastic thinkers, namely Tanluan, Daochuo, Shandao, and others. The religious movement spread to Japan and slowly grew in prominence. Genshin (942-1017) made man of power's Fujiwara no Michinaga (966-1028) convert to Amitabha belief. Hônen (1133–1212) established Pure Land Buddhism as an independent sect in Japan, known as Jôdo Shu.

Today Pure Land is, together with Chan (Zen), the dominant form of Buddhism in China, Korea, Japan, Taiwan, and Vietnam. Contemporary Pure Land traditions see

Amitabha preaching the Dharma in his buddha-field (Sanskrit: buddhakcetra), called the "Pure Land" or "Western Pureland", a region offering respite from karmic transmigration. In such traditions, entering the Pure Land is popularly perceived as equivalent to the attainment of enlightenment. After practitioners attain enlightenment in the Pure Land, they have the choice of becoming a Buddha and entering nirvana or returning to any of the six realms as bodhisattvas to help all living beings in samsara. Thus, adherents believe that Amitabha Buddha provided an alternative path towards attaining enlightenment: the Pure Land Path. In Pure Land Buddhist thought, Enlightenment is difficult to obtain without the assistance of Amitabha Buddha, since people are now living in a degenerate era, known as the Age of Dharma Decline.

Instead of solitary meditative work toward enlightenment, Pure Land Buddhism teaches that devotion to Amitabha leads one to the Pure Land, where enlightenment can be more easily attained. In medieval East Asian culture, this belief was particularly popular among peasants and individuals who were considered "impure", such as hunters, fishermen, those who tan hides, prostitutes and so on. Pure Land Buddhism provided a way to practice Buddhism for those who were not capable of practicing other forms. In fact, in the Larger Sutra of Immeasurable Life the Amitabha Buddha makes 48 vows, and the 18th Vow states that Amitabha will grant rebirth to his Pure Land to anyone who can recite his name as little as 10 times.

It also states, *Excluded, however, are those who commit the five gravest offences and abuse the right Dharma.*

What is Pure Land

The Pure Land is described in the *Limitless Life Sutra*

as a land of beauty that surpasses all other realms. More importantly for the Pure Land practitioner, once one has been "born" into this land (birth occurs painlessly through lotus flowers), one will never again be reborn. In the Pure Land one will be personally instructed by Amitabha Buddha and numerous Bodhisattvas until one reaches full and complete enlightenment. In effect, being born into the Pure Land is akin to achieving enlightenment, through escaping samsara, the Buddhist concept of "the wheel of birth and death."

Pure Land Practice

Practitioners believe that chanting Amitâbha Buddha's name, or the nianfo, during their current life allows them, at this life's end, to be received with their karma by Amitâbha Buddha. The simplicity of this form of veneration has contributed greatly to its popularity throughout East Asia. This practice is called nembutsu in Japanese, or Buddha recitation, or "Being Mindful of the Buddha." An alternate practise found in Pure Land Buddhism is meditation or contemplation of Amitâbha or his Pure Land. The basis for this is found in the Contemplation Sutra, where The Buddha describes to Queen Vaidehi what Amitâbha looks like and how to meditate upon him.

Visualization practises for Amitâbha are more popular among esoteric Buddhist sects, such as Japanese Shingon Buddhism, while the nianfo is more popular among lay followers.

Some have claimed there is evidence of dying people going to the pure land, such as:

(a) Knowing the time of death - some prepare by bathing and reciting the name of the Buddha Amitabha.

(b) The "three saints in the west" (Amitâbha Buddha and the two bodhisattvas, Avalokiteúvara on his right and Mahâsthâmaprâpta on his left), appear and welcome the dying person. Visions of other buddhas or bodhisttvas are disregarded as they may be bad spirits disguising themselves, attempting to stop the person from entering the Pure Land.

(c) Records of practicing Pure Land Buddhists who have died have been known to leave clusters of crystallized bone fragments after cremation.

Remarkably, last part of the body to become cold is the top of the head (posterior fontanelle). In Buddhist teaching, souls who enter the Pure Land leave the body through the fontanelle at the top of the skull. Hence, this part of the body stays warmer longer than the rest of the body.

The *Verses on the Structure of the Eight Consciousnesses*, reads: "to birth in saints the last body temperature in top of head, to deva in eyes, to human in heart, to hungry ghosts in belly, to animals in knee cap, to the hells-realm in sole of feet."

The dying person may demonstrate some, but not necessarily all, of these evidences. For example, his facial expression may be happy, but he may not demonstrate other signs, such as sharira and dreams.

Eastern Pure Land

In Mahayana Buddhism, there are many Buddhas, and each Buddha has a Pure Land. For example, Amitàbha's Pure Land is understood to be in the Western direction, whereas Akcobhya's Pure Land (Abhirati), is in the East.

While recognized by the Japanese Shingon sect, Eastern Pure Land Buddhism is less popular than Western Pure

Land Buddhism. Though there are various traditions devoted to various Pure Lands, Amitabha's is by far the most popular.

Tibetan Pure Land

Tibetan Pure Land Buddhism has a long and innovative history dating from the 8th-9th centuries CE, the times of the Tibetan Empire, with the translation and canonization of the Sanskrit *Sukhâvatîvyûha* sûtras in Tibetan. Tibetan compositions of pure-land prayers and artistic renditions of Sukhâvatî in Central Asia date to that time. Tibetan pure-land literature forms a distinct genre and encompasses a wide range of scriptures, "aspiration prayers to be born in Sukhâvatî", commentaries on the prayers and the sûtras, and meditations and rituals belonging to the Vajrayâna tradition. The incorporation of phowa (mind transference techniques) in pure-land meditations is textually attested in the 14th century, in the *The Standing Blade of Grass* (Tib. *'Pho-ba 'Jag-tshug ma*), a *terma* text allegedly dating to the time of the Tibetan Empire.

A good number of Buddhist treasure texts are dedicated to Buddha Amitâbha and to rituals associated with his pure-land, while the wide acceptance of phowa in Tibetan death rituals may owe its popularity to pure-land Buddhism promoted by all schools of Tibetan Buddhism. The terton Rigdzin Longsal Nyingpo (1625-1682/92 or 1685-1752) of Katok Monastery revealed a terma on pureland. This terma entailed phowa during the bardo of dying, sending the mindstream to a pureland.

This may evidence what some scholars have intimated as examples of successful, popular teachings disseminated from other localities such as China being codified within the Tibetan tradition; terma as cultural innovation.

REFERENCES

Corless, Roger. 1989. 'Pure Land and Pure Perspective: A Tantric Hermeneutic of Sukhâvatî.' *The Pure Land*, New Series, 6: 205-17.

Halkias, T. Georgios. 2009. "Compassionate Aspirations and their fulfilment: Dol-po-pa's A Prayer for Birth in Sukhâvatî ." In *As Long As Space Endures: Essays on the Kâlachakra Tantra in Honor of His Holiness the Dalai Lama*. Ithaca: Snow Lion Publications, pp. 259-275.

_____. 2006. "Pure-Lands and other Visions in Seventeenth-Century Tibet: a Gnam-chos sâdhana for the pure-land Sukhâvatî revealed in 1658 by Gnam-chos Mi-'gyur-rdo-rje (1645-1667)." In *Power, Politics and the Reinvention of Tradition: Tibet in the Seventeenth and Eighteenth Century*, ed. B. Cuevas et al. Leiden: Brill Publishers, pp. 121-151.

Kajihama, Ryoshun. 2002a. Tibet no Jyôdo Shisô no Kenkyû (Japanese. The Study of Pure Land in Tibet). Kyoto: Nagata Bunshôdô.

______.2002b. "3rd rDo Gruchen Rinpoche's Pure Land Thought (III)." *Journal of Indian and Buddhist Studies*, 50/2: 984-87.

______.1996. "3rd rDo Gruchen Rinpoche's Pure Land Thought (II)." *Journal of Indian and Buddhist Studies*, 44/2: 948-52.

______.1994. "3rd rDo Gruchen Rinpoche's Pure Land Thought (I)." *Journal of Indian and Buddhist Studies*, 43/1: 492-98.

Kapstein, Matthew. 2004. "Pure Land Buddhism in Tibet? From Sukhâvatî to the Field of Great Bliss." In *Approaching the Land of Bliss: Religious Praxis in the Cult of Amitâbha*, ed. R. Payne and K. Tanaka. Honolulu: University of Hawaii Press,1-16.

______.1998. "A Pilgrimage of Rebirth Reborn: the 1992 Celebration of the Drigung Powa Chenmo". In *Buddhism in Contemporary Tibet*, ed. M. Goldstein and M. Kapstein, Delhi: Motilal Banarsidass, 95-119.

Mei, Ching Hsuan. 2004. "'Pho ba Liturgy in 14th Century Tibet." *Tibet Journal*, XXIX/2: 47-70.

Silk, Jonathan. 1993. "The Virtues of Amitâbha: A Tibetan Poem from Dunhuang." *Bükkyo Bunka Kenkyüjo Kiyö*, 32.

8

Pre-sectarian Buddhism

It is remarkable that idea of a "pre-sectarian Buddhism" was not studied before Western scholarship on Buddhism began in the 1890s. Both Theravada and Mahayana Buddhists accepted their reliability of their respective canons.

In fact, the term pre-sectarian Buddhism is used by some scholars to refer to the Buddhism that existed before the various subsects of Buddhism came into being. Other terms that have been used to refer to this first period of Buddhism are: *the earliest Buddhism*, *original Buddhism* and *the Buddhism of the Buddha himself.* Some Japanese scholars (such as Nakamura and Hirakawa) use the term *Early Buddhism* to refer to this first period of Buddhism, and refer to the subsequent period of the Early Buddhist Schools as *sectarian Buddhism*. Pre-sectarian Buddhism refers to Buddhism in the period between the first discourse of Gautama Buddha until the first enduring split in the Sangha, which occurred (according to most scholars) between the second Buddhist council and the third Buddhist council.

Professor Hirakawa however, places the first schism after the death of King Asoka. Professor Schopen questions whether there ever was a unified Buddhism which split into sects. Pre-sectarian Buddhism is the Buddhism presupposed by the early Buddhist schools as existing about one hundred years after the Parinirvana of the Buddha. Most scholars do agree that there was a rough body of sacred literature that a relatively early community maintained and transmitted. This may be substantially the Buddhism of the Buddha himself, although this cannot be proved.

According to A.K. Warder, there is no evidence to suggest that it was formulated by anyone other than the Buddha and his immediate followers. Prof. Ronald Davidson however has little confidence that much, if any, of surviving Buddhist scripture is actually the word of the historical Buddha.

It is significant to note that information on Buddhism in the period before the rise of the early Buddhist schools is based on accounts of Buddha's life and teachings in the scriptures of the Theravadin Pali Canon, and the surviving portions of the scriptures of Sarvastivada, Mulasarvastivada, Mahisasaka, Dharmaguptaka and other schools, most of which are only available in a Chinese translation. Some individual scriptures found in Nepal, however, are composed in Sanskrit. Recently the Gandhâran Buddhist Texts were recovered from Afghanistan.

The central body of sutras in these texts is so similar that they are considered to be different recensions of the same text. The accounts in these individual scriptures might be tainted by the particular philosophies of those schools or by translation issues. However, since various recensions of these texts (from various schools) are available, comparisons can be made, and conclusions drawn, to filter out the most obvious of these taints. Comparing the various scriptures, it is even possible to uncover certain features of early

Buddhism (and its environment) that the traditions themselves have forgotten about.

The earliest phase of scriptures, recognized by nearly all scholars (the main exception is Dr Gregory Schopen), is based on a comparison of the Pali Canon with the Chinese Agamas and other surviving portions of other early canons. Some scholars consider that this rough common core of the scriptures of the different schools gives a substantially correct picture of the original teachings of the Buddha. This core is identified as the four main nikayas of the Sutta Pitaka (the Digha Nikaya, Majjhima Nikaya, Samyutta Nikaya and Anguttara Nikaya), together with the main body of monastic rules, the Vinaya Pitaka. Scholars have also claimed that there is a core within this core, referring to some poems and phrases which seem to be the oldest parts of the Sutta Pitaka.

Another body of scholars consider that the question has not been settled one way or another. This last group includes those scholars who claim it is impossible to ever know the teachings of the Buddha, an attitude which has been criticized by Warder to be one of 'extreme caution'.

Pre-sectarian Buddhism was a changing form of Buddhism, with Gautama Buddha defining and refining the proper behavior for monks (Vinaya), with the help of monks like Upali. The rules were frequently amended to allow for certain (harmless) kinds of behavior which was forbidden in a previous version of the rule. The Pre-sectarian Buddhist monks' order grew from a small unknown order of highly dedicated monks (in the year after the attainment of Nirvana) to a large, well-established and well-known order, which needed more formalities and more rules to uphold the correct teachings and discipline. It was relatively sober and the monks were not supposed to go to public festivals (number 7 of the ten precepts), and were expected to refrain from activities such as playing and dancing. The monks were not allowed to show off their supernatural abilities. They were also not allowed to use or receive money, in order to lead a simple life of contentment.

Basically, the beginning the order of monks (Sangha) did not have any monasteries, but already in its first year the Buddha allowed these to be given, after being asked to do so by King Bimbisara. Many of the these monasteries were based in parks or forests, for example Veluvana, Jetavana and Nigrodharama. One of the buildings given was a very well-furnished building, comparable to a palace, called the Migaramatupasada.

In fact, the Buddha, as the leader and main teacher, was the one who decided on the rules to be followed, but the executive power lay with the monastic community as a whole. Buddha forbade the monastic community to make their own rules and gave instructions for the monks to still follow his teaching (doctrine and discipline) after his death. Thus, He did not appoint a successor to have legislative power over the Sangha and the monks. He gave limited powers to the Sangha to unanimously agree to not follow the 'lesser and minor' rules.

At the first Buddhist council the Sangha unanimously agreed to continue following all the rules laid down by Buddha, to prevent any major rules (pacittiya or higher) to be classified as a minor rule and thus be put aside. The second Buddhist council took place about 100 years after the Parinibbana of the Buddha. It was convened to decide on the subject of discipline or Vinaya, and dealt with whether it was allowed to follow adapted rules, thus disregarding the instructions of Gautama Buddha. The adapted rules were integrated within the larger framework of correct procedures, and the offending monks refused to acknowledge their fault. For this reason a council was convened, in which the issue was satisfactorily dealt with, in that the offending monks abandoned their old habits. Shortly after the second Buddhist council the first long-lasting schisms occurred in the Sangha. The second Buddhist council is sometimes considered to be the origin of these schisms, but no direct evidence for this is apparent. The first post-schismatic groups are often stated to be the Sthaviravada and the Mahasanghika.

After the Sangha split into the various early Buddhist schools and the Mahayana, various new doctrines, scriptures and practices arose, composed and developed by monks, concerning issues deemed important at the time. During the time of Pre-sectarian Buddhism, these later elaborations on the teachings had not yet come into existence, and were not part of the established teaching and practice of Buddhism. In later times, the arguments between the various schools were based in these newly introduced teachings, practices and beliefs, and monks sought to validate these newly introduced teachings and concepts by referring to the older texts (Sutta-pitaka and Vinaya-pitaka). Most often, the various new Abhidhamma and Mahayana teachings were bases for arguments between sects.

Some scholars state that unintentional literalism was a major force for change in the early doctrinal history of Buddhism. This means that texts were interpreted paying too much attention to the precise words used and not enough to the speaker's intention, the spirit of the text. Some later doctrinal developments in the early Buddhist schools show scholastic literalism, which is a tendency to take the words and phrases of earlier texts (maybe the Buddha's own words) in such a way as to read in distinctions which it was never intended to make.

Remarkably, following Buddhist scriptures were not existent, or in a very early (insignificant) stage of development:

Abhidhamma: As the last major division of the canon, the Abhidhamma Pitaka has had a checkered history. It was not accepted as canonical by the Mahasanghika school and several other schools. Another school included most of the Khuddaka Nikaya within the Abhidhamma Pitaka. Also, the Pali version of the Abhidhamma is a strictly Theravada collection, and has little in common with the Abhidhamma works recognized by other Buddhist schools. The various Abhidhamma philosophies of the various early schools have no agreement on doctrine and belong to the period of 'Divided Buddhism' (as opposed to Undivided Buddhism). The earliest texts of the Pali Canon (the Sutta Nipata and parts of the Jataka), together with the first four (and early) Nikayas of the Suttapitaka, have no mention of (the texts of) the Abhidhamma Pitaka.

The Abhidhamma is also not mentioned at the report of the First Buddhist Council, directly after the death of the Buddha. This report of the first council does mention the existence of the Vinaya and the five Nikayas (of the Suttapitaka). Although the literature of the various Abhidhamma Pitakas begun as a kind of commentarial supplement upon the earlier teachings in the Suttapitaka, it soon led to new doctrinal and textual developments and became the focus of a new form of scholarly monastic life. The various Abhidhamma works were starting to be composed from about 200 years after the passing away of the Buddha.

Traditionally, it is believed (in Theravadin culture) that the Abhidhamma was taught by Buddha to his late mother who was living in Tusita heaven. However, this is rejected by scholars, who believe that only small parts of the Abhidhamma literature may have been existent in a very early form.

Some schools of Buddhism had important disagreements on subjects of Abhidhamma, while having a largely similar Sutta-pitaka and Vinaya-pitaka. The arguments and conflicts between them were thus often on matters of philosophical Abhidhammic origin, not on matters concerning the actual words and teachings of Buddha. One impetus for composing new scriptures like the Adhidhammas of the various schools, according to some scholars, was that Buddha left no clear statement about the ontological status of the world - about what *really* exists. Subsequently, later Buddhists have themselves defined what exists and what not (in the Abhidhammic scriptures), leading to disagreements.

Khuddaka Nikaya: 'The Khuddaka Nikaya can easily be divided into two strata, one being early and the other late. The texts Sutta Nipata, Itivuttaka, Dhammapada, Therigatha (Theragatha), Udana, and Jataka tales belong to the early stratum. The texts Khuddakapatha, Vimanavatthu, Petavatthu, Niddesa, Patisambhida, Apadana, Buddhavamsa and Cariyapitaka can be categorized in the later stratum.'

In fact, the texts in the early stratum date from before the second council (earlier than 100 years after Buddha's parinibbana), while the later stratum is from after the second council, which means they are definitely later additions to the Sutta Pitaka, and that they might not have been the original teachings by the Buddha, but later compositions by disciples.

The following books of the Khuddaka Nikaya can thus be regarded as later additions:

(a) the Khuddakapatha

(b) the Vimanavatthu

(c) the Petavatthu

(d) the Niddesa

(e) the Patisambhida

(f) the Apadana

(g) the Buddhavamsa

(h) the Cariyapitaka

(i) the Milindapanha, which is part of the Burmese Khuddaka Nikaya.

(j) the Buddhavamsa

Remarkably, the original verses of the Jatakas are recognized as the earliest part of the Canon, but the accompanying (and more famous) Jataka Stories are purely commentarial, an obvious later addition.

Parivara: The Parivara, the last book of the Vinaya Pitaka, is a later addition to the Vinaya Pitaka.

Other Later Writings

- all literature of the Mahayana (the Mahayana Sutras).
- all commentarial works (atthakatha) of Theravada and other early Buddhist schools.

9

Nichiren Buddhism

It is remarkable to note the Nichiren Buddhism is a branch of Buddhism based on the teachings of the 13th century Japanese monk Nichiren (1222–1282). Various forms of Nichiren Buddhism have had great influence among certain sections of Japanese society at different times in the country's history, such as among the merchants of Kyoto in Japan's Middle Ages and among some ultranationalists during the pre-World War II era.

Nichiren Buddhism is generally noted for its focus on the Lotus Sutra and an attendant belief that all people have an innate Buddha nature and are therefore inherently capable of attaining enlightenment in their current form and present lifetime. It is also noted for positioning itself in opposition to other forms of Japanese Buddhism—in particular the Zen, Pure Land, esoteric, Shingon, and Ritsu schools, which Nichiren saw as deviating from the orthodoxy of Mahayana Buddhism.

Nichiren Buddhism is a comprehensive term covering several major schools and many sub-schools, as well as several of Japan's new religions. An evangelical streak is evinced by some schools' practice of *shakubuku,* efforts to convert others by refuting their current beliefs and convincing them of the validity of Nichiren's teachings. Nichiren Buddhists believe that the spread of Nichiren's teachings and their effect on practitioners' lives will eventually bring about a peaceful, just, and prosperous society.

From the age of 16 until 32, Nichiren studied in numerous temples in Japan, especially Mt. Hiei (Enryakuji) and Mt. Kôya, in his day the major centers of Buddhist study, in the Kyoto–Nara area. He eventually concluded that the highest teachings of Shakyamuni Buddha (563?–483?BC) were to be found in the Lotus Sutra. The mantra he expounded on 28 April 1253, Nam-Myôhô-Renge-Kyô, expresses his devotion to that body of teachings. During his lifetime Nichiren stridently maintained that the contemporary teachings of Buddhism taught by other sects (particularly Shin, Zen, Shingon, and Ritsu) were mistaken in their interpretations of the correct path to enlightenment and therefore refuted them publicly and vociferously. In doing so, he provoked the ire of the country's rulers and of the priests of the sects he criticized; he was subjected to persecution which included an attempted beheading and at least two exiles.

Some Nichiren schools see the incident of the attempted beheading as marking a turning point in Nichiren's teaching, since Nichiren began inscribing the Gohonzon and wrote a number of major doctrinal treatises during his subsequent three-year exile on Sado Island in the Japan Sea.

After a pardon and his return from exile, Nichiren moved to Mt. Minobu in today's Yamanashi Prefecture, where he and his disciples built a temple, Tharonja. Nichiren spent most of the rest of his life here training disciples.

Today, Nichiren Buddhism is not a single denomination. It began to branch into different schools within several years of Nichiren's passing, before which Nichiren had named *six senior priests* (*rokurôsô*) whom he wanted to transmit his teachings to future generations: Nisshô, Nichirô, Nikô, Nitchô, Nichiji, and Nikkô.

Each started a lineage of schools, but Nichiji eventually travelled to the Asian continent (ca. 1295) and was never heard from again, and Nitchô later in life (1302) rejoined and became a follower of Nikkô. The reasons for the splits are numerous, entangled, and subject to different interpretations depending on which school is telling the story; suffice it to say that the senior priests had different understandings of what Nichiren's lifetime of teaching was about. Although the former five remained loosely affiliated to varying degrees, the last—Nikkô—made a clean break by leaving Kuon-ji in 1289. He had come to the conclusion that Nikô and the others were embarking on paths to heresy that he could not stem.

Kuon-ji eventually became the central temple of today's Nichiren Shu, one of the two largest branches and the one encompassing the numerous minor schools of the Minobu branch into which most of the schools started by Nisshô, Nichirô, and Nichiji have been subsumed. The other dominant branch is centered at Taiseki-ji, the head temple of today's Nichiren Shoshu school. Taiseki-ji, which Nikkô founded in 1290 after leaving Kuon-ji, was the starting point for the other schools of the Kômon-ha or Fuji-ha, from the locality) branch.

Other traditional Nichiren schools include several sub-schools that call themselves just Hokke Shû, the Honmon Butsuryû Shû, and the Kempon Hokke Shû. Several of Japan's new religions are also sub-sects of or otherwise based on one or another of the traditional Nichiren schools.

The Reiyûkai, Risshô Kôsei Kai, and Nipponzan Myôhôji Sangha stem from one or another of the Kuon-ji/Minobu branch schools, whereas Soka Gakkai, Shôshinkai, and Kenshôkai trace their origins to the Nichiren Shoshu school.

Major Nichiren Buddhist Schools

- Nichiren Shû: Sozan Minobuzan Kuon-ji
- Nichiren Shôshû: Sôhonzan Taiseki-ji
- Honmon Butsuryû Shû
- Kempon Hokke Shu: Sôhonzan Myôman-ji
- Hokkeshû, Honmon Ryû
- Hokkeshû, Jinmon Ryû
- Hokkeshû, Shinmon Ryû
- Honmon Hokke Shû: Daihonzan Myôren-ji
- Nichiren Honshû: Honzan Yôbô-ji
- Nichiren Shû Fuju-fuse-ha: Sozan Myôkaku-ji
- Nichiren Hokke Shû
- Hokke Nichiren Shû
- Hompa Nichiren Shû
- Honke Nichiren Shû (Hyôgo)
- Fuju-fuse Nichiren Kômon Shû
- Honke Nichiren Shû (Kyôto)
- Shôbô Hokke Shû
- Honmon Kyôô Shû
- Nichiren Kômon Shû

[Note: Head temple names are given in Roman letters only when the reading could be confirmed. Japanese characters preceded by "ja:" link to articles in the Japanese Wikipedia.]

Non-traditional Schools

- Reiyûkai (Spiritual-Friendship-Association) Founded in 1920 by Kakutaro Kubo and Kimi Kotani, Reiyûkai considers itself the grandfather of lay-based new religions devoted to the Lotus Sutra and ancestor veneration.
- Risshô Kôsei Kai
- Nipponzan Myôhôji
- Kokuchukai | Kokuchûkai
- Shôshinkai
- Fuji Taisekiji Kenshôkai (also, just *Kenshôkai*)
- Honmon Shôshû
- Sôka Gakkai (also, Soka Gakkai International (SGI))

[Note: Though many sources (e.g., Britannica online; *Illustrated*, p. 1443; *Cambridge*, p. 175; *Iwanami*, p. 679) characterize Sôka Gakkai as one of Japan's new religions or as a lay-followers organization of Nichiren Shoshu (to which it has not been affiliated since the early 1990s). Sôka Gakkai and its constituent organizations position themselves as lay organizations whose purpose is to support practitioners of Nichiren Buddhism.]

Doctrine and Practices

Much of Nichiren Shoshu's underlying teachings are, overtly, extensions of Tendai thought, including much of its worldview and its rationale for criticism of Buddhist schools that do not acknowledge the designation by historical Buddha Shakyamuni of the Lotus Sutra to be Buddhism's highest teaching. For example, Nichiren Shoshu doctrine adopts or extends Tendai's classification of the Buddhist sutras into five time periods and eight categories its theory of 3,000 interpenetrating realms within a single life-moment, and its view of the Three Truths (NæŠ: *Santai*). Because of these similarities, as well as space considerations, this article will confine itself to discussion of the hows and whys of Nichiren Shoshu's central doctrine: How it views Nichiren Daishonin and his lifetime of teaching, and why its believers practice the way they do.

Nichiren was a prolific writer. His personal communications and writings to his followers as well as numerous treatises detail his view of the correct form of practice for the *Latter Day of the Law* (*Mappô*); lay out his views on other Buddhist schools, particularly those of influence during his lifetime; and elucidate his interpretations of Buddhist teachings that preceded his. These writings are collectively known as *Gosho* (*go* is an honorific prefix designating respect; *sho* means *writings*) in some schools and *go-ibun* ("left-behind writings") in others.

Over 700 of them, some complete and some only in fragments, have been passed down through the centuries in compilations, as copies, and even many in the original. Some are also available in English translation, most notably in *Letters of Nichiren* and *Selected Writings of Nichiren* in the *Translations from the Asian Classics* series.

REFERENCES

1. *A Dictionary of Buddhist Terms and Concepts*. Nichiren Shoshu International Center, 1983 (Out of print).
2. *Letters of Nichiren*. Burton Watson et al., trans.; Philip B. Yampolsky, ed. Columbia University Press, 1996.
3. *Selected Writings of Nichiren*. Burton Watson et al., trans.; Philip B. Yampolsky, ed. Columbia University Press, 1990.

10

Shingon Buddhism

Shingon Buddhism arose in Japan's Heian period (794-1185) when the monk Kûkai went to China in 804 and studied tantric practices in the city of Xi'an under Huiguo and returned with many texts and art works. In time, he developed his own synthesis of esoteric practice and doctrine, centered on the universal Buddha Vairocana (or, more accurately, Mahavairocana Tathagata). He established a monastery on Mount Kôya (Koyasan), which became the base of the Shingon sect of Buddhism.

Remarkably, Shingon Buddhism is one of the mainstream major schools of Japanese Buddhism and one of the few surviving Buddhist esoteric lineages. It is often called "Japanese Esoteric Buddhism", or "Orthodox Esoteric Buddhism". The word *shingon* is the Japanese reading of the kanji for the Chinese word *zhçnyán*, literally meaning "true words", which in turn is the Chinese translation of the Sanskrit word *mantra*.

Shingon enjoyed immense popularity during the Heian Period, particularly among the Heian nobility, and contributed greatly to the art and literature of the time, as well as influencing other communities, such as the Tendai sect on Mt. Hiei.

Also, Shingon's emphasis on ritual found support in the Kyoto nobility, particularly the Fujiwara clan. This favor allotted Shingon several politically powerful temples in the capital, where rituals for the imperial family and nation were regularly performed. Many of these temples such as Toji and Daigoji in the South of Kyoto and Jingoji and Ninnaji in the Northwest became ritual centers establishing their own particular ritual lineages. Like the Tendai School that branched into the Jôdo, and Nichiren Schools in the Kamakura period, Shingon also divided into two major branches: Kogi Shingon (,*Old Shingon*?) and Shingi Shingon (*New Shingon*?).

This division primarily arose out of a political dispute between Kakuban and his faction of priests centered at the Denbô-in Hall and the leadership at Kongôbuji, the head of Mt. Kôya. Kakuban, who was originally ordained at Ninnaji in Kyoto, studied at several temple-centers (including the Tendai temple complex at Onjiyôji) before going to Mt. Kôya. Through his connections, he managed to gain the favor of high ranking nobles in Kyoto, which helped him to be appointed abbot of Mt. Kôya. The leadership at Kongôbuji, however, opposed the appointment on the premise that Kakuban had not originally been ordained on Mt. Kôya. After several conflicts Kakuban and his faction of priests left the mountain for Mt. Negoro to the northwest, where they constructed a new temple complex, now known as Negoroji. After the death of Kakuban in 1143, the Negoro faction returned to Mt. Kôya.

However in 1288, the conflict between Kongôbuji and the Denbôe came to a head once again. Led by Raiyu, the Denbôe priests once again left Mt. Kôya, this time establishing their headquarters on Mt. Negoro. This exodus marked the beginning of the Shingi Shingon School at Mt. Negoro, which was the center of Shingi Shingon until sacked by Hideyoshi Toyotomi in 1585.

During the initial stages of his predication in Japan, the Catholic missionary Francis Xavier was welcomed by the Shingon monks since he used the word *Dainichi* for the Christian God. As Xavier learned more about the religious nuances of the word, he changed to *Deusu* from the Latin and Portuguese *Deus*. The monks also realized by that point that Xavier was preaching a rival religion.

Main Teachings

The teachings of Shingon are based on early tantric Buddhist texts, the Mahavairocana Tantra and the Vajrasekhara Sutra. These two mystical teachings are expressed in the two main mandalas of Shingon, The Mandalas of The Two Realms - The Womb Realm (Skt. Garbhadhatu, Jap. Taizokai) mandala and the Diamond Realm (Skt. Vajradhatu, Jap. Kongokai) mandala. These two mandalas are considered to be a compact expression of the entirety of the Dharma, and form the root of Vajrayana Buddhism. In Shingon temples, these two mandalas are always mounted one on each side of the central altar. Tantric Buddhism is concerned with the rituals and meditative practices that lead to enlightenment.

According to the Shingon doctrine, enlightenment is not a distant, foreign reality that can take aeons to approach but a real possibility within this very life, based on the spiritual potential of every living being, known generally as Buddha-nature. If cultivated, this luminous nature manifests as innate wisdom. With the help of a genuine teacher and through proper training of the body, speech, and mind, we can reclaim and liberate this enlightened capacity for the benefit of ourselves and others. Kûkai also systematized and categorized the teachings he inherited from Huiguo into ten stages or levels of spiritual realisation. He wrote at length on the difference between exoteric mainstream Mahayana Buddhism and esoteric Tantric Buddhism.

The differences between exoteric and esoteric can be summarised as:

1. Esoteric teachings are preached by the Dharmakaya. Buddha which Kûkai identifies as Mahavairocana. Exoteric teachings are preached by the Nirmanakaya. Buddha, which in our world and aeon, is the historic Gautama Buddha or one of the Sambhoghakaya Buddhas.
2. Exoteric Buddhism holds that the ultimate state of Buddhahood is ineffable, and that nothing can be said of it. Esoteric Buddhism holds that while nothing can be said of it verbally, it is readily communicated via esoteric rituals which involve the use of mantras, mudras, and mandalas.
3. Kûkai held that exoteric doctrines were merely provisional, skillful means (Skt. Upâya) on the part of the Buddhas to help beings according to their capacity to understand the Truth. The esoteric doctrines by comparison are the Truth itself, and are a direct communication of the "inner experience of the Dharmakaya's enlightenment". A simple way to put it would be to say that when Gautama Buddha attained enlightenment in his earthly Nirmanakaya body, he realized that the Dharmakaya body is actually reality in its totality and that totality is Mahavairocana.
4. Some exoteric schools in the late Nara and early

> Heian Japan held (or were portrayed by Shingon adherents as holding) that attaining Buddhahood is possible but requires a huge amount of time (three incalculable aeons) of practice to achieve, whereas esoteric Buddhism teaches that Buddhahood can be attained in this lifetime by anyone.

Kûkai held, along with the Chinese Huayan school that all phenomena could be expressed as 'letters' in a 'World-text'. Mantra, mudra, and mandala are special because they constitute the 'language' through which the Dharmakaya (i.e. Reality itself) communicates. Although portrayed through the use of anthropomorphic metaphors, Shingon does not see the Dharmakaya Buddha as a god, or creator. The Dharmakaya is in fact a symbol for the true nature of things which is impermanent and empty of any essence. The teachings were passed from Mahavairocana.

It is important to note that during Kûkai's time, Tantric Buddhism was still in its early stages of development in India and would not develop into the "School of Vajrayana" as we know it today until several centuries later. Many prominent Indo-Tibetan tantras like The Guhyasamaja Tantra and The Kalachakra Tantra developed over this later period were never transmitted to Japan. Also, although Tibetan Buddhism and Shingon share similar teachings and practices, they are actually quite different as a whole. Thus, there is debate on whether Shingon should be classified under Vajrayana in terms of doctrine.

However, based on the doctrine of The Three Vehicles (Skt. Triyana), Shingon is clearly Vajrayana by virtue of its tantric and esoteric nature. Nevertheless, one should always bear in mind that even though Shingon is a Vajrayana vehicle, it had little to do with its development as a subset of Buddhism.

In Shingon, Mahavairocana Tathagata is the universal or primordial Buddha that is the basis of all phenomena, present in each and all of them, and not existing independently or externally to them. The goal of Shingon is the realization that one's nature is identical with Mahavairocana, a goal that is achieved through initiation (for ordained followers), meditation and esoteric ritual practices. This realization depends on receiving the secret doctrine of Shingon, transmitted orally to initiates by the school's masters. Body, speech, and mind participate simultaneously in the subsequent process of revealing one's nature: the body through devotional gestures (mudra) and the use of ritual instruments, speech through sacred formulas (mantra), and mind through meditation.

Shingon places special emphasis on the Thirteen Buddhas, a grouping of various Buddhas and boddhisattvas:

(a) Acala Vidyaraja

(b) Shakyamuni Buddha

(c) Manjusri Bodhisattva

(d) Samantabhadra Bodhisattva

(e) Kcitigarbha Bodhisattva

(f) Maitreya Bodhisattva

(g) Bhaisajyaguru Buddha

(h) Avalokitesvara Bodhisattva

(i) Mahasthamaprapta Bodhisattva

(j) Amitabha Buddha

(k) Akshobhya Buddha

(l) Mahavairocana Buddha

(m) Akasagarbha Bodhisattva

Mahavairocana is the Universal Principle which underlies all Buddhist teachings, according to Shingon Buddhism, so other Buddhist figures can be thought of as manifestations with certain roles and attributes. Each Buddhist figure is symbolized by its own Sanskrit "seed" letter as well.

One feature that Shingon shares in common with the other surviving school of Japanese Esoteric Buddhism (Tendai) is the use of *seed-syllables* or *bija* (*bîja*) along with anthropomorphic and symbolic representations, to express Buddhist deities in their mandalas. There are four types of mandalas: anthropomorphic representation), the seed-syllable mandala or the *samaya-man ala* representations of the vows of the deities in the form of articles they hold or their mudras), and the *karma-ma, ala* representing the activities of the deities in the three-dimensional form of statues, etc. An ancient Indian Sanskrit syllabary script known as *Siddham* (Shittan or Bonji) is used to write mantras.

A core meditative practice of Shingon is *ajikan*, "Meditating on the Letter 'A'", which uses the siddham letter representing the sound "Ah." Other Shingon meditations are *Gachirinkan* ("full moon" visualization), *Gojigonjingan* ("visualization of the five elements arrayed in the body" from the *Mahavairocana Tantra*) and *Gosôjôjingan* (*pañcâbhisabodhi* "series of five meditations to attain Buddhahood" from the *Sarvatathâgatatattva-sagraha Tantra*, also known as the *Vajrasekhara Sutra)*.

The essence of Shingon Mantrayana practice is to experience Reality by emulating the inner realization of the Dharmakaya through the meditative ritual use of mantra, mudra and visualization of mandala (ie. the three mysteries). All Shingon followers gradually develop a teacher-student relationship, whereby a teacher learns the disposition of the student and teaches practices accordingly. For lay practitioners, there is no initiation ceremony beyond the *Kechien Kanjô*, which is normally offered only at Mt. Koya but can also be offered by larger temples under masters permitted to transmit the empowerment. It is not required for all laypersons to take.

Notably, the case of disciples wishing to train to become Shingon teachers or acharyas (ajari, the process is more complex and requires initiations in various mandalas, rituals and so on. In either case, the stress is on finding a qualified and willing mentor who will guide you through Shingon practice at a gradual pace. Apart from prayers and reading of sutras, there are some basic mantras and meditative techniques for laypersons to practice on their own but the bulk of Shingon practices are tantric rituals involving complex invocations, hand gestures, ritual implements and visualizations all rich in hidden symbolism. Almost all of these practices require the devotee to undergo initiation or *abhisheka* (Jap. *Kanjô* Lp˜) into each of these practices under the guidance of a master before they may begin to learn and practice them.

As with all schools of Vajrayana, great emphasis is placed on the empowerment and oral transmission of teachings from teacher to student. Undergoing these practices on one's own without empowerment and guidance is extremely frowned upon not only because it is considered a serious offence but also because it can be dangerous to the practitioner if not done properly.

Homa Fire Ritual: The Homa Ritual of consecrated fire is unique to Vajrayana and Esoteric Buddhism and is perhaps also the most mystical and cognitively powerful. It stems from the Vedic Agnihotra Ritual and is performed by qualified priests and acharyas for the benefit of individuals, the state or all sentient beings in general. The consecrated fire is believed to have a powerful cleansing effect spiritually and psychologically. The central deity invoked in this ritual is usually Acala. The ritual is performed for the purpose of destroying negative energies, detrimental thoughts and desires, and for the making of secular requests and blessings. In most Shingon temples, this ritual is performed daily in the morning or the afternoon. Larger scale ceremonies often include the constant beating of taiko drums and mass chanting of the mantra of Acala by priests and lay practitioners.

Flames can sometimes reach a few meters high. The combination of the ritual's visuals and sounds can be trance-inducing and make for a profound experience. Esoteric Buddhism is also practiced, in the Japanese Tendai School, founded at around the same time as the Shingon School in the early 9th century (Heian period). The general term for Esoteric Buddhism in Japan is Mikkyô (literally "secret teachings").

In order to differentiate between the two schools, Shingon practices are also known as Tomitsu and Tendai esoteric practices as Taimitsu. In China and countries with large Chinese populations such as Taiwan, Malaysia and Singapore, Chinese Esoteric Buddhism is usually known as Tángmì which means 'Tang Dynasty Esoteric Buddhism' or Mìzông 'The Esoteric School' when referring to Esoteric Buddhism as a whole including the Tibetan, Chinese and Japanese traditions.

Pantheon

In Orthodox Esoteric Buddhism, divine beings are grouped into six classes.

- Buddhas (Butsu)
- Bodhisattvas (Bosatsu)
- Wisdom Kings or Vidyarajas (Myôô)
- Deities or Devas (Ten)
- Avatars (Keshin)
- Patriarchs (Soshi).

The Five Great Wisdom Kings

The Five Great Wisdom Kings are wrathful manifestations of the Five Dhyani Buddhas.

- Acala or Acalanatha (Fudô Myôô) "The Immovable One" - Manifestation of Buddha Mahavairocana
- Amrtakundalin (Gundari Myôô) "The Dispenser of Heavenly Nectar" - Manifestation of Buddha Ratnasambhava
- Trailokyavijaya (Gozanze Myôô) "The Conqueror of The Three Planes" - Manifestation of Buddha Akshobhya
- Yamântaka (Daitoku Myôô) "The Defeater of Death" - Manifestation of Buddha Amitabha
- Vajrayaksa (Kongo Yasha Myôô) "The Devourer of Demons" - Manifestation of Buddha Amoghasiddi

Other well-known Wisdom Kings

- Ragaraja (Aizen Myôô)
- Mahamayuri (Kujaku Myôô)
- Hayagriva (Batô Kannon)
- Ucchusma (Ususama Myôô)
- Atavaka (Daigensui Myôô)

The Twelve Guardian Deities (Deva)

- Brahmâ (Bonten) - Lord of the Heavens ; Guardian of the Heavens (upward direction)
- Indra (Taishakuten) - Lord of the TrâyastriCœa Heaven and The Thirty Three Devas ; Guardian of the East
- VaruGa (Suiten) - Lord of Water ; Guardian of the West
- Vaishravana (Bishamonten or Tamonten) - Lord of Wealth ; Guardian of the North
- Yama (Enmaten) - Lord of the Underworld ; Guardian of the South
- Agni (Katen) - Lord of Fire ; Guardian of the South East
- Rakshasa (Rasetsuten) - Lord of Demons ; Guardian of the South West
- Shiva or Maheshvara (Daijizaiten or Ishanaten) - Lord of The Desire Realms ; Guardian of the North East
- Vâyu (Futen)- Lord of Wind ; Guardian of the North West
- Sûrya (Nitten) - Lord of the Sun
- Chandra (Gatten) - Lord of the Moon
- Prthivi (Jiten) - Lord of the Earth ; Guardian of the Earth (downward direction)

Other Important Deities (Deva)

- Marici (Marishi-Ten) - Patron deity of Warriors
- Mahakala (Daikokuten) - Patron deity of Wealth

- Saraswati (Benzaiten) - Patron deity of Knowledge, Art and Music
- Ganesha (Kangiten) Patron deity of Bliss and Remover of Obstacles
- Skanda (Idaten or Kumaraten) Protector of Buddhist Monasteries and Monks

Branches of Shingon

- Kôyasan
- Tôji
- Zentsûji-ha
- Daigo-ha
- Omuro-ha
- Daikakuji-ha
- Sennyûji-ha
- Yamashina-ha
- Shigisan
- Nakayamadera-ha
- Sanbôshû
- Sumadera-ha
- Chizan-ha
- Buzan-ha
- Shingi
- Ritsushû
- Kokubunji-ha
- Inunaki-ha

11

Tibetan Buddhism

Tibet, the land of Lamas is an abode of Buddhism. Here in this chapter we will light on some salient feature of Tibetan school of Buddhism.

Basically, Tibetan Buddhism is the body of Buddhist religious doctrine and institutions characteristic of Tibet and certain regions of the Himalayas, including northern Nepal, Bhutan, and India (particularly in Arunachal Pradesh, Ladakh, Dharamsala, Lahaul and Spiti in Himachal Pradesh, and Sikkim). It is the state religion of Bhutan. It is also practiced in Mongolia and parts of Russia (Kalmykia, Buryatia, and Tuva) and Northeast China.

Texts recognized as scripture and commentary are contained in the Tibetan Buddhist canon, such that Tibetan is a spiritual language of these areas. In the wake of the 1959 Tibetan uprising, a Tibetan diaspora has made Tibetan Buddhism more widely accessible to the rest of the world.

It has since spread to many Western countries, where the tradition has gained popularity. Among its prominent exponents is the 14th Dalai Lama of Tibet. The number of its adherents is estimated to be between ten and twenty million.

Tibetan Buddhism comprises the teachings of the three vehicles of Buddhism: the Foundational Vehicle, Mahâyâna, and Vajrayâna. The Mahâyâna goal of spiritual development is to achieve the enlightenment of Buddhahood in order to most efficiently help all other sentient beings attain this state.

The motivation in it is the bodhicitta mind of enlightenment — an altruistic intention to become enlightened for the sake of all sentient beings. Bodhisattvas are revered beings who have conceived the will and vow to dedicate their lives with bodhicitta for the sake of all beings. Tibetan Buddhism teaches methods for achieving Buddahood more quickly by including the Vajrayâna path in Mahâyâna.

In fact, Buddhahood is defined as a state free of the obstructions to liberation as well as those to omniscience. When, in Buddhahood, one is freed from all mental obscurations, one is said to attain a state of continuous bliss mixed with a simultaneous cognition of emptiness, the true nature of reality. In this state, all limitations on one's ability to help other living beings are removed. It is said that there are countless beings who have attained Buddhahood. Buddhas spontaneously, naturally and continuously perform activities to benefit all sentient beings. However it is believed that sentient beings' karmas limit the ability of the Buddhas to help them.

Thus, although Buddhas possess no limitation from their side on their ability to help others, sentient beings continue to experience suffering as a result of the limitations of their own former negative actions.

Introspection as the mark of a Buddhist is embodied in the Tibetan term for Buddhist: literally, "internalist". More precisely, Tibetans specify two alternative criteria for being

Buddhist - a) formal: having taken refuge and b) in belief: acceptance of the four marks of existence.

Transmission and Realisation

It is pertinent to note that emphasis on oral transmission as more important than the printed word derives from the earliest period of Indian Buddhism, when it allowed teachings to be kept from those who should not hear them. Hearing a teaching (transmission) readies the hearer for realisation based on it. The person from whom one hears the teaching should have heard it as one link in a succession of listeners going back to the original speaker: the Buddha in the case of a sutra or the author in the case of a book.

Then the hearing constitutes an authentic lineage of transmission. Authenticity of the oral lineage is a prerequisite for realisation, hence the importance of lineages. Merely reading about a teaching is helpful but no substitute for receiving a transmission on it. Listening to a text recited aloud by someone who holds the lineage for transmission of that text makes oneself also a holder of that lineage and the more ready for realization of the teaching in it.

Oral transmissions by lineage holders traditionally can take place in small groups or mass gatherings of listeners and may last for seconds (in the case of a mantra, for example) or months (as in the case of a section of the canon). A transmission can even occur without actually hearing, as in Asanga's visions of Maitreya.

Spontaneous realisation on the basis of transmission is possible but rare. Normally an intermediate step is needed in the form of analytic meditation, i.e., thinking about what one has heard. As part of this process, entertaining doubts and engaging in internal debate over them is encouraged in some traditions.

Analytic meditation is just one of two general methods of meditation. When it achieves the quality of realisation, one is encouraged to switch to "focused" or "fixation" meditation. In this the mind is stabilised on that realisation for periods long enough to gradually habituate it to it.

A person's capacity for analytic meditation can be trained with logic. The capacity for successful focused meditation can be trained through calm abiding. A meditation routine may involve alternating sessions of analytic meditation to achieve deeper levels of realization, and focused meditation to consolidate them. The deepest level of realization is Buddhahood itself.

Two characteristic aspects of Tibetan Buddhism are skepticism and devotion to the guru which have led it into conflict with Chinese socialism and so invited the destruction of the Tibetan intelligentsia under Mao. An attitude of critical skepticism is encouraged to promote abilities in analytic meditation.

However, as in other Buddhist traditions, an attitude of reverence for the teacher is also highly prized. In favour of skepticism towards Buddhist doctrines in general, Tibetans are fond of quoting sutra to the effect that one should test the Buddha's words as one would the quality of gold. On the other hand, at the beginning of a public teaching, a lama will do prostrations to the throne on which he will teach due to its symbolism, or to an image of the Buddha behind that throne, then students will do prostrations to the lama after he is seated. Merit accrues when one's interactions with the teacher are imbued with such reverence in the form of guru devotion, a code of practices governing them that derives from Indian sources.

By such things as avoiding disturbance to the peace of

mind of one's teacher, and wholeheartedly following his prescriptions, much merit accrues and this can significantly help improve one's practice.

In fact, there is a general sense in which any Tibetan Buddhist teacher is called a lama. A student may have taken teachings from many authorities and revere them all as lamas in this general sense. However, he will typically have one held in special esteem as his own root guru and is encouraged to view the other teachers who are less dear to him, however more exalted their status, as embodied in and subsumed by the root guru.

Often the teacher the student sees as root guru is simply the one who first introduced him to Buddhism, but a student may also change his personal view of which particular teacher is his root guru any number of times. The opposing principles of skepticism and guru devotion are reconciled with the Tibetan injunction to scrutinise a prospective guru thoroughly before finally adopting him as such without reservation. A Buddhist may study with a lama for decades before finally accepting him as his own guru.

Vajrayâna is said to be the fastest method for attaining Buddhahood but for unqualified practitioners it can be dangerous. To engage in it one must receive an appropriate initiation (also known as an "empowerment") from a lama who is fully qualified to give it.

From the time one has resolved to accept such an initiation, the utmost sustained effort in guru devotion is essential.

The aim of preliminary practices (*ngöndro*) is to start the student on the correct path for such higher teachings.

Just as Sutrayâna preceded Vajrayâna historically in India, so sutra practices constitute those that are preliminary to tantric ones. Preliminary practices include all *Sutrayâna* activities that yield merit like hearing teachings, prostrations, offerings, prayers and acts of kindness and compassion, but chief among the preliminary practices are realizations through meditation on the three principle stages of the path: renunciation, the altruistic bodhicitta wish to attain enlightenment and the wisdom realizing emptiness.

For a person without the basis of these three in particular to practice Vajrayâna can be like a small child trying to ride an unbroken horse. While the practices of Vajrayâna are not known in Sutrayâna, all Sutrayâna practices are common to Vajrayâna. Without training in the preliminary practices, the ubiquity of allusions to them in Vajrayâna is meaningless and even successful Vajrayâna initiation becomes impossible. The merit acquired in the preliminary practices facilitates progress in Vajrayâna. While many Buddhists may spend a lifetime exclusively on sutra practices, however, an amalgam of the two to some degree is common. For, example, in order to train in calm abiding, one might use a tantric visualisation as the meditation object.

Esotericism

In Vajrayâna particularly, Tibetan Buddhists subscribe to a voluntary code of self-censorship, whereby the uninitiated do not seek and are not provided with information about it. This self-censorship may be applied more or less strictly depending on circumstances such as the material involved. A depiction of a mandala may be less public than that of a deity. That of a higher tantric deity may be less public than that of a lower. The degree to which information on Vajrayâna is now public in western languages is controversial among Tibetan Buddhists.

Basically, Buddhism has always had a taste for esotericism since its earliest period in India. Tibetans today maintain greater or lesser degrees of confidentiality also with information on the *vinaya* and emptiness specifically. In Buddhist teachings generally, too, there is caution about revealing information to people who may be unready for it. Esoteric values in Buddhism have made it at odds with the values of Christian missionary activity, for example in contemporary Mongolia.

Some commentators have emphasised Tibetan innovations such as the system of incarnate lamas, but such genuine innovations have been few. True to its roots in the *Pâla* system of North India, however, Tibetan Buddhism carried on a tradition of eclectic accumulation and systematisation of diverse Buddhist elements, and pursued their synthesis. Prominent among these achievements are the Stages of the Path and motivational training.

Tenet Systems in Tibetan Buddhism

Tibetan Buddhists practice one or more understandings of the true nature of reality, the emptiness of inherent existence of all things. Emptiness is propounded according to four classical Indian schools of philosophical tenets.

Two belong to the older path of the Foundation Vehicle:

- Vaibhacika (Tib. *bye-brag smra-ba*)
- Sautrântika (Tib. *mdo-sde-pa*)

In fact, the primary source for the former is the Abhidharma-koœa by Vasubandhu and its commentaries. The Abhidharmakoúa is also an important source for the Sautrântikas. Dignâga and Dharmakîrti are the most prominent exponents.

The other two are Mahayana (Skt. *Greater Vehicle*) (Tib. *theg-chen*):

- Yogâcâra, also called Cittamâtra (Tib. *sems-tsam-pa*), *Mind-Only*
- Madhyamaka (Tib. *dbu-ma-pa*)

Yogacârins base their views on texts from Maitreya, AsaEga and Vasubandhu, Madhyamakas on Nâgârjuna and Âryadeva. There is a further classification of Madhyamaka into Svatantrika-Madhyamaka and PrasaEgika-Madhyamaka.

The former stems from Bhavaviveka, Úântarakcita and Kamalaaúîla, and the latter from Buddhapâlita and Candrakîrti. The tenet system is used in the monasteries and colleges to teach Buddhist philosophy in a systematic and progressive fashion, each philosophical view being more subtle than its predecessor.

Therefore the four schools can be seen as a gradual path from a rather easy-to-grasp, "realistic" philosophical point of view, to more and more complex and subtle views on the ultimate nature of reality, that is on emptiness and dependent arising, culminating in the philosophy of the Mâdhyamikas, which is widely believed to present the most sophisticated point of view.

According to a Tibetan legendary tradition, Buddhist scriptures including the Kâran avyûhasûtra and relics including the *cintamani* arrived in southern Tibet in the fifth century during the reign of Lha Thothori Nyantsen, the 28th king of Tibet. The tale is miraculous: the objects fell from the sky on the roof of the king's palace, but it may have a historical background in the form of the arrival of Buddhist missionaries. The earliest well-documented influence of Buddhism in Tibet dates from the reign of king Songtsän Gampo, who died in 650. He married a Chinese Tang Dynasty Buddhist princess, Wencheng, who came to Tibet with a statue of Shakyamuni Buddha.

According to a Tibetan legendary tradition, Songtsän Gampo also married a Nepalese Buddhist princess, Bhrikuti; but Bhrikuti, who bears the name of a goddess, is not mentioned in reliable sources. Songtsän Gampo founded the first Buddhist temples. By the second half of the 8th century he was already regarded as an embodiment of the bodhisattva Avalokitesvara. The successors of Songtsän Gampo were less enthusiastic about the propagation of Buddhism but in the 8th century, King Trisong Detsen (755-797) established it as the official religion of the state. He invited Indian Buddhist scholars to his court. In his age the famous tantric mystic Padmasambhâva arrived in Tibet according to the Tibetan tradition. In addition to writing a number of important scriptures, some of which he hid for future *tertons* to find, Padmasambhâva, along with Úântarakcita, established the Nyingma school. The outlines of the history of Buddhism in Tibet from this time are well-known. At this early time also, from the south came the influence of scholars under the Pâla dynasty in the Indian state of Magadha.

They had achieved a blend of Mahayana and Vajrayana that has come to characterize all forms of Tibetan Buddhism. Their teaching in sutra centred on the *Abhisamayâlankâra*, a fourth century Yogacârin text, but prominent among them were the Mâdhyamika scholars Úântarakcita and Kamalaúîla. A third influence was that of the Sarvâstivâdins from Kashmir in the south west and Khotan in the north west. Although they did not succeed in maintaining a presence in Tibet, their texts found their way into the

Tibetan Buddhist canon, providing the Tibetans with almost all of their primary sources about the Foundation Vehicle. A subsect of this school, Mûlasarvâstivâda was the source of the Tibetan vinaya. A fourth influence from China in the east came in the form of Chan.

According to A. W. Barber of the University of Calgary, Chan Buddhism was introduced to the Nyingmapa in three principal streams: the teachings of Master Kim, Kim Ho-shang, (Chin ho shang) transmitted by *Sang Shi* in ca. 750 CE; the lineage of Master Wu Chu of the Pao T'ang School was transmitted within Tibet by Ye-shes Wangpo; and the teaching from Mo Ho Yen, (Tibetan: *Hwa shang Mahayana*) that were a synthesis of the Northern School of Chan and the Pao T'ang School.

Tibetan king *Khri srong lde btsan* (742–797) invited the Ch'an master Mo-ho-yen (whose name consists of the same Chinese characters used to transliterate "Mahayana") to transmit the Dharma at Samye Monastery. Mo-ho-yen had been disseminating Dharma in the Tun-huang locale, but, according to Tibetan sources, lost an important philosophical debate on the nature of emptiness with the Indian master Kamalasîla, and the king declared Kamalasîla's philosophy should form the basis for Tibetan Buddhism. However, a Chinese source says their side won, and some scholars conclude that the entire episode is fictitious. Pioneering Buddhologist Giuseppe Tucci speculated that Hwashang's ideas were preserved by the Nyingmapas in the form of dzogchen teachings. Whichever may be the case, Tibetan Buddhists today trace their spiritual roots from Indian masters such as Padmasambhâva, Atiœa, Tilopa, Naropa and their later Tibetan students.

From the outset Buddhism was opposed by the native

shamanistic Bön religion, which had the support of the aristocracy, but with royal patronage it thrived to a peak under King Rälpachän (817-836).

Terminology in translation was standardised around 825, enabling a translation methodology that was highly literal. Despite a reversal in Buddhist influence which began under King Langdarma (836-842), the following centuries saw a colossal effort in collecting available Indian sources, many of which are now extant only in Tibetan translation. Tibetan Buddhism exerted a strong influence from the 11th century CE among the peoples of Central Asia, especially in Mongolia and Manchuria.

It was adopted as an official state religion by the Mongol Yuan dynasty and the Manchu Qing dynasty that ruled China. Coinciding with the early discoveries of "hidden treasures" (*terma*), the 11th century saw a revival of Buddhist influence originating in the far east and far west of Tibet. In the west, Rinchen Zangpo (958-1055) was active as a translator and founded temples and monasteries.

Prominent scholars and teachers were again invited from India. In 1042 Atiœa arrived in Tibet at the invitation of a west Tibetan king. This renowned exponent of the Pâla form of Buddhism from the Indian university of Vikramasîla later moved to central Tibet.

There his chief disciple, Dromtonpa founded the Kadampa school of Tibetan Buddhism, under whose influence the New Translation schools of today evolved.

Major Schools

Tibetan Buddhism has four main traditions:

(a) Nyingma(pa), "the Ancient Ones". This is the oldest, the original order founded by Padmasambhâva and

Úântarakcita. Whereas other schools categorize their teachings into the three vehicles: The Foundation Vehicle, Mahâyâna and Vajrayâna, the Nyingma tradition classifies its into nine vehicles, among the highest of which is that known as *Atiyoga* or Dzogchen ("Great Perfection"). Hidden treasures (*terma*) are of particular significance to this tradition.

(b) Kagyu(pa), "Lineage of the (Buddha's) Word". This is an oral tradition which is very much concerned with the experiential dimension of meditation. Its most famous exponent was Milarepa, an eleventh century mystic.

It contains one major and one minor subsect. The first, the Dagpo Kagyu, encompasses those Kagyu schools that trace back to the Indian master Naropa via Marpa, Milarepa and Gampopa and consists of four major sub-sects: the Karma Kagyu, headed by a Karmapa, the Tsalpa Kagyu, the Barom Kagyu, and Pagtru Kagyu.

There are further eight minor sub-sects, all of which trace their root to Pagtru Kagyu and the most notable of which are the Drikung Kagyu and the Drukpa Kagyu. The once-obscure Shangpa Kagyu, which was famously represented by the 20th century teacher Kalu Rinpoche, traces its history back to the Indian master Naropa via Niguma, Sukhasiddhi and Kyungpo Neljor.

(c) Sakya(pa), "Grey Earth". This school very much represents the scholarly tradition. Headed by the Sakya Trizin, this tradition was founded by Khon Konchog Gyalpo, a disciple of the great translator Drokmi Lotsawa and traces it's lineage to the Indian master Virupa. A renowned exponent, Sakya Pandita

1182–1251CE was the great grandson of Khon Konchog Gyalpo.

(d) Gelug(pa), "Way of Virtue". Originally a reformist movement, this tradition is particularly known for its emphasis on logic and debate. Its spiritual head is the Ganden Tripa and its temporal one the Dalai Lama. The Dalai Lama is regarded as the embodiment of the Bodhisattva of Compassion Successive Dalai Lamas ruled Tibet from the mid-17th to mid-20th centuries. The order was founded in the 14th to 15th century by Je Tsongkhapa, renowned for both his scholasticism and his virtue.

These major schools are sometimes said to constitute the "Old Translation" and "New Translation" traditions, the latter following from the historical *Kadampa* lineage of translations and tantric lineages. Another common differentiation is into "Red Hat" and "Yellow Hat" schools.

Besides these major schools, there is a minor one, the Jonang. The Jonangpa were suppressed by the rival Gelugpa in the 1600s and were once thought extinct, but are now known to survive in Eastern Tibet.

There is also an ecumenical movement known as Rimé.

Monasticism

Although there were many householder-yogis in Tibet, monasticism was the foundation of Buddhism in Tibet. There were over 6,000 monasteries in Tibet, but nearly all were ransacked and destroyed by Red Guards during the Cultural Revolution. Most of the major ones have been at least partially re-established but many still remain in ruins. In Mongolia during the 1920s, approximately one third of the male population were monks, though many lived outside monasteries.

By the beginning of the 20th century about 750 monasteries were functioning in Mongolia. These monasteries were largely dismantled during Communist rule, but many have been reestablished during the Buddhist revival in Mongolia which followed the fall of Communism. Monasteries generally adhere to one particular school. Some of the major centers in each tradition are as follows:

Nyingma

The Nyingma lineage is said to have "six mother monasteries," although the composition of the six has changed over time:

- Dorje Drak
- Dzogchen Monastery
- Kathok
- Mindroling
- Palyul
- Shechen

Also of note is

- Samye — the first monastery in Tibet, established by Padmasambhâva and Úântarakcita

Kagyu

Many Kagyu monasteries are in Kham, eastern Tibet. Tsurphu, one of the most important, is in central Tibet, as is Ralung and Drikung.

- Palpung Monastery — the seat of the Tai Situpa and Jamgon Kongtrul
- Ralung Monastery — the seat of the Gyalwang Drukpa

- Surmang Monastery — the seat of the Trungpa tülkus
- Tsurphu Monastery — the seat of H.H. the Gyalwa Karmapa

Sakya

- Sakya Monastery — the seat of H.H. the Sakya Trizin

Gelug

The three most important centers of the Gelugpa lineage are Ganden, Sera and Drepung Monasteries, near Lhasa:

- Ganden Monastery — the seat of the Ganden Tripa
- Drepung Monastery — the home monastery of the Dalai Lama
- Sera Monastery

Three other monasteries have particularly important regional influence:

- Tashilhunpo Monastery in Shigatse — founded by the first Dalai Lama, this monastery is now the seat of the Panchen Lama
- Labrang Monastery in eastern Amdo
- Kumbum Jampaling in central Amdo

Great spiritual and historical importance is also placed on:

- The Jokhang Temple in Lhasa — said to have been built by King Songtsen Gampo in 647 AD, a major pilgrimage site

Today, Tibetan Buddhism is adhered to widely in the

Tibetan Plateau, Nepal, Bhutan, Mongolia, Kalmykia (on the north-west shore of the Caspian), Siberia (central Russia, specifically Buryatia and Chita Oblast), and the Russian Far East (concentrated in Tuva).

The Indian regions of Sikkim and Ladakh, both formerly independent kingdoms, are also home to significant Tibetan Buddhist populations. In the wake of the Tibetan diaspora, Tibetan Buddhism has gained adherents in the West and throughout the world. Celebrity practitioners include Brandon Boyd, Richard Gere, Adam Yauch, Jet Li, Sharon Stone, Allen Ginsberg, Philip Glass and Steven Seagal.

REFERENCES

1. Coleman, Graham, ed. (1993). *A Handbook of Tibetan Culture*. Boston: Shambhala Publications, Inc.
2. Conze, Edward (1993). *A Short History of Buddhism* (2nd ed.). Oneworld.
3. Dhargyey, Geshe Ngawang; ed. Alexander Berzin, based on oral trans. by Sharpa Tulku (3rd edn, 1978). *Tibetan Tradition of Mental Development*. Dharmsala: Library of Tibetan Works and Archives. [A pithy lam-rim by a geshe appointed in 1973.
4. Dhargyey, Geshe Ngawang; ed. Alexander Berzin, based on oral trans. by Sharpa Tulku (1982). *An Anthology of Well-Spoken Advice on the Graded Paths of the Mind, Vol. I*. Dharmsala: Library of Tibetan Works and Archives.
5. Hopkins, Jeffrey (1996). *Meditation on Emptiness*. Boston: Wisdom.
6. Lati Rinpoche; trans. & ed.: Elizabeth Napper (1980). *Mind in Tibetan Buddhism: Oral Commentary on Ge-shay Jam-bel-sam-pel's "Presentation of Awareness and Knowledge Composite of All the Important Points Opener of the Eye of New Intelligence*. Valois, NY: Snow Lion.
7. Mullin, Glenn H. (1998). *Living in the Face of Death: The Tibetan Tradition*. 2008 reprint: Snow Lion Publications, Ithica, New York.

8. Nyanaponika Thera (1965). *The Heart of Buddhist Meditation*. Boston: Weiser.
9. Pabongka Rinpoche; Ed. Trijang Rinpoche, transl. Michael Richards (3rd edn. 2006). *Liberation in the Palm of Your Hand, A Concise Discourse on the Path to Enlightenment*. Somerville, MA: Wisdom.
10. Powers, John. *History as Propaganda: Tibetan Exiles versus the People's Republic of China* (2004) Oxford University Press.
11. Ringu Tulku. *The Ri-Me Philosophy of Jamgon Kongtrul the Great: A Study of the Buddhist Lineages of Tibet*. Shambhala.
12. Smith, E. Gene (2001). *Among Tibetan Texts: History and Literature of the Himalayan Plateau*. Boston: Wisdom Publications.
13. Sopa, Geshe Lhundup; Jeffrey Hopkins (1977). *Practice and Theory of Tibetan Buddhism*. New Delhi: B.I. Publications.

12

Concept of God in Buddhism

> "The love of wealth makes bitter men;
> the love of God, better men."
>
> —*W.L. Hudson*

God and god realisation is the key element of every religion. First it is significant to note that since the time of the Buddha, the refutation of the existence of a creator has been seen as a key point in distinguishing Buddhist from non-Buddhist views. Buddhism is usually considered a religion, but is also commonly described as a "spiritual philosophy", because it generally lacks an absolute creator god. The Buddhist approach is empirical and based on experience. In the Four Noble Truths, the Buddha analyzed the problem of suffering, diagnosed its root cause and prescribed a method to dispel suffering.

He taught that through insight into the nature of existence and the wisdom of "not-self" or "selflessness" (*anatta*) all sentient beings following the noble eightfold path can dispel ignorance and thereby suffering. Hence Buddhism does not hinge upon the concept of a Creator God but upon the personal practice of ethics, meditation, and wisdom. Buddhist philosophy can also be contrasted with Hindu ideas of an ultimate Self, the definition of which varies between sects.

But, in some Buddhist traditions, veneration of the Buddha as a teacher of Dharma is significant and an important part of spiritual development. While according to Pali Buddhism, the Buddha rejected being deified, in some streams of Mahayana Buddhism Gautama Buddha is worshipped as 'an omnipotent divinity endowed with numerous supernatural attributes and qualities'. and a number of Buddhist tantric scriptures promulgate the notion of Buddha as 'Primordial Lord', as the omnipresent and eternal foundation of all that exists.

Supernatural

While many Buddhist traditions do not deny the existence of supernatural beings (e.g., the *devas*, of which many are discussed in Buddhist scripture), it does not ascribe powers, in the typical Western sense, for creation, salvation or judgement, to the "gods". They are regarded as having the power to affect worldly events in much the same way as humans and animals have the power to do so. Just as humans can affect the world more than animals, *devas* can affect the world more than humans. While gods may be more powerful than humans, none of them are absolute (unsurpassed).

Most importantly, gods, like humans, are also suffering in samsara, the ongoing cycle of death and subsequent rebirth. Gods have not attained nirvana, and are still subject to emotions, including jealousy, anger, delusion, sorrow, etc. Thus, since a Buddha shows the way to nirvana, a Buddha is called "the teacher of the gods and humans." According to the Pali Canon the gods have powers to affect only so far as their realm of influence or control allows them. In this sense therefore, they are no closer to nirvana than humans and no wiser in the ultimate sense. A dialogue between the king Pasenadi Kosala, his general Vidudabha and the historical Buddha reveals a lot about the relatively weaker position of gods in Buddhism. The Pali Canon also attributes supernatural powers to enlightened beings (Buddhas), that even gods may not have.

In a dialogue between king Ajatasattu and the Buddha, enlightened beings are ascribed supranormal powers (like human flight, walking on water etc.), clairaudience, mind reading, recollection of past lives of oneself and others. Yet, according to the Buddha, an enlightened person realizes the futility of these powers and instead unbinds himself completely from *samsara* through discernment.

Buddhism on Creation

Reflecting a common understanding of the Buddha's earliest teachings, Nyanaponika Thera asserts:

> "From a study of the discourses of the Buddha preserved in the Pali canon, it will be seen that the idea of a personal deity, a creator god conceived to be eternal and omnipotent, is incompatible with the Buddha's teachings. On the other hand, conceptions of an impersonal godhead of any description, such as world-soul, etc., are not excluded by the Buddha's teachings on Anatta, non-self or unsubstantiality. ... In Buddhist literature, the belief in a creator god (issara-nimmana-vada) is frequently mentioned and rejected, along with other causes wrongly adduced to explain the origin of the world."

Besides, nowhere in the Pali Canon, are Buddhas ascribed powers of creation, salvation and judgement. In fact, Buddhism is critical of all theories on the origin of the universe and holds the belief in creation as a fetter binding one to samsara. However, the Aggañña Sutta does contain a detailed account of the Buddha describing the origin of human life on earth. In this text, the Buddha provides an explanation of the caste system alternate to the one contained in the Vedas, and shows why one caste is not really any better than the other.

According to scholar Richard Gombrich, the sutta gives strong evidence that it was conceived entirely as a satire of pre-existing beliefs, and he and scholar David Kalupahana have asserted that the primary intent of this text is to satirize and debunk the brahminical claims regarding the divine nature of the caste system, showing that it is nothing but a human convention. Strictly speaking, the sutta is not a cosmogony, as in Buddhism, an absolute beginning is inconceivable.

Since the earliest times Buddhists have, however, taken it seriously as an account of the origins of society and kingship. Gombrich, however, finds it to be a parody of brahminical cosmogony as presented in the *Rigvedic* "Hymn of creation" (RV X, 129) and BAU 1, 2. He states: "The Buddha never intended to propound a cosmogony. If we take a close look at the *Aggañña Sutta,* there are considerable incoherencies if it is taken seriously as an explanatory account - though once it is perceived to be a parody these inconsistencies are of no account." In particular, he finds that it violates the basic Buddhist theory of how the law of karma operates. However, scholar Rupert Gethin strongly disagrees, stating:

> While certain of the details of the Aggainia-sutta's account of the evolution of human society may be, as Gombrich has persuasively argued, satirical in intent, there is nothing in the Nikayas to suggest that these basic cosmological principles that I have identified should be so understood; there is nothing to suggest that the Aggafinia-sutta's introductory formula describing the expansion and contraction of the world is merely a joke. We should surely expect early Buddhism and indeed the Buddha to have some specific ideas about the nature of the round of rebirth,

> and essentially this is what the cosmological details presented in the Aggafifia-sutta and elsewhere in Nikayas constitute ... far from being out of key with what we can understand of Buddhist thought from the rest of the Nikayas, the cosmogonic views offered by the Aggañña Sutta in fact harmonize very well with it . .I would go further and say that something along the lines of the Aggañña myth is actually required by it.

Remarkably, in Buddhism, the focus is primarily on the effect the belief in theories of creation and a creator have on the human mind. The Buddhist attitude towards every view is one of critical examination from the perspective of what effect the belief has on the mind and whether the belief binds one to samsara or not. The Buddha declared that "it is not possible to know or determine the first beginning of the cycle of existence of beings who wander therein deluded by ignorance and obsessed by craving." Speculation about the origin and extent of the universe is generally discouraged in early Buddhism.

Theravada

Huston Smith describes early Buddhism as psychological rather than metaphysical. Unlike theistic religions, which are founded on notions of God and related creation myths, Buddhism begins with the human condition as enumerated in the Four Noble Truths. Thus while most other religions attempt to pass a blanket judgement on the goodness of a pre-fallen world (e.g. 'He then looked at the world and saw that it was good.' Book of Genesis, Old Testament, Christian Bible) and therefore derive the greatness of its Creator.

Early Buddhism denies that the question is even worth asking to begin with. Instead it places emphasis on the human condition of clinging and the insubstantial nature of the world. This approach is often even in contrast with many of the Mahayana forms of Buddhism. No being, whether a god or an enlightened being (including the historical Buddha) is ascribed powers of creation, granting salvation and judgement.

According to the Pali Canon, omnipotence cannot be ascribed to any being. Further, in Theravada Buddhism, there are no lands or heavens where a being is guaranteed nirvana, instead he can attain nirvana within a very short time, though nothing conclusive could be said about the effort required for that.

In this sense therefore, there is no equivalent of the Mahayana "Pure Land" or magical abode of Buddhas where one is guaranteed to be enlightened, in Early Buddhist tradition. However, Theravada Buddhism does mention the 'Pure Abodes' (pali: Sudhavasasa) in which Non-Returners (pali: Anagami) are born and there they attain Nirbana.

Mahayana

Like Theravada Buddhism Mahayana Buddhism posits no Creator or ruler God. In the Avatamsaka Sutra it says, "If you want to understand all the Buddhas of the past, present, and future, then you should view the whole universe as being created by Heart."

In some major traditions of Mahayana Buddhism (the Tathagatagarbha and Pure Land streams of teaching) there is a notion of the Buddha as the omnipresent, omniscient, liberative essence of reality, and Buddhas are spoken of as generators of vast "pure lands", "Buddha lands", or "Buddha paradises", in which beings will unfailingly attain Nirvana.

Vajrayana

It is pertinent to note that Tibetan schools of Buddhism also refer to two truths, absolute and relative. Relative truth is simply a truth that is relative to another condition, exaclty as one would expect, and ultimate truth is described as an experience of emptiness, or rhater looking into a concept and finding it has no firm entitiy.

There are many philosophical viewpoints, but unique to the Vajrayana perspective is emptiness as an experience.

Is Buddha God

Although an absolute creator god is absent in most forms of Buddhism, veneration or worship of the Buddha and other Buddhas does play a major role in all forms of Buddhism. While, in Buddhism all beings may strive for Buddhahood, striving to become a god or God in a monotheistic context (like in Abrahamic religions) would be futile or senseless, even heretical, due to a strict distinction between humanity and divinity. Throughout the schools of Buddhism, it is taught that being born in the human realm is best for realizing full enlightenment, whereas being born as a god presents one with too much pleasure and too many distractions to provide any motivation for serious insight meditation.

Doctrines of theosis have played an important role in Christian thought, and there are a number of theistic variations of Hinduism where a practitioner can strive to become the godhead (for example Vedanta), but from a Buddhist perspective, such attainment would be disadvantageous to the attainment of nirvana. In Buddhism, one venerates Buddhas and sages for their virtues, sacrifices, and struggles for perfect enlightenment, and as teachers who are embodiments of the Dhamma.

In Buddhism, this supreme victory of the human ability for perfect gnosis is celebrated in the concept of human saints known as Arahants which literally means "worthy of offerings" or "worthy of worship" because this sage overcomes all defilements and obtains perfect gnosis to obtain Nirvana.

Perry Schmidt-Leukel comments on how some portrayals of the Buddha within Western understanding deprive him of certain 'divine' features, which are in fact found in the earlier scriptures and in certain Eastern contexts. Schmidt-Leukel writes:

> What a difference between the presentation of the Buddha within the genuine context of religious veneration, as in [the Doi Suthep Thai] temple, and the image of the Buddha - currently so widespread in the West - according to which the Buddha was simply a human being, free from all divine features! Indeed this modern view does not at all correspond to the description of the Buddha in the classical Buddhist scriptures.

There's some uncertainty whether such worship has any effects beyond purely spiritual. East Asian doctrines, particularly the flavor of Zen popular in the West, teach that the Buddha and other Buddhas are immutable and therefore cannot or do not intervene in human affairs; at best, prayer to them may facilitate one's own enlightenment, even that due to conscious efforts of the one who prays rather than through the intervention of the supreme being. For that and other reasons, Buddha worship is rarely, if ever, practiced in Mahayana.

Buddha worship is common among laymen in Theravada countries such as Thailand, and it often assumes forms more reminiscent of prayers to gods and saints in Christianity or pagan religions, where worshippers may ask Buddha for help in practical matters. At the same time, this objection does not apply to worship of Bodhisattvas. Prayer to and meditation on Bodhisattvas such as Avalokitesvara are integral elements of Tibetan Buddhism.

Thought as Creator

In Theravada Buddhism, there is no Supreme creator. Yet thoughts (or mind, perceptions, etc.; Pali *manas*, *mano* in combined form) are the causes and conditions of the way we view the world.

The opening phrase of the Dhammapada expresses in a few words the most profound understanding in Buddhism of the role of thought in the creation of our perception of the things (*dhamma*) with which we construct our worldview. In modern parlance it expresses a psychology of phenomonologically ideal realism.

Manopubbangammâ Dhammâ

Manosemmhâ manomayâ

Manasâ ce padummhena

These words are of such integral importance to understanding the Buddhist view of the role of thinking in the construction of a worldview that no single English translation should be relied upon. For example, many English translations insert the pronoun "we" into the lines which does not appear in the original Pali.

To demonstrate the variety of English translations:

We are what we think.
All that we are arises with our thoughts.
With our thoughts we make the world.
Preceded by perception are mental states.
For them is perception supreme.
From perception have they sprung.

> All mental phenomena are preceded by mind,
> Mind is their master,
> they are produced by mind.

In Theravada Buddhism there is no "designer" who is outside of the design. The recognition of a "design" (i.e., pattern recognition at all levels of mentation, perception, mental complexes, etc.) is the function of *manas* (thinking mind) and is otherwise known in Buddhist psychology as the Sixth Consciousness.

It is this role of the Sixth Consciousness in creating the fundamental patterns for the building blocks of a worldview that makes thought the "creator" of the world. All the notions we have about ourselves and our world are fundamentally incorrect notions that become the root cause of ignorance. In Theravada Buddhism, the term *the world* does not refer to an objective empirical world accepted as real, but to the process of objectification of a world that we experience.

In Theravada Buddhism the world arises moment by moment, and no thing exists beyond the thought-moment of its existence, but that thinking makes it seem to be so by stringing together thought-moments (for example, using memory and associations) into a tapestry of the illusion of a world. So in Theravada Buddhism, the words *the world* refers to *all this mass of stress* created by the delusions of our thought-designs interpreting, configuring, and constructing the world of experience (i.e., the first Five Consciousnesses). It is noteworthy therefore that while creation in most other religions, as perceived by a person who objectifies themselves as a being, or separate entity, is the act of a divine being and viewed as a purely positive event, while in Theravada Buddhism, neither is creation divine nor is it only positive, but necessarily both positive and negative, plus and minus, in equal proportion.

That is, when the undifferentiated mind (i.e., the Eighth Consciousnesses) discriminates itself (i.e., the functioning of the Seventh Consciousnesses), that discrimination is itself the activity of mind functioning in both plus and minus capacities. This discrimination function must necessarily include both poles of every "opposition" or "polarity" that is discriminated. When the thinking process (*manas*) then attempts to configure a design out of the multiplicity of oppositions, it naturally falls on or grasps at one side of the apparent opposition in distinction to the other side in order to create a sense of solidity or fixation to the world. By such "taking sides" or "one-sidedness", thinking makes itself appear supreme (*semmha*) in its own world, thus the designation *manosemmhâ* in line two of the *Dhammapada* above.

In the Buddhist view, liberation occurs when our thinking mind (*manas*) comes down off its self-created throne and sees that the world it creates is illusory and that all things or patterns (i.e., *dhammas*) are not other than discrimination of Mind as the waves are the discrimination of the ocean.

This Mind that is discriminated is designated in positive language as the Tathagata, Dharmakaya, Tathagatagarbha, Buddha Nature, Suchness, Thusness, etc. and in negative language as Sunyata, Emptiness, Non-dual, No-Mind, etc. The statement "From consciousness as a requisite condition comes name-&-form" repeatedly occurs throughout the Pali canons, indicating that the Buddha had meant the world physically arises from consciousness.

Remarkably, in early Buddhism, the Buddha clearly states that "reliance and belief" in creation by a supreme being leads to lack of effort and inaction: This is a significant hindrance in the path to liberation in the Buddha's view. It may be noted that the Buddha did not criticize veneration of the noble, veneration of the wise and learned, but only said that the belief in the existence of a creator God fetters the mind to samsara.

Having approached the priests and contemplatives who hold that...

> 'Whatever a person experiences... is all caused by a supreme being's act of creation,'
>
> I said to them: 'Is it true that you hold that... "Whatever a person experiences... is all caused by a supreme being's act of creation?"'
>
> Thus asked by me, they admitted, 'Yes.'
>
> Then I said to them, 'Then in that case, a person is a killer of living beings because of a supreme being's act of creation. A person is a thief... unchaste... a liar... a divisive speaker... a harsh speaker... an idle chatterer... greedy... malicious... a holder of wrong views because of a supreme being's act of creation.'

When one falls back on creation by a supreme being as being essential, monks, there is no desire, no effort [at the thought], 'This should be done. This shouldn't be done.' When one can't pin down as a truth or reality what should and shouldn't be done, one dwells bewildered and unprotected. One cannot righteously refer to oneself as a contemplative. This was my second righteous refutation of those priests and contemplative who hold to such teachings, such views.

It is also noteworthy that gods in Buddhism have no role to play in liberation.

Sir Charles Eliot describes god in early Buddhism as such:

> The attitude of early Buddhism to the spirit world — the hosts of deities and demons who people this and other spheres. Their existence is assumed, but the truths of religion are not dependent on them, and attempts to use their influence by sacrifices and oracles are deprecated as vulgar practices similar to juggling.

> The systems of philosophy then in vogue were mostly not theistic, and, strange as the words may sound, religion had little to do with the gods. If this be thought to rest on a mistranslation, it is certainly true that the dhamma had very little to do with devas.

Often as the Devas figure in early Buddhist stories, the significance of their appearance nearly always lies in their relations with the Buddha or his disciples. Of mere mythology, such as the dealings of Brahma and Indra with other gods, there is little. In fact the gods, though freely invoked as accessories, are not taken seriously, and there are some extremely curious passages in which Gotama seems to laugh at them, much as the sceptics of the 18th century laughed at Jehovah. Thus in the [Pali Canon] Kevaddha Sutta he relates how a monk who was puzzled by a metaphysical problem applied to various gods and finally accosted Brahma himself in the presence of all his retinue.

After hearing the question, which was "Where do the elements cease and leave no trace behind?" Brahma replies, "I am the Great Brahma, the Supreme, the Mighty, the All-seeing, the Ruler, the Lord of all, the Controller, the Creator, the Chief of all, appointing to each his place, the Ancient of days, the Father of all that are and are to be." "But," said the monk, "I did not ask you, friend, whether you were indeed all you now say, but I ask you where the four elements cease and leave no trace." Then the Great Brahma took him by the arm and led him aside and said, "These gods think I know and understand everything. Therefore I gave no answer in their presence. But I do not know the answer to your question and you had better go and ask the Buddha."

Basically, even more curiously ironic is the account given of the origin of Brahma. There comes a time when this world system passes away and then certain beings are reborn in the "World of Radiance" and remain there a long time. Sooner or later, the world system begins to evolve again and the palace of Brahma appears, but it is empty. Then some being whose time is up falls from the "World of Radiance" and comes to life in the palace and remains there alone.

At last he wishes for company, and it so happens that other beings whose time is up fall from the "World of Radiance" and join him. And the first being thinks that he is Great Brahma, the Creator, because when he felt lonely and wished for companions other beings appeared. And the other beings accept this view.

And at last one of Brahma's retinue falls from that state and is born in the human world and, if he can remember his previous birth, he reflects that he is transitory but that Brahma still remains and from this he draws the erroneous conclusion that Brahma is eternal. The Brahmins of the day apparently claimed that they were the link between humans and the devas. Often this would place the priestly class at an advantageous position. But the Pâli suttas dismiss the folly of those religious teachers who would lead others to what they themselves do not personally know, as "foolish talk", or "ridiculous, mere words, a vain and empty thing".

Brahma in the Pali Text

Brahma is among the common gods found in the Pali Canon. Brahma (in common with all other devas) is subject to change, final decline and death, just as are all other sentient beings in samsara (the plane of continual reincarnation and suffering).

In fact there are several different Brahma worlds and several kinds of Brahmas in Buddhism, all of which however are just beings stuck in samsara for a long while. Instead of belief in such a would-be Creator God as Brahma (a benign heavenly being who is in reality not yet free from self-delusion and the processes of rebirth), the wise are encouraged to practise the Dharma (spiritual truth) of the Buddha, in which the Noble Eightfold Path are paramount and are said to bring spiritual Liberation and Awakening.

Many of the other gods in the Pali Canon find a common mythological role in Hindu literature. Some common gods and goddesses are Indra, Aapo (Varuna), Vayo (Vayu), Tejo (Agni), Surya, Pajapati (Prajapati), Soma, Yasa, Venhu (Visnu), Mahadeva (Siva), Vijja (Saraswati), Usha, Pathavi (Prithvi) Sri (Lakshmi) Kuvera (Kubera), several yakkhas (Yakshas), gandhabbas (Gandharvas), Nâgas, garula (Garuda), sons of Bali, Veroca, etc.

While in Hindu texts some of these gods and goddesses are considered embodiments of the Supreme Being, to early Buddhists this is a ridiculous idea. In the Buddha's view all gods and goddesses were bound to samsara. The world of gods according to the Buddha presents a being with too many pleasures and distractions.

Remarkably, one of the views emerging in the time of the Buddha and seen even today was the view that even though the world was not created by a creator God, there is a driving force, a guiding principle behind the workings of the world. As an example, in ancient India, some Hindu sects considered God to be the dispenser of the results of action. According to the Buddha, this view was very dangerous in two ways.

One of the primary reasons is that this places a limitation in ones understanding of the mechanism of karma. Understanding the mechanism of karma is central to the understanding the Dharma leading to the cessation of stress and hence to complete unbinding (*nirvana*).

In fact, when the Buddha attained enlightenment, he first used his insightful awareness to view his past lives and the past and future lives of all other beings and observed the law of karma in action. Belief that a Supreme God is the force behind this law of nature places a significant road-block in spiritual progress, thus disabling the person from understanding the mechanism of karma, in terms of paticcasamuppada (or dependent causality). The second reason the Buddha considered this notion as egregious is that this belief makes God a dispenser of the results of our actions. Given this, we could try to bribe God or as was common in those days and even today, one would worship God (or confess) to ask for forgiveness.

According to the Buddha, this only makes a person irresponsible. If he were solely responsible for the results of his own actions (as he truly is) he will have no one to ask for pardon. The tendency of the human mind to look for such a God is mainly due to its tendency to indulge and yet expect to be forgiven.

However, only when we understand that we are entirely responsible for our own actions, and that results accrue as a law of nature and not due to some benign or judgmental being, will we understand the importance of skillful action and reflection that leads to happiness and escape from samsara. Another view quite popular today which was also present at the time of the Buddha in India was that God is the principle of the law of nature that causes events to occur in a causal manner. In this belief he is not considered a being whose behaviour could be influenced by human endeavour, but nevertheless was a personified image that 'governs' the world. However this is essentially an egregious personification of the laws of causality that the Buddha ascribed to the workings of the world.

According to the Buddha, the law of causality could be described briefly as:

> When this arises, that arises
> When this ceases, that ceases.

As such detailed exposition of the dependent causality was needed to understand the more subtle function of the mind-body complex of the human world. The law of causality is not intended to explain the workings of every single phenomenon in the world, but to understand the nature of samsara, the round of birth and death and karma. Personifying this law of nature into a God is of no special benefit as seen from the Buddhist standpoint.

Mahayana and Tantric Mystical Doctrines

Mahayana Buddhism, unlike Theravada, talks of Mind — using terms such as "the womb of the Thus-come One" — in a manner that is mistaken by some to indicate an "eternal entity". Such positive statements arose as a way to relate to the common misunderstanding of emptiness as nothingness, that is a nihilistic view of reality. The affirmation of emptiness by positive terminology appears quite radical when compared with early Buddhism's avoidance of "atman" and "god" terminology. Theravada, the oldest surviving school of Buddhism, generally does not subscribe to the idea of referring to the emptiness of mind with positive terminology. According to the Pali Canon, there is no eternal, all-pervading entity that is the source of all energy. Several Theravada scholars criticize the Mahayana scholars as having resorted to the same Vedantic ideas of eternal entities that the Buddha had rejected. From the Mahayana view, to the extent that any Mahayana practitioner actually asserts an "eternal entity" then this Theravada criticism is warranted. However, also from the Mahayana view, the Theravada criticism of Mahayana's use of postitive terminology as an assertion of "eternal entity" is itself a misperception of Mahayana and of Buddha's teaching.

C.D. Sebastian writes in his study of tathagatagarbha doctrine that Mahayana Buddhism is not merely intellectual, but also encompasses the sphere of devotion. Buddha is taken as the Supreme Reality - a kind of God who assumed human form in order to benefit all humanity:

> 'Mahayana Buddhism is not only intellectual, but also it is devotional ... in Mahayana, Buddha was taken as God, as Supreme Reality itself that descended on the earth in human form for the good of mankind. The concept of Buddha (as equal to God in theistic systems) was never as a creator but as Divine Love that out of compassion (*karuna*) embodied itself in human form to uplift suffering humanity. He was worshipped with fervent devotion... He represents the Absolute (*paramartha satya*), devoid of all plurality (*sarva-prapancanta-vinirmukta*) and has no beginning, middle and end ... Buddha ... is eternal, immutable ... As such He represents Dharmakaya.'

Tathagata and Dharmakaya as God

It is pertinent to note that in some Mahayana traditions,

the Buddha is indeed worshipped as a virtual divinity who is possessed of supernatural qualities and powers. Dr. Guang Xing writes:

> "The Buddha worshipped by Mahayanist followers is an omnipotent divinity endowed with numerous supernatural attributes and qualities ...[He] is described almost as an omnipotent and almighty godhead.".

Buddhist scholar, Dr. B. Alan Wallace, has also indicated that saying that Buddhism as a whole is 'non-theistic' may be an over-simplification. Wallace discerns similarities between some forms of Vajrayana Buddhism and notions of a divine 'ground of being' and creation. He writes: 'a careful analysis of Vajrayana Buddhist cosmogony, specifically as presented in the Atiyoga tradition of Indo-Tibetan Buddhism, which presents itself as the culmination of all Buddhist teachings, reveals a theory of a transcendent ground of being and a process of creation that bear remarkable similarities with views presented in Vedanta and Neoplatonic Western Christian theories of creation.'

In fact, Wallace sees these views as so similar that they seem almost to be different manifestations of the same theory. He comments: 'Vajrayana Buddhism, Vedanta, and Neoplatonic Christianity have so much in common that they could almost be regarded as varying interpretations of a single theory.' Vedantic statements regarding an invariant substratum are, however, rejected by the Buddha of the earliest scriptures as "pernicious views." In fact, regarding attempts of Brahmins to merge with a professed eternal substratum (known as Brahman), the Buddha stated that such people were worrying about something that is "non-existent" (*asati*).

Western analogues of aspects the thought of the Buddha as recorded in the earliest texts have only developed in modern times. In particular, early Buddhism has been compared to process philosophy (which existed in ancient Greece, but was eclipsed in Western thought by substance-attribute ontology until modern times), phenomenology, and deconstructionism.

According to the tathagatagarbha sutras, the Buddha also taught the existence of a spiritual essence called the tathagagatagarbha or Buddha-nature, which is present in all beings and phenomena.

Dr. B. Alan Wallace writes of this doctrine:

> 'the essential nature of the whole of samsara and nirvana is the absolute space (*dhatu*) of the *tathagatagarbha*, but this space is not to be confused with a mere absence of matter. Rather, this absolute space is imbued with all the infinite knowledge, compassion, power, and enlightened activities of the Buddha. Moreover, this luminous space is that which causes the phenomenal world to appear, and it is none other than the nature of one's own mind, which by nature is clear light.'

Writing on the Yogachara school of Buddhism, Dr. A.K. Chatterjee remarks:

> 'The Absolute is a non-dual consciousness. The duality of the subject and object does not pertain to it. It is said to be void (*sunya*), devoid of duality; in itself it is perfectly real, in fact the only reality ...There is no consciousness *of* the Absolute; Consciousness *is* the Absolute.'

While this is a traditional Tibetan interpretation of Yogacara views, it has been rejected by modern Western scholarship, namely by Kochumuttom, Anacker, Kalupahana, Dunne, Lusthaus, Powers, and Wayman.. Scholar Dan Lusthaus writes:

> "They [Yogacarins] did not focus on consciousness to assert it as ultimately real (Yogâcâra claims consciousness is

> only conventionally real since it arises from moment to moment due to fluctuating causes and conditions), but rather because it is the cause of the karmic problem they are seeking to eliminate."

According to the earliest Buddhist scriptures, the Buddha placed the belief in an unchanging consciousness on par with denying the necessity of the practical foundation of monasticism, celibacy. The Buddha says of a monk holding the former view that this misunderstanding "both damages himself and generates much demerit."

Gombrich writes: "A fundamental difference between the Buddha's view and the Upanishadic view is that the Buddha never confused epistemology with ontology ... The Buddha did not reify consciousness. Vinnana is one of the five khandha, and is a process, not a thing: consciousness is always consciousness *of*". The clearest statement that consciousness is simply a process is the description of it as "dependently originated" (*paticca-samuppanna*).

A further name for the irreducible, time-and-space-transcending mysterious Truth or Essence of Buddhic Reality spoken of in some Mahayana and tantric texts is the Dharmakaya (Body of Truth). Of this the Zen master (Zen Buddhism is a Mahayana school), Sokei-An, says:

> ... *dharmakaya* [is] the equivalent of God ...

The Buddha also speaks of no time and no space, where if I make a sound there is in that single moment a million years. It is spaceless like radio waves, like electric space - intrinsic. The Buddha said that there is a mirror that reflects consciousness. In this electric space a million miles and a pinpoint - a million years and a moment - are exactly the same. It is pure essence ... We call it 'original consciousness' - 'original *akasha*' - perhaps God in the

Christian sense. I am afraid of speaking about anything that is not familiar to me. No one can know what IT is ...

The same Zen adept, Sokei-An, further comments:

> The creative power of the universe is not a human being; it is Buddha. The one who sees, and the one who hears, is not this eye or ear, but the one who is *this* consciousness. *This One* is Buddha. *This One* appears in every mind. *This One* is common to all sentient beings, and is God.

The Rinzai Zen Buddhist master, Soyen Shaku, speaking to Americans at the beginning of the 20th century, discusses how in essence the idea of God is not absent from Buddhism, when understood as ultimate, true Reality:

> "At the outset, let me state that Buddhism is not atheistic as the term is ordinarily understood. It has certainly a God, the highest reality and truth, through which and in which this universe exists. However, the followers of Buddhism usually avoid the term God, for it savors so much of Christianity, whose spirit is not always exactly in accord with the Buddhist interpretation of religious experience ... To define more exactly the Buddhist notion of the highest being, it may be convenient to borrow the term very happily coined by a modern German scholar, 'panentheism', according to which God is ... all and one and more than the totality of existence .... As I mentioned before, Buddhists do not make use of the term God, which characteristically belongs to Christian terminology. An equivalent most commonly used is Dharmakaya ... When the Dharmakaya is most concretely conceived it becomes the Buddha, or Tathagata ..."

Primordial Buddhas

Theories regarding a self-existent "ground of being" were common in India prior to the Buddha, and were rejected by him: "The Buddha, however, refusing to admit any metaphysical principle as a common thread holding the moments of encountered phenomena together, rejects the Upanishadic notion of an immutable substance or principle underlying the world and the person and producing phenomena out of its inherent power, be it 'being', atman, brahman, or 'god.'" In later Mahayana literature, however, the idea of an eternal, all-pervading, all-knowing, immaculate, uncreated and deathless Ground of Being (the *dharmadhatu*, inherently linked to the *sattvadhatu*, the realm of beings), which is the Awakened Mind (*bodhicitta*) or Dharmakaya ("body of Truth") of the Buddha himself, is attributed to the Buddha in a number of Mahayana sutras, and is found in various tantras as well.

In some Mahayana texts, such a principle is occasionally presented as manifesting in a more personalised form as a primordial buddha, such as Samantabhadra, Vajradhara, Vairochana, and Adi-Buddha, among others. In some Buddhist tantric and Dzogchen scriptures, too, this immanent and transcendent Dharmakaya (the ultimate essence of the Buddha's being) is portrayed as the primordial Buddha, Samantabhadra, worshipped as the primordial lord.

In a study of Dzogchen, Dr. Sam van Schaik mentions how Samantabhadra Buddha is indeed seen as 'the heart essence of all buddhas, the Primordial Lord, the noble Victorious One, Samantabhadra'. Dr. Schaik indicates that Samantabhadra is not to be viewed as some kind of separate *mindstream*, apart from the mindstreams of sentient beings, but should be known as a universal nirvanic principle termed the Awakened Mind (*bodhi-citta*) and present in all.

Dr. Schaik quotes from the tantric texts, *Experiencing the Enlightened Mind of Samantabhadra* and *The Subsequent Tantra of Great Perfection Instruction* to portray

Samantabhadra as an uncreated, reflexive, radiant, pure and vital Knowing (gnosis) which is present in all things:

> 'The essence of all phenomena is the awakened mind; the mind of all buddhas is the awakened mind; and the life-force of all sentient beings is the awakened mind, too ... This unfabricated gnosis of the present moment is the reflexive luminosity, naked and stainless, the Primordial Lord himself.'

In the Mahavairocana Sutra, the essence of Vairocana, who is viewed in that scripture as the supreme Buddha, is said to be symbolised by the letter "A", which is claimed to reside in the hearts of all beings and of which Buddha Vairocana declares that "[the mystic letter 'A'] is placed in the heart location:

> it is Lord and Master of all,
> and it pervades entirely
> all the animate and inanimate.
> 'A' is the highest life-energy...

The text refers to Vairocana Buddha as the "Bhagavat" ("Blessed One," a term traditionally linked in Indian discourse with "the Divine"), "Master of the Dharma, *the Sage who is completely perfect, who is all-pervasive, who encompasses all world systems, who is All-Knowing, the Lord Vairocana".*

The Tantric text, *The Sarva-Tathagata-Tattva-Samgraha*, characterizes Vairocana as follows:

> He is universal Goodness, beneficial,
>
> destroyer [of suffering], the great Lord of Happiness, sky womb, Great Luminosity ... the great All-perceiving Lord ... He is without beginning or end ... [He is] Vishnu [God] ... Protector of the world, the sky, the earth ... The elements, the good benefactor of beings, All things ... the Blessed

> Rest, Eternal ... The Self of all the Buddhas ... Pre-eminent over all, and master of the world.

The Shingon Buddhist monk, Dohan, regarded the two great Buddhas, Amida and Vairocana, as one and the same Dharmakaya Buddha and as the true nature at the core of all beings and phenomena.

There are several realisations that can accrue to the Shingon practitioner of which Dohan speaks in this connection, as Dr. James Sanford points out: there is the realisation that Amida is the Dharmakaya Buddha, Vairocana; then there is the realisation that Amida as Vairocana is eternally manifest within this universe of time and space; and finally there is the innermost realisation that Amida is the true nature, material and spiritual, of all beings, that he is 'the omnivalent wisdom-body, that he is the unborn, unmanifest, unchanging reality that rests quietly at the core of all phenomena'.

Similar God-like descriptions are encountered in the *All-Creating King Tantra* (Kunjed Gyalpo Tantra), where the universal Mind of Awakening (in its mode as "Samantabhadra Buddha") declares of itself:

> I am the core of all that exists. I am the seed of all that exists. I am the cause of all that exists. I am the trunk of all that exists. I am the foundation of all that exists. I am the root of existence. I am "the core" because I contain all phenomena. I am "the seed" because I give birth to everything. I am "the cause" because all comes from me. I am "the trunk" because the ramifications of every event sprout from me. I am "the foundation" because all abides in me. I am called "the root" because I am everything.

It is remarkable that *Karandavyuha Sutra* presents the great bodhisattva, Avalokitesvara, as a kind of supreme lord of the cosmos. A striking feature of Avalokitesvara in this sutra is his creative power, as he is said to be the progenitor of various heavenly bodies and divinities.

Dr. Alexander Studholme, in his monograph on the sutra, writes:

> 'The sun and moon are said to be born from the bodhisattva's eyes, Mahesvara [Siva] from his brow, Brahma from his shoulders, Narayana [Vishnu] from his heart, Sarasvati from his teeth, the winds from his mouth, the earth from his feet and the sky from his stomach.'

Avalokitesvara himself is linked in the versified version of the sutra to the first Buddha, the Adi Buddha, who is 'svayambhu' (self-existent, not born from anything or anyone). Dr. Studholme comments:

> 'Avalokitesvara himself, the verse sutra adds, is an emanation of the *Adibuddha*, or 'primordial Buddha', a term that is explicitly said to be synoymous with *Svayambhu* and *Adinatha*, 'primordial lord'.'

That primordial Buddha, Âdibuddha (Adi-Buddha), figures prominently in the Kalachakra tantra. Âdibuddha is believed to be a primordial, self-existent, self-created Buddha who is the personification of Shunyata or emptiness [freedom from confining substance or conceptual graspability) enshrining the infinitely Knowing Mind of Great Compassion; all phenomena lack true separate existence yet still appear, and their basis is the undifferentiated and inconceivable Mind of Buddha (empty of all defects and ignorance).

However, all these seemingly godlike figures (Samantabhadra, Vairochana, Vajradhara, etc.) are traditionally understood to be personifications of emptiness and compassion – the ungraspable, limitless, invisible, inconceivable, unimpeded benevolent Reality of Buddha-Mind and the true nature of all phenomena.

Some Buddhists see the above quote from Samantabhadra Buddha as radically subjective psychology, while still others will insist that the words mean what they say and do communicate the sense of an actual sustaining force or spiritual essence behind and within all phenomena.

Shin Buddhism

In Shin Buddhism, Amida Buddha is viewed as the eternal Buddha who manifested as Shakyamuni in India and who is the personification of Nirvana itself. The Shin Buddhist priest, John Paraskevopoulos, in his monograph on Shin Buddhism, writes:

> 'In Shin Buddhism, Nirvana or Ultimate Reality (also known as the "Dharma-Body" or *Dharmakaya* in the original Sanskrit) has assumed a more concrete form as (a) the Buddha of Infinite Light (*Amitabha*) and Infinite Life (*Amitayus*)and (b) the "Pure Land" or "Land of Utmost Bliss" (*Sukhavati*), the realm over which this Buddha is said to preside ... Amida is the Eternal Buddha who is said to have taken form as Shakyamuni and his teachings in order to become known to us in ways we can readily comprehend.'

John Paraskevopoulos elucidates the notion of Nirvana, of which Amida is an embodiment, in the following terms:

> '... [Nirvana's] more positive connotation is that of a higher state of being, the dispelling of illusion and the corresponding joy of liberation. An early Buddhist scripture describes Nirvana as: ... the far shore, the subtle, the very difficult to see, the undisintegrating, the unmanifest, the peaceful, the deathless, the sublime, the auspicious, the secure, the destruction of craving, the wonderful, the amazing, the unailing, the unafflicted, dispassion, purity, freedom, the island, the shelter, the asylum, the refuge ... (*Samyutta Nikaya*)'

This Nirvana is seen as eternal and of one nature,

indeed as the essence of all things. Paraskevopoulos tells of how the *Mahaparinirvana Sutra* speaks of Nirvana as eternal, pure, blissful and true self:

> 'In Mahayana Buddhism it is taught that there is fundamentally one reality which, in its highest and purest dimension, is experienced as Nirvana. It is also known, as we have seen, as the Dharma-Body (considered as the ultimate form of Being) or "Suchness" (*Tathata* in Sanskrit) when viewed as the essence of all things ... "The Dharma-Body is eternity, bliss, true self and purity. It is forever free of all birth, ageing, sickness and death" (*Nirvana Sutra*)'.

To attain this Self, however, it is needful to transcend the 'small self' and its pettiness with the help of an 'external' agency, Amida Buddha. This is the view promulgated by the Jodo Shinshu founding Buddhist master, Shinran Shonin. John Paraskevopoulos comments on this:

> 'Shinran's great insight was that we cannot conquer the self by the self. Some kind of external agency is required: (a) to help us to shed light on our ego as it really is in all its petty and baneful guises; and (b) to enable us to subdue the small 'self' with a view to realising the Great Self by awakening to Amida's light.'

When that Great Self of Amida's light is realised, Shin Buddhism is able to see the Infinite which transcends the care-worn mundane. John Paraskevopoulos concludes his monograph on Shin Buddhism thus:

> 'It is time we discarded the tired view of Buddhism as a dry and forensic rationalism , lacking in warmth and devotion ... By hearing the call of Amida Buddha we become awakened to true reality and its unfathomable working ... to live a life that dances jubilantly in the resplendent light of the Infinite.'

One of the Mahayana Sutras, the Lankavatara Sutra,

states that the notions of a sovereign God, Atman are figments of the imagination or manifestations of the mind and can also be an impediment to perfection as this leads to attachment to the concept of God:

> All such notions as causation, succession, atoms, primary elements, that make up personality, personal soul, Supreme Spirit, Sovereign God, Creator, are all figments of the imagination and manifestations of mind.

No, Mahamati, the Tathágata's doctrine of the Womb of Tathágata-hood is not the same as the philosopher's Atman.

Instead of a personal creator God, the sutra speaks of creative Mind, and of Suchness (*tathata* - universal Truth-as-it-is), which is defined as: "... this Suchness may be characterised as Truth, Reality, exact knowledge, limit, source, self-substance, the Unattainable".

Moreover, the same sutra also sees the Buddha reveal that he is the unrecognised One who is actually being addressed when beings project from their unawakened minds notions of Divinity and address themselves to "God". The many names for such ultimate Being or Truth are in fact said by the Buddha to be unwitting appellations of the Buddha himself.

He states:

> The same can be said of myself as I appear in this world of patience before ignorant people and where I am known by uncounted trillions of names. They address me by different names not realizing that they are all names of the one Tathagata. Some recognize me as Sun, as Moon; some as a reincarnation of the ancient sages; some as one of "ten powers"; some as Rama, some as Indra, and some as Varuna. Still there are others who speak of me as The Un-born, as Emptiness, as "Suchness," as Truth, as Reality,

> as Ultimate Principle; still there are others who see me as Dharmakaya, as Nirvana, as the Eternal; some speak of me as sameness, as non-duality, as un-dying, as formless; some think of me as the doctrine of Buddha-causation, or of Emancipation, or of the Noble Path; and some think of me as Divine Mind and Noble Wisdom.
>
> Thus in this world and in other worlds am I known by these uncounted names, but they all see me as the moon is seen in the water.

Though they all honor, praise and esteem me, they do not fully understand the meaning and significance of the words they use; not having their own self-realization of Truth they cling to the words of their canonical books, or to what has been told to them, or to what they have imagined, and fail to see that the name they are using is only one of the many names of the Tathagata.

In their studies they follow the mere words of the text vainly trying to gain the true meaning, instead of having confidence in the one "text" where self-confirming Truth is revealed, that is, having confidence in the self-realization of noble Wisdom.

In the "Sagathakam" section of the sutra (which contains some striking statements contradictory of earlier chapters of the sutra), one also reads of the reality of the pure Self (atman), which (while not identical to the atman of the Hindus) is equated with the Tathagatagarbha (Buddha-Essence):

> The *atma* [Self] characterised with purity is the state of self-realisation; this is the Tathagatagarbha, which does not belong to the realm of the theorisers.

This Tathagatagarbha is in the *Lankavatara Sutra* identified with the root or all-containing Consciousness of all beings, the Alaya-vijnana. This Tathagatagarbha-

Alayavijnana is stated not to belong to the realm of speculation, but can be understood directly by

> those Bodhisatva-Mahasattvas [great Bodhisattvas] who like you [Mahamati] are endowed with subtle, fine, penetrative thought-power and whose understanding is in accordance with the meaning ...

Such an all-containing Buddhic Matrix (Tathagatagarbha) or basis of universal consciousness (Alayavijnana) has resonances with a conception of divinity which posits the latter as the underlying reality behind and within all things. This "Self" is in some Mahayana Buddhist scriptures and tantras equated with the original, primal, all-sustaining cosmic Buddha himself (viewed either as Samantabhadra or Mahavairochana).

Zen and the One Mind

The Zen Teachings of Huang Po gives a detailed description of the one mind, which can be argued is the essence of a God.

The Master said to me: All the Buddhas and all sentient beings are nothing but the One Mind, beside which nothing exists.

This Mind, which is without beginning, is unborn and indestructible.

It is not green nor yellow, and has neither form nor appearance.

It does not belong to the categories of things which exist or do not exist, nor can it be thought of in terms of new or old.

It is neither long nor short, big nor small, for it transcends all limits, measures, names, traces, and comparisons.

It is that which you see before you — begin to reason about it and you at once fall into error.

It is like the boundless void which cannot be fathomed or measured.

The One Mind alone is the Buddha, and there is no distinction between the Buddha and the sentient things, but that sentient beings are attached to forms and so seek externally for Buddhahood.

By their very seeking they lose it, for that is using the Buddha to seek for the Buddha and using mind to grasp Mind.

Even though they do their utmost for a full eon, they will not be able to attain to it.

They do not know that, if they put a stop to conceptual thought and forget their anxiety, the Buddha will appear before them, for this Mind is the Buddha and the Buddha is all living beings. It is not the less for being manifested in ordinary beings, nor is it greater for being manifested in the Buddhas.

Though not believing in a creator God, Buddhists inherited the Indian cosmology of the time which includes various types of 'god' realms such as the Heaven of the Thirty-Three, the Four Great Kings, and so on. Deva-realms are part of the various possible types of existence in the Buddhist cosmology. Rebirth as a deva is attributed to virtuous actions performed in previous lives. Beings that had meditated are thought to be reborn in more and more subtle realms with increasingly vast life spans, in accord with their meditative ability. In particular, the highest deva realms are pointed out as false paths in meditation that the meditator should be aware of. Like any existence within the cycle of rebirth (samsara), a life as a deva is only temporary. At the time of death, a large part of the former deva's good karma has been expended, leaving mostly negative karma and a likely rebirth in one of the three lower realms.

REFERENCES

1. A.K. Chatterjee, *The Yogacara Idealism*, Motilal, Delhi, 1975, pp. 133-134
2. B. Alan Wallace, "Is Buddhism Really Non-Theistic?" Lecture delivered at the National Conference of the American Academy of Religion, Boston, Mass., Nov., 1999. sbinstitute.com/.../Is%20Buddhism%20Really%20Nontheistic_.pdf p. 1, accessed 14 August 2009
3. B. Alan Wallace, *Contemplative Science*. Columbia University Press, 2007, pp. 97-98.
4. David J. Kalupahana, *Mûlamadhyamakakârikâ of Nâgârjuna: The Philosophy of the Middle Way*. Reprint by Motilal Banarsidass Publ., 1991, p. 61.
5. David Kalupahana, *Causality: The Central Philosophy of Buddhism*. The University Press of Hawaii, 1975, pp. 111-112.
6. Dr. Guang Xing, *The Three Bodies of the Buddha: The Origin and Development of the Trikaya Theory*, Routledge Curzon, Oxford, 2005, p. 1.
7. Gethin, Rupert. "Cosmology and meditation: from the Anganna Sutta to the Mahayana" in Williams, Paul. *Buddhism, Vol. II*. Routledge 2004. pp. 104, 126.
8. Guang Xing, *The Three Bodies of the Buddha: The Origin and Development of the Trikaya Theory*, RoutledgeCurzon, Oxford, 2005, pp.1 and 85
9. Hajime Nakamura, *A History of Early Vedânta Philosophy: Part One*. Reprint by Motilal Banarsidass Publ., 1990, page 139.
10. Helmuth von Glasenapp, *Vedanta and Buddhism: A comparative study*, The Wheel, Publication No. 2, Kandy, 1978.

11. Jay L. Garfield, *Empty Words: Buddhist Philosophy and Cross-Cultural Interpretation*, Oxford University Press: 2001.
12. Johnson, Peter (2001). "The Ten Titles of the Buddha". http://www.tientai.net/teachings/dharma/buddha/10titles.htm. Retrieved 2008-09-12.
13. Kannakatthala Sutta, (MN-90)
14. M. Walshe: *The Long Discourses of the Buddha*, p. 407: "On Knowledge of Beginnings", Somerville, MASS, 1995.
15. Mahasi Sayadaw, *Thoughts on the Dhamma,* The Wheel Publication No. 298/300, Kandy BPS, 1983.
16. Manu Bazzano, *Buddha is dead: Nietzsche and the dawn of European Zen*. Sussex Academic Press, 2006, pp. 62-63.
17. Noa Ronkin, *Early Buddhist Metaphysics.* Routledge, 2005.
18. Professor Perry Schmidt-Leukel, 'Buddha and Christ as Mediators of the Transcendent', in *Buddhism and Christianity in Dialogue*, ed. by Professor Perry Schmidt-Leukel, SCM Press, Norfolk, 2005, p. 152
19. Richard Gombrich, *How Buddhism began: the Conditioned Genesis of the Early Teachings.* Continuum International Publishing Group, 1996, p. 82.
20. Richard Gombrich, *How Buddhism began: the Conditioned Genesis of the Early Teachings.* Continuum International Publishing Group, 1996, p. 81.
21. Richard Gombrich, *How Buddhism began: the conditioned genesis of the early teachings.* Continuum International Publishing Group, 1996, p. 43.
22. Richard Gombrich, *Theravada Buddhism: A Social History from Ancient Benares to Modern Colombo.* Routledge and Kegan Paul, 1988, p. 85.
23. *Sacred Writings, Buddhism: The Dhammapada*, Translated by John Ross Carter and Mahindha Palihawadana, pp. 13, 89. 1992. Quality Paperback Book Club, New York.

Bibliography

Alan Wallace, B., *Contemplative Science.* Columbia University Press, 2007.

Armstrong, Karen, *Buddha.* Penguin Books, 2001.

Beal, *Catena of Buddhist Scriptures from the Chinese*, (London, 1871).

Bechert, Heinz & Richard Gombrich (ed.), *The World of Buddhism*, Thames & Hudson, 1984.

Bhagwan Das, *"Revival of Buddhism in India and Role of Dr. Baba Saheb B.R. Ambedkar"* (Dalit Today Prakashan, 18/455, Indira Nagar, Lucknow, U.P., India, 1998).

Bob Hudson, *The Origins of Bagan*, Thesis for University of Sydney,2004.

Buswell, Robert E. (ed.), *Encyclopedia of Buddhism.* MacMillan Reference Books, 2003.

Chatterjee, A.K., *The Yogacara Idealism*, Motilal, Delhi, 1975, pp. 133-134

Connolly & Hamilton, *Indian Insights*, (ed.) Luzac, London, 1997.

Coogan, Michael D. (ed.) (2003). *The Illustrated Guide to World Religions.* Oxford University Press.

Corless, Roger, 'Pure Land and Pure Perspective: A Tantric Hermeneutic of Sukhâvatî.' *The Pure Land*, New Series, 1989.

Cousins, L.S. (1996), "The dating of the historical Buddha: a review article", *Journal of the Royal Asiatic Society* (3)6(1): 57–63.

Damien Keown Dictionary of Buddhism (Oxford University Press, 2003).

David J. Kalupahana, *Mûlamadhyamakakârikâ of Nâgârjuna: The Philosophy of the Middle Way.* Reprint by Motilal Banarsidass Publ., 1991.

David Kalupahana, *Causality: The Central Philosophy of Buddhism.* The University Press of Hawaii, 1975.

Davidson, Ronald M., *Indian Esoteric Buddhism: A Social History of the Tantric Movement.* New York: Columbia University Press, 2003.

de Give, Bernard, *Les rapports de l'Inde et de l'Occident des origines au règne d'Asoka.* Les Indes savants, 2006.

Donath, Dorothy C., *Buddhism for the West: Theravâda, Mahâyâna and Vajrayâna; a comprehensive review of Buddhist history, philosophy, and teachings from the time of the Buddha to the present day.* Julian Press, 1971.

Dr. Guang Xing, *The Three Bodies of the Buddha: The Origin and Development of the Trikaya Theory,* Routledge Curzon, Oxford, 2005.

Elizabeth Moore, "Interpreting Pyu material culture: Royal chronologies and finger-marked bricks," *Myanmar Historical Research Journal,* No(13) June 2004.

Etienne Lamotte, *History Of Indian Buddhism,* Peeters Publishers: 1988.

Gethin, Rupert, *Foundations of Buddhism.* Oxford University Press, 1998.

Gethin, Rupert. "Cosmology and meditation: from the Anganna Sutta to the Mahayana" in Williams, Paul. *Buddhism, Vol. II*. Routledge, 2004.

Gombrich, Richard F. (1988; 6th reprint, 2002). *Theravâda Buddhism: A Social History from Ancient Benares to Modern Colombo* (London: Routledge).

Guang Xing, *The Three Bodies of the Buddha: The Origin and Development of the Trikaya Theory*, RoutledgeCurzon, Oxford, 2005.

Gunaratana, Bhante Henepola, *Mindfulness in Plain English*. Wisdom Publications, 2002.

Gyatso, Geshe Kelsang. *Introduction to Buddhism*: An Explanation of the Buddhist Way of Life, Tharpa Publications (2nd. ed., 2001, US ed. 2008)

Hajime Nakamura, *A History of Early Vedânta Philosophy: Part One*. Reprint by Motilal Banarsidass Publ., 1990.

Halkias, T. Georgios. "Compassionate Aspirations and their fulfilment: Dol-po-pa's A Prayer for Birth in Sukhâvatî ." In *As Long As Space Endures: Essays on the Kâlachakra Tantra in Honor of His Holiness the Dalai Lama*. Ithaca: Snow Lion Publications, 2009.

Harvey, *Introduction to Buddhism*, Cambridge University Press, 1990.

Harvey, Peter, *An Introduction to Buddhism: Teachings, History and Practices*. Cambridge University Press, 1990.

Helmuth von Glasenapp, *Vedanta and Buddhism: A comparative study,* The Wheel, Publication No. 2, Kandy, 1978.

Hirakawa Akira (translated and edited by Paul Groner), *A History Of India Buddhism*, Motilal Banarsidass Publishers, Delhi, 1993.

Jay L. Garfield, *Empty Words: Buddhist Philosophy and Cross-Cultural Interpretation*, Oxford University Press: 2001.

John Boardman, *The Diffusion of Classical Art in Antiquity*, Princeton University Press, 1994.

Johnson, Peter, "The Ten Titles of the Buddha", 2001.

Kapstein, Matthew, "Pure Land Buddhism in Tibet? From Sukhâvatî to the Field of Great Bliss." In *Approaching the Land of Bliss: Religious Praxis in the Cult of Amitâbha*, ed. R. Payne and K. Tanaka. Honolulu: University of Hawaii Press, 2004.

Kevin Lynch, *The Way of The Tiger: A Buddhist's Guide To Achieving Nirvana*, Yojimbo Temple, 2005.

Mahasi Sayadaw, *Thoughts on the Dhamma,* The Wheel Publication No. 298/300, Kandy BPS, 1983.

Manu Bazzano, *Buddha is dead: Nietzsche and the dawn of European Zen*. Sussex Academic Press, 2006.

Mario D'Amato,"Mapping the Mahâyâna: Some Historical and Doctrinal Issues". *Religion Compass* 2008.

Mei, Ching Hsuan, "'Pho ba Liturgy in 14th Century Tibet." *Tibet Journal*, 2004.

Mettanando Bhikkhu and Oskar von Hinueber, "The Cause of the Buddha's Death"; Vol. XXVI of the Journal of the Pali Text Society, 2000.

Michael Carrithers, *The Buddha,* 1983, pages 13, 14. Found in *Founders of Faith,* Oxford University Press, 1986.

Morgan, Kenneth W. (ed), *The Path of the Buddha:*

Buddhism Interpreted by Buddhists, Ronald Press, New York, 1956.

Narada, *A Manual of Buddhism*. Buddha Educational Foundation, 1992.

Nattier, Jan, *A Few Good Men: The Bodhisattva Path according to The Inquiry of Ugra (Ugrapariprccha)*. University of Hawai'i Press, 2003.

Noa Ronkin, *Early Buddhist Metaphysics*. Routledge, 2005.

Peter Harvey, *The Selfless Mind*. Curzon Press, 1995.

Professor Perry Schmidt-Leukel, 'Buddha and Christ as Mediators of the Transcendent', in *Buddhism and Christianity in Dialogue*, ed. by Professor Perry Schmidt-Leukel, SCM Press, Norfolk, 2005.

Randall Collins, *The Sociology of Philosophies: A Global Theory of Intellectual Change*. Harvard University Press, 2000.

Richard Foltz *Religions of the Silk Road* by (St. Martin's Griffin, New York, 1999).

Richard Gombrich, *How Buddhism began: the Conditioned Genesis of the Early Teachings*. Continuum International Publishing Group, 1996.

Richard Gombrich, *How Buddhism began: the Conditioned Genesis of the Early Teachings*. Continuum International Publishing Group, 1996.

Richard Gombrich, *How Buddhism began: the conditioned genesis of the early teachings*. Continuum International Publishing Group, 1996.

Richard Gombrich, *Theravada Buddhism: A Social History from Ancient Benares to Modern Colombo*. Routledge and Kegan Paul, 1988.

Richard Gombrich, *Theravada Buddhism: A Social History from Ancient Benares to Modern Colombo.* Routledge and Kegan Paul, 1988.

Robinson, Richard H. and Willard L. Johnson (1970; 3rd ed., 1982). *The Buddhist Religion: A Historical Introduction* (Belmont, CA: Wadsworth Publishing).

Romila Thapar, *The Penguin History of Early India: From Origins to AD 1300.* Penguin Books, 2002.

Sacred Writings, Buddhism: The Dhammapada, Translated by John Ross Carter and Mahindha Palihawadana, 1992.

Schopen, G. "The inscription on the Kusan image of Amitabha and the character of the early Mahayana in India", *Journal of the International Association of Buddhist Studies 10*, 1990.

Shaw, Sarah. "Buddhist Meditation Practices in the West". Department of Continuing Education, Oxford University.

Sinha, H.P., *Bhâratîya Darshan kî rûprekhâ (Features of Indian Philosophy)*. Motilal Banarasidas Publ., 1993.

Smith, Hudson. Novak, Philip. Buddhism. New York: HarperCollins Publishers, 2003.

Stanley Jeyaraja Tambiah, *Buddhism Betrayed?* The University of Chicago Press, 1992.

Sue Hamilton, *Early Buddhism: A New Approach: The I of the Beholder.* Routledge, 2000.

Thanissaro Bhikkhu (2001). *Refuge: An Introduction to the Buddha, Dhamma, & Sangha (3rd ed., rev.).*

Thich Nhat Hanh, *The Heart of the Buddha's Teaching*, Broadway Books, 1974.

Thomas McEvilley, *"The Shape of Ancient Thought. Comparative studies in Greek and Indian Philosophies"* (Allworth Press, New York, 2002).

Thurman, Robert A. F., *Holy Teaching of Vimalakirti: Mahayana Scripture*. Pennsylvania State University Press, 1976.

Ven. Elgiriye Indaratana Maha Thera, *Vandana: The Album of Pali Devotional Chanting and Hymns*, 2002.

Walshe, M., *The Long Discourses of the Buddha*, p. 407: "On Knowledge of Beginnings", Somerville, MASS, 1995.

Walshe, Maurice *The Long Discourses of the Buddha: A Translation of the Digha Nikaya*, 1995, Boston: Wisdom Publications.

Warder, A.K., Indian Buddhism Motilal Banarsidass: 2000.

Index

●●●